THE CULTURALIST CHALLENGE
TO LIBERAL REPUBLICANISM

MCGILL-QUEEN'S STUDIES IN THE HISTORY OF IDEAS
Series Editor: Philip J. Cercone

THE CULTURALIST CHALLENGE
TO LIBERAL REPUBLICANISM

Michael Lusztig

McGill-Queen's University Press
Montreal & Kingston • London • Chicago

© McGill-Queen's University Press 2017

ISBN 978-0-7735-5104-6 (cloth)
ISBN 978-0-7735-5105-3 (paper)
ISBN 978-0-7735-5170-1 (ePDF)
ISBN 978-0-7735-5171-8 (ePUB)

Legal deposit third quarter 2017
Bibliothèque nationale du Québec

Printed in Canada on acid-free paper that is 100% ancient forest free
(100% post-consumer recycled), processed chlorine free

McGill-Queen's University Press acknowledges the support of the Canada
Council for the Arts for our publishing program. We also acknowledge the
financial support of the Government of Canada through the Canada Book
Fund for our publishing activities.

Library and Archives Canada Cataloguing in Publication

Lusztig, Michael, 1962–, author
    The culturalist challenge to liberal republicanism / Michael Lusztig.

(McGill-Queen's studies in the history of ideas; 72)
Includes bibliographical references and index.
Issued in print and electronic formats.
ISBN 978-0-7735-5104-6 (cloth). – ISBN 978-0-7735-5105-3 (paper). –
ISBN 978-0-7735-5170-1 (ePDF). – ISBN 978-0-7735-5171-8 (ePUB)

1. Republicanism. 2. Liberalism. 3. Culture. I. Title. II. Series:
McGill-Queen's studies in the history of ideas; 72

JC423.L87 2017   321.8   C2017-902068-4
                                                     C2017-902069-2

This book was typeset by Marquis Interscript in 10/12 New Baskerville.

To the memory of Peter A. Lusztig

Contents

Acknowledgments

In writing this book I am fortunate to have had a great deal of support – professional, financial, and personal. Professionally this book benefited from interactions with friends and colleagues. In particular I would like to thank Patrick James, Cal Jillson, Joseph Kobylka, the late Dennis Simon, and Matthew Wilson for their helpful suggestions. Christine Carberry and Erica Kenney read the entire manuscript. They, as well as three anonymous reviewers for McGill-Queen's University Press, provided detailed and provocative comments that greatly improved the quality of the work. Jacqueline Mason at McGill-Queen's University Press was incredibly supportive in guiding the book through the editorial process, gently nudging me in the right direction in terms of tone and balance.

I would also like to thank the John Goodwin Tower Center for Political Studies at Southern Methodist University, which provided financial assistance through a Colin Powell Fellowship. Similar thanks go to Dedman College at SMU for course relief that greatly facilitated the research process.

Finally I thank my wife, Christine Carberry, for her constant support, and my family for always listening to my ideas, however much they might have disagreed with them. My dad took particular interest in the project and I fondly recall our lively debates over issues of multiculturalism. The book is dedicated to his memory.

THE CULTURALIST CHALLENGE
TO LIBERAL REPUBLICANISM

1

The End of History or the End of the World?

In 1989, with the impending end of the Cold War, Francis Fukuyama created significant academic controversy with his proclamation that we had reached the end of history. By the end of history, Fukuyama means an evolutionary end point, of institutionalizing liberal democratic governance, representing the pinnacle of humanity's socio-political achievements. It was a bold proclamation, and not without merit. With fascism long vanquished, and communism crumbling, the new world order proclaimed by then president Bush appeared to be one characterized by an inevitable global progress toward liberal democracy. Economic and political development in East Asia, not to mention a budding movement toward free markets and free politics that would manifest itself in 1990s Latin America, gave credence to the idea that the nature of the realm of freedom that Marx understood to be historically determined would not be communist, but liberal (Fukuyama 1989; 2002).

A less optimistic picture of the robustness of liberal democratic regimes has been painted by any number of prognosticators who, in some way or another, can be classified as republicans. If liberals have proclaimed the end of history, republicans from Plato to Robert Bork have warned of the metaphorical end of the world (or at least the end of the regime). Indeed, republicanism begins with the premise that all regimes are destined to fail, that regime longevity is not to be confused with regime immortality. Which "side" is correct? Are we on the precipice of the end of history or the end of the world?

Not surprisingly, the answer here is neither. Although saying that the end is not imminent is not the same thing as saying that there are no straws in the wind. I have no intention here of predicting one end or the other. More interesting to me is a survey of the landscape – what values inform liberal democratic regimes and what challenges exist to preserve those values. I identify benign challenges and malignant threats. I seek to distinguish between prescriptions presented by well-intentioned advocates of social justice and those undertaken by forces hostile to the survival of particular liberal democracies and even liberal democracy in general.[1] Although I am interested in these hostile cultures, I am even more interested in the challenge posed by well-intentioned and loyal citizens who question the prioritization of some values over others within liberal democracies. Before unpacking the argument any further, however, we need to return to the end of history and, indeed, get a handle on what we mean by history.

History

The western political tradition is inextricably tied to our understanding of time and place. History, whether whether we see it as the product of random sequences of events or of a larger cosmic process, has influenced our understanding of politics. If the former, history is particular, a succession of discrete moments in time linked, certainly, to preceding events, but lacking universal principles that tie these moments into a cohesive or purposive whole. If the latter, history is universal. *Universal* histories are directional, adopting either recursive or eschatological (progressive) properties. We thus can conceive history as an endless feedback loop or we can understand it as a story with a beginning, middle, and end.

The quintessential example of a recursive universal history is found in the classical philosophy of antiquity. These philosophers and historians understood that the natural cycle of birth and death attached to all organisms, animate and inanimate alike. History thus was destined to repeat itself with (depending on the philosopher) greater or lesser fidelity to the precise sequence of past events (Frost 1952; Pocock 1975, esp. 77–80).[2]

---

1 We should be clear on a couple of points. The first is that Fukuyama does not really mean that the world has reached the end of history. There is too much dislocation and too many unstable regimes to declare global liberation from the clutches of history. While he probably does (or at least did) mean that the developed world had reached the end of history, even here he equivocates. In the conclusion of his book (2002), Fukuyama challenges the entire premise of a sustainable end of history, suggesting that such an environment ultimately may prove insufficient for anyone seeking to risk their lives in pursuit of principle and ambition.

2 Politically, this well-known *kyklos* assumes that civil society begins with the emergence of a great man, one who is more courageous and wise and honourable than the rest. It is this man whose people will anoint him king, and his prestige will be such that his heirs and

Eschatological universal histories are also common. Christian theology and Marxist philosophy, for example, both rely on eschatological historical progression. More pertinent to present purposes, Hegel (1977) sees human existence in terms of gradual stages of development toward the ultimate objective of freedom. Such progression manifests through regime types that gradually expand the scope of freedom, from the despot, who enjoys singular freedom and mastery over others, to increasingly pluralized forms of government that extend the realm of freedom (Smith 1989, 4; Fukuyama 2002, 60–5). In the terminal phase mastery and slavery cease to exist in a political context. It is governed by the sovereignty of law which institutionalizes the universality of dignity, protecting the external freedoms of all individuals and guiding them toward liberation from internal constraints on their liberty (Hegel 1977, chs. I–V; Taylor 1988/1989, 864; Smith 1989, 5).

Critical to our understanding is modern liberal democratic government's relationship to history. Its antecedents can be traced to two philosophic traditions, liberalism and republicanism. Liberals' first-order social value is the protection and preservation of liberty whereas republicans' first-order social value is virtue or obligation. It is the liberal worldview that informs a reasonable basis for an eschatological end of history. Unlike republicanism, liberalism is predicated on the assumption of regime robustness, even immortality (although see Walsh 1997, ch.1). There are credible claims for such robustness.

---

their heirs will rule in hereditary succession. With time, however, a monarchy becomes indulgent and ostentatious. Kings build great monuments to themselves and flaunt their wealth and privilege. When inevitable jealousies arise and harden into resentment, kings are obliged to secure their reigns through tyranny. Ultimately the revolutionary impulse prevails, and tyrannies are overthrown. The leaders of these revolutions, who enjoy the sympathy of the people, ascend to power and govern as an aristocracy. But as with the heirs of monarchy, subsequent generations of aristocrats succumb to debauchery and avarice. Governance turns from benign aristocracy to oligarchy, and the people become just as dissatisfied with oligarchical rule as they had been with royal tyranny. With the overthrow of oligarchy, and with the memory of tyranny still at the forefront of their consciousness, the people construct a democracy whereby freedom and equality are the watchwords. But inevitably, that system breaks down as well. Societies need leaders and there will emerge a class of professional politicians, competing with each other through bribery and corruption for the privilege of holding high office. Camps emerge as society fractures into factions held together by the promise of material enrichment at the expense of others. Ultimately civil society breaks down only to be rescued from the darkness by a great man of courage and character as the cycle begins anew (Aristotle 1962, bk. V; Polybius 1889, bk.VI, esp. ss. 3–9).

Liberal Robustness

A critically important claim is the economic structure of liberal, or free market, economies. Free markets create avenues for economic ambition that would otherwise not exist for those not already privileged. In a free market economy, a broad range of individuals acquire a stake in the system, either through the assets they need to protect, or through the reasonable prospect of acquiring assets. This outlet for economic ambition and the commitment to a system that fosters that ambition and protects the rewards accrued through it works against the propensity for revolution because revolutions are fought by those barred from reaping the rewards of the prevailing economic and political systems. No one revolts against a system in which she might reasonably expect to benefit. Free markets are beneficial, moreover, insofar as they facilitate both economic and sociopolitical mobility. This mobility represents a sort of lubricant, preventing the system from seizing up. It serves as a buffer between having (and using whatever force is necessary to keep having) and not having (and using whatever force is necessary to start having) (Lipset 1959; 1981).

Another claim for liberal robustness is that liberalism represents a hedge against instability through war. Liberal democratic leaders have an incentive to be responsive to the preferences of those they govern. And for citizens who have a stake in the stability of the regime, international aggression runs counter to their interests. Indeed, Kant suggests, a rational people will find war a "bad business."[3] War obviates the economic benefits extracted through the free market, and just as important, peace enhances such benefits. Thus, Onéal and Russett (1997) find that international trade between nations reduces their propensity for militarized conflict. Such international cooperation is a function of the fact that liberal economies share a number of relevant commonalities. These include a basic free market structure, an incentive for economic specialization that fosters state interdependence, and a cosmopolitan political culture that militates against aggression as a means of resolving conflicts among similarly situated states (Fukuyama 2002, esp. ch. 26; see also Kant 1795; Keohane and Nye 1977; Doyle 1986; Russett 1993).

---

3 This is because, Kant argues, citizens "must fight themselves; they must hand over the costs of war from their own property; they must do their poor best to make good the devastation it leaves behind; and finally, as a crowning ill, they have to accept a burden of debt that will embitter even peace itself, and which they can never pay off on account of the new wars which are always impending" (1795, 122–3).

The robustness of liberal regimes is also the product of a crucial cognitive dimension that we can think of as the universalization of dignity. With its emphasis on individual rights and equality, liberalism satisfies the deep-seated human need for esteem or recognition of inherent worth. Recognition has always been critical both to the fulfillment of the human condition (hence Plato's inclusion of the *thymos* as an element of the soul (1974, 440c–e)) and to politics. It is why Hegel sees historical evolution as primarily a struggle for recognition (Hegel 1977, ch. 4). Individual rights, including the liberty from which liberalism derives its name, represent ways of claiming and protecting human dignity. From the liberal perspective, rights accrue to each individual equally and hence reflect the mandate that each individual enjoys an undifferentiated claim to human dignity.

Such a claim is a relatively modern phenomenon. Before the Enlightenment, differential claims to human dignity legitimated hierarchical forms of government. A differential claim to human dignity was conceived as honour – a reward for virtue motivated by the desire to be respected and deferred to in the eyes of others (Olsthoorn 2005). Honour thus was a spur to greatness, a means to wealth and high office. It was also a means to institutionalized privilege. Inevitably, however, recognition born of great deeds evolved into recognition based on birth. The differential claim to dignity thus came to represent a shared (class-based) good reflecting social stratification, privilege, deference, and chauvinism. The veneer of nobility and concomitant rectitude legitimated the dominance of particular classes of citizens as recognized through a social hierarchy that bound the slave, metaphorical or literal, to the will of his master. It is for this reason that a differential claim to dignity represented the fundamental obstacle to liberty; and it is the stepwise transition from enslavement to emancipation that informs the course of modern history.

Vestiges of differential claims to human dignity survived the Enlightenment. Although their social privileges have been greatly circumscribed, Western European countries still feature hereditary aristocracies, and other honours, including knighthoods, are still used to signify great deeds. More perniciously, differential claims to human dignity have taken the form of differentiating among groups of people distinguished by innate or ascriptive characteristics, such as race, ethnicity, religion, gender, and sexual orientation, all of which were viewed as having a lesser claim to human dignity.

In theory, a universal claim to dignity lies at the heart of liberal republicanism. Universality is based on the assumption that all individuals have equal moral claims to have their dignity recognized and affirmed.

This recognition and affirmation manifests itself in three principal ways. The first is a recognition by individuals (subjects) that their moral claims to dignity are contingent on the moral claims of others, such that a sense of community is informed by intersubjectivity, the reciprocal duties and obligations that each are owed and owe to one another by virtue of their humanity. The second is a mandate by the state to treat all individuals equally before the law. The third is the protection of the moral claims of all individuals by legal enforcement of natural rights, which travel with all individuals from a state of nature into a civil society.

... OR THE END OF THE WORLD?

Unlike liberalism, traditional (or pre-liberal) republicanism is not imbued with a great sense of long-term optimism. Indeed, rather than leading us to the end of history, traditional republicanism seeks only to avoid the metaphorical end of the world. That political regimes would succeed one another in a predictable, recursive pattern was well understood in ancient times. In the ancient world, republicanism represented a means of, if not wholly halting the cyclical process, at least slowing it down. It was an organic conception of political life in which the virtues associated with different classes of citizens were brought to bear for the greater good.

The merits of this structure served as the very backbone of Roman republicanism (Fink 1945, ch. 1; Pocock 1975, 79). Indeed, Rome has long stood as a metaphor for republican life. Its brilliant ascent and sudden decline represented the embodiment of the cycle of both life and all that is created by humanity. Ultimately, its republican structure of mixed government could not arrest the cyclical process of regime change. Rome thus stood for most republicans as a beacon of caution, a warning that the best a republican system could hope to achieve was a longer life for the republic before it inevitably disintegrated into licentiousness and anarchy.

This inevitability was born of the fact that good governance demanded good people – men of virtue – to lead the government. But unlike self-interest – the life-blood of the liberal regime – virtue (or what we think of as obligation) is not an inexhaustible good. Virtue is vulnerable in the face of corrupting influences that entice men to put their particular interests ahead of the greater good. Ultimately, republican virtue falls victim to the corrosive influence of corruption and the regime sickens and dies.

Republican virtue has manifold characteristics, most fundamentally, fidelity to the moral good. The source and nature of this moral good is subject to some debate among traditional republicans. However, from antiquity through the Protestant Reformation there was a general consensus that moral wisdom was beyond the reach of most individuals and thus demanded good laws constructed by good men, creating a critical social distinction between the great and the many that mandated a hierarchical structure of governance. And while the civic humanism of Aristotle and the Renaissance republicans would come to be less beholden to the greatness of the great, it was not until the Enlightenment that republicanism would abandon the twin pillars of moral exogeneity and political hierarchy manifest in traditional republicanism.

In addition to the moral dimension of virtue, there is also a civic or political element that manifests itself in the imperative for social cohesion. Social cohesion does not demand social consensus, as all familiar with the rough and tumble of the Roman Republic will recall. But it does mandate a sense of what, lacking a better term, we will call "usness," or an overarching sense of belonging to a discrete and meaningful social entity. Usness serves to build trust among citizens, to provide a common set of principles that unite a people whatever else might divide them, and to define a people.[4] A sense of usness places obligations upon citizens: to be trustworthy, to contribute to the construction of (and live in accordance with) laws that derive from common principles, and to remain faithful to the principles that define a people. In other words, with usness comes the imperative for civic virtue or obligation or commitment to the greater good.[5] It is for this reason that, at least before the liberal republicanism of the modern era, usness could not accommodate factionalism, which was understood to be the very representation of corruption.

Finally, republican virtue also has a personal dimension. The hallmark of a just republican society is that every person be able to live his or her best life, the life that fulfills her unique purpose as a human being, makes life meaningful, and represents what we will later call an authentic life. Whatever we wish to call it, realizing the good life depends on a social environment that guides us toward a virtuous existence; there

4 For republicans, usness might be understood as what in modern times we call national identity and social capital.

5 Civic obligation can be measured in a number of ways. Most prominently in modern political science, we can conceive civic obligation in terms of what Almond and Verba (1965, ch. 1) call a participant political culture featuring high levels of social and political trust and high levels of political efficacy. The commitment to the greater good is sometimes understood in terms of self-sacrifice, or subordinating the private good to the public good. But for many republicans, the distinction between private and public good represents a false dichotomy. It is to the benefit of everyone that the republic be virtuous in both a moral and a civic sense.

is thus a recursive relationship between the good life and the good society. People live their most authentic life when their talents or capacities or excellences are recognized and developed through education and habituation.

The great republican breakthrough on regime mortality, and one of the philosophical modifications that eased republicanism's reconciliation with liberalism, was the shift in the emphasis on great men to the emphasis on great systems of government. This shift did not obviate the imperative for a virtuous citizenry; it merely weakened the necessity for good leadership. Although the institutional dimension of government was hardly lost on traditional republicans, it was left to more modern republicans (most famously Machiavelli, Harrington, and Madison) to delegitimize the hierarchical element of republican politics by sacrificing the great man to the impersonal mandate of government in which rules and incentive structures replaced moral wisdom as the foundation of good government.[6] Indeed, it was this purging of political hierarchy that made modern liberal republicanism so much more robust than fascism and communism, the systems of government it vanquished in the twentieth century.

While liberalism and republicanism may have found common ground with the dawning of the Enlightenment, liberal republicans today are still some distance from achieving consensus on the end of history. Pessimism about regime mortality has remained a persistent theme in modern politics. It has informed a good deal of scholarship on post-industrial liberal republics and the United States in particular. Some of this literature turns on geopolitical stability that is the result of American economic and political hegemony (Gilpin 1983; Kennedy 1988); some focuses on the inevitability of special interests overwhelming government's capacity to govern for the greater good (Brittan 1975; Olson 1982); some explores the erosion of the bonds of civil society (Glendon 1991; Taylor 1991c); and some predict demise based on deviation from sound religious or secular moral principles (Bellah 1975; Bork 1997). Among the more recent causes for concern are those associated with a looming demographic crisis (Teitelbaum and Winter 1986; Frey 1996; Peterson 1999). Indeed, unfavourable demographics, high welfare spending, and the imperative for an emergent identity politics have

---

6 It is possible to overstate this point. None of these early institutionalists discount virtue in its entirety. Indeed, generally they see institutions as a means of sustaining virtue rather than replacing it altogether. Whatever the mechanism, however, the fact remains that institutions are what keeps officials, in Harrington's words, "mannerly at the public table" (1770, 44).

served to expose liberal republics to the prospect of regime destabilization that belies the end of history.

THIS BOOK

This book does not claim to predict whatever it is that we are coming to the end of but it does seek to put the contending perspectives into context by assessing the challenges that affect the (im)mortality of modern liberal republics. To do so, it is important to establish that liberal republicanism – an oxymoron – exists as a cogent philosophy. It is just as important to understand the prevailing metaphysics that inform liberal republicanism. In other words, it is necessary to understand what a good or just liberal republican society looks like. Because justice lies at the heart of liberal republicanism, the first portion of the book is dedicated to a discussion of four dimensions – individual or social – that contribute to a liberal republican conception of justice: equality, liberty, obligation, and purpose. Confoundingly, the component philosophies of liberalism and republicanism have traditionally understood each of these four values in ways antithetical to one another.

At the risk of oversimplification, the *liberal* part of liberal republicanism – the part that distinguishes it from classical or traditional republicanism – is the imperative to universalize human dignity. It is only reasonable to speak of the liberal form of republicanism after the Enlightenment and the establishment of the principle that all individuals are equal before the law, and all have an equal moral claim to the rights and civil privileges that serve to recognize and affirm human dignity.

It is this commitment to formal equality as a means of universalizing human dignity that creates tension between liberal republicanism and culturalism. Culturalism represents a cluster of ideas that revolve around the idea that human dignity is sensitive to cultural context. Unlike the message implicit in liberal ideology that informs the commitment to formal equality – that a person is a person is a person – culturalism holds that social identity is a fundamental element of human dignity and it is therefore unreasonable to treat each individual as an equal, rights-bearing citizen without first securing the protection and preservation of the cultural identity that gives meaning to her life.

The second half of this book (chapters 5 to 9) unpacks the logic of culturalism and assesses the challenges and threats it poses to liberal republican regime stability. Culturalism constitutes a reaction against the dominance of the dominant cultural group within liberal republican societies. While culturalists understand the nature of this dominant group slightly differently, suggesting that the dominant group consists of straight White males is close enough to the mark. In challenging the dominance of the dominant cultural group, different types of culturalism are manifest. The most benign forms are dedicated to universalizing human dignity, but in a way that recognizes and affirms the importance of cultural identity as a means to human dignity.

More malignant forms of culturalism concern themselves less with the universalization of human dignity than with replacing the prevailing cultural hierarchy with a new cultural hierarchy. The problem, in other words, is not that some cultural identities are marginalized. It is that the *wrong* cultural identities are marginalized. Thus, this second, more radical strand of culturalism seeks to appropriate the dominant position enjoyed by the erstwhile dominant group.

Layout

The two halves of the book make up a complementary whole. However, given the wide range of issues covered, for readers interested only in liberal democratic theory on the one hand, or the threat to liberal democratic regimes on the other, each half can be read and understood on its own. Chapter 2 begins the process of reconciling the four component values in a liberal republican theory of justice. It is dedicated to exploring the slow emergence of a democratic theory that recognizes the moral equality of all individuals. It traces the egalitarian impulse, if we may call it that, from its roots in ancient Greece, through the Scottish and German Enlightenments. The upshot is that a general commitment to human equality was born of a fundamental shift in western civilization's understanding of moral agency. Hierarchical forms of government traditionally were predicated upon the idea of moral exogeneity (although see Ajzenstat 1985, esp. 132). That is, the moral capacity of citizens to live a good life was contingent on moral wisdom they could acquire only through the guidance and direction of great men. The great revolutionary contribution of the Enlightenment was to demonstrate that all human beings enjoyed moral self-sufficiency. More than anything else, it is the general recognition of this moral capacity that mandates the liberal republican imperative that all individuals have an equal claim to dignity merely by virtue of their humanity.

In chapter 3 the analysis turns to reconciling the three remaining values: liberty, obligation, and purpose. The chapter holds that classical liberalism conceives liberty too narrowly, and as a consequence takes too restrictive a view of obligation and purpose.[7] I take classical liberalism to

---

7 I use "liberalism" and "liberals" as heuristics as a way of articulating a cogent philosophical position that real-world thinkers tap into to some degree or another. That few thinkers beyond strict libertarians buy into the heuristic in its entirety does not affect the

reflect liberty in its negative form – that is, freedom from external con-straint which constitutes the logical extension of freedom of will (Berlin 1991).[8] By contrast, liberal republicanism holds that not all constraints are external and that indeed ignorance, fear, a lack of self-confidence, and other internal constraints represent meaningful obstacles to living good, authentic lives. Liberal republicans thus hold that enthusiasm for negative liberty must be tempered by the need for the internal freedom generally conceived as *positive* liberty.

This qualification to the nature of liberty, however, has further impli-cations. One pertains to obligation. Classical liberal contractarianism is predicated on a thin theory of obligation in which social obligations are thought of as little more than reciprocal considerations. By contrast, the imperative for positive liberty broadens the liberal republican mandate to include what we can think of as intersubjective or moral obligation – the affirmative obligation we owe to others to aid them in pursuit of a good life (see Damico 1984, esp. 548–9; Nock 1995).

Finally, classical liberalism envisions a minimalist role for the state, as one that exists to no broader purpose than to protect individual rights. However, to satisfy the thicker theory of obligation mandated by liberal republicanism, the liberal republican state is more teleological – it exists to a broader purpose than merely preserving rights.

Chapter 4 explores the liberal republican conception of justice. It con-ceives liberal republican justice broadly – accommodating theorists as diverse as Emerson and Rawls. It also looks systemically at the values and rules that sustain justice. Of particular importance are values. The

---

utility of the heuristic. Indeed, my point in Chapter 3 is that the internal logic of "liberal-ism" is so restrictive, that – as it pertains to purpose, for example – it cannot reasonably be said to exist outside of its heuristic form. To say this differently, in my quest to reconcile liberalism and republicanism into a cogent political philosophy, I make the claim that lib-eralism on its own does not really exist without borrowing from the logic of another (albeit more empirically applicable) heuristic: "republicanism."

8 External constraint is usually taken to be the product of agency, such that one pre-vents another from exercising her freedom. However, circumstances such as a lack of eco-nomic resources, for example, can also be seen as external constraints upon liberty (e.g., Gewirth 2007, 222–4). Hence Anatole France's famous point that anyone is free to sleep under a bridge, although the poor are more likely to avail themselves of the option. Skinner argues that one of the great intellectual feats of classical liberalism has been to appropriate this negative understanding of liberty to the exclusion of all other meanings. Thus, "it would be no exaggeration to say that this assumption – that the only coherent idea of liberty is the negative one of being unconstrained – has underpinned the entire development of modern contractarian political thought" (Skinner 1984, 194). More bluntly, Flew maintains that in liberal thought it is this negative conception of liberty that "wears the trousers." (2001, 9; see also Geise 1989, 837, although see MacCallum 1991; Hababi 1995).

chapter identifies three types of values, classified as primary, secondary, and tertiary. *Primary* values are common to all countries of a particular regime type. For example, all liberal republics are defined by common primary values. These include the imperative for rights, reflecting a people's collective right to determine how they are constituted and governed; commitment to the equality of all human beings; a sense of moral obligation manifested along a number of dimensions, including tolerance, freedom to participate in public life; and an affirmative mandate on the part of both state and society to establish the sorts of rules, tolerant institutions, and reasonable practices that provide every individual with opportunities to make optimal and authentic life choices.

Secondary values, by contrast, are particularistic. They are the values that inform a country's national identity and create a sense of common citizenship, or usness. Secondary values represent the common purpose that unite otherwise disparate people into a sense of intersubjective obligation that constitutes nationhood. These are the values of a civil religion; they inform the sort of bridging social capital that extends a sense of usness to even diverse groups of citizens.

As with culturalists, liberal republicans have been cognizant of the imperative to ensure that usness not be construed too narrowly. *Tertiary* values are thus a hedge against the conflation of usness with sameness; they represent the particular values of discrete subnational cultural communities. This is why, for example, particularly in large and culturally diverse nations, liberal republics have relied on federalism to preserve the tertiary values of geographic, or spatial, communities.

Chapter 5 highlights the specific differences between liberal republican and culturalist theories of justice. In particular, it focuses on the most common type of culturalism – *multi*culturalism. Both liberal republicanism and multiculturalism accept the imperative for tertiary values. However, unlike liberal republicans, who seek to preserve the tertiary values of geographic, or spatial, communities, culturalists are concerned with preserving the values of ascriptively informed, *essentialist* communities. Multiculturalists hold that spatial representation of subnational values simply reinforces cultural dominance by an ascriptive group that informs the dominant cultural values of all or most relevant spatial communities in liberal republican societies.

Even more problematic from the multiculturalist perspective is liberal republicanism's understanding of *in*justice, which is conceived wholly as a product of individual agency. This understanding implies that because the injustice is agent-specific, so too is the remedy. By contrast, multiculturalists understand injustice in structural or cultural terms. Here injustice is inherent in the internalized norms and values that, however unconsciously, colour the cultural status quo, reflecting the worldview of the dominant culture, creating an understanding of the (large N) Normal, and assigning the tertiary values of subordinate cultures to the abnormal or marginal. Thus, culturalists understand liberal republicanism to be overly narrow and insufficiently rigorous in its commitment to tertiary values. Put differently, liberal republicans can be thought to privilege usness (secondary values) over differentiation (tertiary values), whereas multicultural justice reverses the order.

There are real costs to this. Kenneth and Mamie Clark's famous doll tests of the 1940s and 1950s are testament to the injustice of community values that encourage all citizens to measure up as best they can to the ideals of Whiteness, maleness, and straightness as a means to success in the various dimensions of public life. The hegemony of the Normal contributes to other social pathologies. One is negatively biased self-assessment of task-competence. Closely related is the so-called stereotype threat, whereby the fear of reinforcing negative stereotypes of one's own cultural group places added, often overwhelming, pressure on members of subordinate communities. Finally, a third pathology is that the cultural dominance of a single cultural group forces the members of subordinate cultural communities to choose between material, political, and economic success on the one hand, and preservation of their essentialist cultural norms on the other. It is worth noting that since members of the dominant culture are far less likely to suffer from cultural self-hatred, or inefficacious views of task-competence, or stereotype threat, or a trade-off between achievement and cultural identity, a strong case can be made that liberal republican justice does an incomplete job of universalizing dignity at best.

Chapter 6 is a systematic examination of culturalism. It conceives culturalism as a continuum along which multiculturalism represents the benign polar position. The other pole is occupied by the most malignant form of culturalism, which I call *versoculturalism*. Versoculturalism represents a cultural revolution in the sense that it seeks to displace one set of (regime-defining) primary values with another. It is versoculturalists who represent the emergent threat to the potential for regime immortality implicit in the end of history.

Intermediary positions along the continuum bear mention here as well. The first is *cultural separatism*. Cultural separatists are those whose cultural ambitions are either inconsistent with those of the dominant culture or that have been rejected by the dominant culture and who seek to maintain cultural separation as a means of preserving cultural identity. Although cultural separatism suggests an underlying cultural pathology, it is generally not a threat to regime stability. In extreme cases, however, cultural separatism can manifest itself in a desire for secession, which obviously increases the threat level for liberal republics.

A second intermediate position is *status-seeking*. Status seekers aim to demonstrate the superiority of their claim to cultural recognition – and the political perquisites that come with it – over other subordinate cultural communities. For this reason, status-seeking can occasionally serve as a gateway for more radical forms of culturalism as marginalized cultural communities compete in what Brodie (1996) calls the "market for status."

On the more radical side of the continuum we have what we might think of as *cultural contestants*. Contestants are those who seek either to appropriate a country's secondary values, effectively becoming the new dominant cultural community, or to set up their cultural values as a parallel dominant culture. The marginalization of the French culture in Louisiana is an example of the first; the "two solitudes" of English and French Canada is an example of the second.

Chapters 7 and 8 amplify the points made in the preceding chapter. While versoculturalism and multiculturalism are presented as discrete manifestations of culturalism, chapters 7 and 8 also highlight the interactive effect, particularly in the context of increasing immigration in liberal republican societies. This interactive effect can manifest itself in different ways. One is that benign forms of culturalism, such as multiculturalism, can serve as effective camouflage for versoculturalism. Because cultural revolutionaries rarely advertise their presence in host societies, the benign forms of culturalism can be a useful way to mobilize a versoculturalist constituency while minimizing the risk of a cultural backlash in the host society. Second, versoculturalists may not start their political lives as cultural revolutionaries; they may emerge through progressive radicalization until frustrated multiculturalists come to see cultural appropriation as the only means of realizing their cultural objectives.

Chapter 7 traces the rise of culturalism through the civil rights and post-material eras and illustrates the relationship between culturalism, welfare, fertility rates, immigration, and the decline of the assimilative imperative in liberal republics. It also explores two case studies. The first assesses the effect of Mexican immigration on secondary values in the United States. On the face of it, Mexican immigration represents the threat of cultural contestation. Since the immigration reform of 1965, Mexican immigration into the United States has dwarfed that of any other country. Hispanicization of education and media, slower rates of acculturation, high levels of heritage-cultural affinity, and geographic clustering all speak to the threat that Mexican immigration might well be a prelude to the construction of a parallel set of secondary values in

America. On the other hand, there is evidence that by the third or fourth generation, two-thirds to three-quarters of Mexican immigrants have become thoroughly acculturated. Indeed, if we look at patriotism as an indicator of usness, Americans of Mexican heritage are indistinguishable from members of the dominant community.

The second case study examines the threat of appropriation of primary values through Islamic immigration in Europe. Here the stakes are higher and the prospects, while not yet dire, are grounds for some concern. At issue is the cultural dominance of liberal republican values on the one hand, and fundamentalist sharia law on the other. A significant cultural divide exists between host and (Islamic) heritage cultures in Europe. It is not just episodic extremist violence that is troublesome. The value cleavage is reinforced by a class divide that sees almost half of young Muslims unemployed in France and Germany. By the end of the twentieth century, Muslims in the Netherlands were over five times as likely to be unemployed as native Dutch. Almost half of British Muslims believe that there is a natural conflict between being a devout Muslim and living in a modern society. Many European cities are sufficiently ghettoized that there are defined neighbourhoods that police and municipal officials have more or less ceded to Muslim leaders, who have proclaimed non-Muslims to be unwelcome.

The European response to Islamic immigration has been characterized by separate, although equally problematic, strategies. Some countries (France and Germany are historically good examples) long maintained a sort of cultural chauvinism that relegated Muslims to the socio-political margins of society. Others, and here we may speak of Britain and the Netherlands as paradigmatic examples, took an opposite tack, resisting any form of acculturation that obliged members of the heritage community to accept the values of the host society. In light of the manifest failure of both strategies, European countries have more actively sought to integrate Muslims into the cultural mainstream. Given the entrenched nature of Islamic fundamentalism in many European cities, however, it promises to be a long, hard battle for hearts and minds in Europe.

Chapter 8 explores the relationship between rules and values. Two sorts of rules are used in the governance of liberal republican societies: constitutional rules and legislative rules. Legislative rules give substance to the (largely) procedural constitutional rules and have many virtues. They encourage citizens to participate in politics. They mitigate the effects of factionalization in that they encourage the construction of issue-specific social alliances. They promote compromise by permitting issue linkage so that groups make concessions on one issue in exchange for concessions on another. And finally, legislative rules militate against the stakes associated with victory along any one issue dimension. Indeed, legislative rules are impermanent and can accommodate shifting social attitudes, making political debate and dialogue particularly efficacious.

Constitutional rules are of two types. The first is formal, the second informal. Formal constitutional rules are those constructed through constitutional framing or formal amendment to the constitution. Informal constitutional rules are conventional or jurisprudential. As with legislative rules, informal constitutional rules provide substantive interpretations to procedural rules. In chapter 8, status seekers are presented as those who prefer constitutional rules to legislative rules so they can identify which cultural groups are entitled to special recognition and affirm their cultural importance, and how that special recognition manifests itself. The chapter explores the implications of constitutional status-seeking, particularly as it pertains to the role of courts in gratifying the demands of status-seeking groups. Specifically, it examines two issue areas – abortion and free speech – discussing the relative merits of regulating such issues through legislative or constitutional rules.

The conclusion briefly examines another potential challenge to liberal republicanism – the idea that the philosophy is not as cohesive as I have considered it to be here. Indeed, a growing cultural self-absorption – noted by both Bellah (1975) and Bork (1997) – appears to be somewhat eroding the moral obligation required by liberal republicanism. While this challenge is important to consider, it is equally clear that the history of liberal republicanism has seen periodic ebbing and flowing between periods of more atomistic and more communitarian cultural preferences.

The book concludes that the perception of danger can be distorted by the immediacy of the threat. Thus, the culturalist challenge may be magnified by our current perspective. States have always faced challenges to their security, and culturalism could conceivably become a serious one. The threat is not all that menacing at this stage, but that is not to say that distant potential threats bear no watching. The book is not a clarion call for reinvigorated nativism or chauvinism of any variety. Culturalism is a challenge to liberal republicanism, but (at least in its most benign, multiculturalist, form) it can actually serve to strengthen liberal republics by emphasizing the imperative to ensure that liberal republics do not define what it means to be "people like us" too narrowly. Indeed, it is not going too far to say that benign culturalism is an ameliorative to liberal republicanism, although an ameliorative that brings with it the sorts of challenges this book explores in greater depth.

2

Greatness, Goodness, and Equality

IN THE LAST CHAPTER I SUGGESTED that liberal republicanism is an oxymoron. It is collective-individualism, hierarchical-equality, ends-oriented process, self-interested obligation, and restricted liberty. Traditionally and unsurprisingly, therefore, liberalism and republicanism have been treated as discrete political philosophies that operate at best in an uneasy detente (e.g., Hartz 1955; Pocock 1975; MacIntyre 1981; Geise 1989; Skinner 1990; Ward 1991; Rodgers 1992; McCormick 2003). As such, before we can meaningfully discuss the challenges that liberal republics face, it is necessary to establish that liberal republicanism itself is a meaningful concept. I will undertake that task in this chapter and the next.

Before wading into the conceptual morass of liberal republicanism, it is important to establish some basic assumptions. As stated in chapter 1, I use the term liberalism to encompass all philosophies that assign primacy to liberty. That is, liberals privilege liberty ahead of all competing social values. Unless otherwise qualified, I use liberal and liberalism in the ideal-typical, classical sense.[1] Liberalism is about individual self-determination. This has implications for both capacity and opportunity. With respect to *capacity*, liberalism is predicated on the assumption that individuals are innately capable of self-fulfillment by virtue of their own moral agency. In other words, liberals reject the traditional

---

1 Defining liberalism is notoriously difficult. Walsh suggests that liberalism's "self-understanding from the start has been defined by the opponent to which it is opposed. First it was feudalism and aristocratic privilege, then it was absolutism and arbitrary rule, and in our own time the forces of totalitarian democracy. Deprived of a foe it seems perennially inclined to relax its discipline .... The inability to maintain anything like an equilibrium, in other words, is a problem that lies deep within the nature of the liberal ethos" (Walsh 1997, 22–3).

republican idea that moral wisdom is external to most of humanity. With respect to *opportunity*, liberals understand freedom in its negative form – as freedom from external constraint in all life choices that do not directly and negatively affect the rights of others. Taken together, capacity and opportunity permit individuals to determine for themselves their own conceptions of the good life – the life that permits us to fulfill the human condition. Ultimately, capacity and opportunity obviate the imperative for the sort of political hierarchy that long characterized traditional republicanism.

The assumption that individuals are morally endogenous – capable of determining their own means to the good life – has implications for civil society. Liberals envision a social context in which individual interaction is mediated by mutual self-interest and in which rational individuals owe one another little more than an obligation to uphold the laws that protect their rights. Because society exists simply as a vehicle that facilitates the fulfillment of self-sufficient individuals, it retains a narrow social purpose the scope of which is procedural and not substantive. Liberalism is thus means-oriented and not ends-oriented.

By contrast, republicanism – once again, I use the term republican in its traditional or classical sense, unless otherwise qualified – is a collectivist philosophy that mandates a first-order duty to virtue, conceived here broadly as moral obligation. Republicanism holds that virtue is acquired through laws that reflect moral principles best distilled through the wisdom of political elites. Indeed, because republicans do not see everyone as equally capable of acquiring wisdom, they believe that the governing process should represent a balance between those who propose laws and those who ratify them. Those who propose are the great, imbued with moral wisdom and the capacity to govern. Those who ratify are the many, with insufficient capacity for the moral wisdom required for good governance. In contrast to classical liberalism then, traditional republicanism is both organic and hierarchical; organic in the sense that societies operate best when individuals contribute their various talents in the mode to which they are best suited, and hierarchical in the sense that governing elites acquire their status through general recognition of their superior moral wisdom.

Traditional republicanism differs from liberalism in other ways as well. With respect to liberty, for example, republicans are less concerned with negative liberty than the (positive) liberty that represents freedom from internal constraints. Whether these constraints are ignorance, or fear, or a lack of self-confidence, they preclude individuals from making their best choices. Liberation in the positive sense demands a citizenry dedicated to inculcating enlightenment, security, and confidence.

Such dedication demands a broader theory of obligation than does liberalism. The thin theory of obligation that informs liberalism mandates citizens merely to respect one another's rights and autonomy. The thicker republican theory of obligation has implications for the role of the state. The thinness of the liberal theory of obligation demands a state with limited social purpose. Specifically, the liberal state exists as a sort of night watchman, standing guard over the rights of its citizens (Nozick 1974, 25). By contrast, the thicker republican theory of obligation brings with it broader social purpose. The state serves to coordinate the affirmative obligation that citizens have toward one another born of the imperative to protect liberty in the positive sense.

To summarize, liberalism and republicanism can be said to differ along four crucial dimensions – equality, liberty, obligation, and purpose. If there is to be a meaningful theory of liberal republicanism, it must be demonstrated how these four differences have been reconciled. Such reconciliation has occurred in two distinct ways. The first is philosophical evolution. With respect to equality, reconciliation demanded acceptance of the idea that individuals are moral agents – that is, that all individuals are endowed with innate moral capacity. Such acceptance was a long time in coming, and this chapter traces its historical evolution from antiquity through the Enlightenment.

The second way reconciliation occurs is logical and empirical. Liberal democracies simply are not structured according to the principles of classical liberalism. In other words, a truly classical liberal society could not function without borrowing critical assumptions from republican theory. The assumption that individuals are self-sufficient in living their best lives is based on the assumption that individuals are inherently free from internal constraints. This assumption in turn permits the thin theory of liberal obligation and the limited social purpose of the liberal state. Chapter 3 is dedicated to demonstrating the perils of such an assumption. In doing so, it argues that liberalism must accept a broader theory of obligation than liberals are willing to concede. Finally, chapter 3 argues that the limited social purpose of the night watchman state would not permit it to make reasonable decisions in protecting individual rights. For now, however, I would like to focus on the evolution of equality. In particular, this chapter focuses on the progressive acceptance of egalitarianism in both republican philosophy and Christian theology.

Historically, both philosophy and Christian theology have adopted a dim view of human moral capacity. The frailty of this capacity – the idea that moral agency must be infused through law or divine grace – mandated social and political hierarchy as a delivery mechanism for goodness. Beginning with the secular humanism of the Renaissance and the

Protestantism of the Reformation, however, republican and Christian views on human moral competence – and hence equality – began to change. This change culminated in the fundamental assumption that all individuals are morally self-sufficient. That is, each individual enjoys an innate moral capacity, which in turn precludes the imperative for political hierarchy.

This latent egalitarianism was bolstered by the arrival of the commercial age. Commercialism not only broadened opportunities for social and political advancement, but operated according to the strictly egalitarian and (as is argued below) virtue-enhancing rules of the free market. The chapter concludes with a brief examination of the early American republic and its synthesis of the republican, Christian, and liberal values discussed in this chapter.

THE ANCIENT AND MEDIEVAL WORLD: GREATNESS, GOODNESS, AND THE IMPERATIVE FOR HIERARCHY

In the ancient Greek and Roman worlds, republicans understood political status in terms of honour and honour in terms of virtuous action. Honour was a spur to greatness. Demonstrating great virtue represented qualification to hold high political office so the most virtuous men competed with one another to demonstrate their virtue. Reserving high office for those most fit to occupy it ensured that virtue seeped downward from the top, infusing the laws and social structure with the character of greatness (Cicero 2008a, bk. I, 2; bk. V, 4; 2008b, bk. II, 15–17; 1891, *De Har.* 19).

Typically, greatness was understood in a physical sense, e.g., the great demonstrated the courage and leadership and judgment to wage effective warfare. Such men inspired confidence and made for effective leaders, particularly during the pre-social Homeric age in which chieftains enjoyed no formal–legal bases of support. Classical Greek political philosophy challenged the physical basis of greatness, locating it instead in metaphysical excellence. Greatness, to put this differently, was a byproduct of *goodness*. Goodness, in turn, was manifest in love of knowledge (philosophy) or moral wisdom.

The obvious prototype is Socrates. The Socratic philosopher is a statesman; his objective is justice, and the means to justice is good governance. Justice for Socrates is not to be found, as the aristocratic devotees of Homer would have it, in the ability of the strong to assert themselves (Plato 1974, 338c, 358a). Nor does Socrates agree with Glaucon that justice is but a shield protecting the weak from the strong (358e–9e). Both circumstances represent deviations from justice in its true Form

(Saxonhouse 2012, 43). Instead, justice is born of a balanced soul and knowledge of the self, processes aided by sound social construction and good laws.

For Socrates, sound social construction mandates a division of labour in which some govern and some are governed. The republic exists for the public good, but the public good does not mandate collective governance. As Plato's Eleatic Stranger echoes, justice suffers from too many hands in the construction as surely as from too much rigidity in the law. From this perspective true justice is not to be found in the evolutionary give-and-take of democratic politics but is reflected in the knowledge of a singular philosopher whose wisdom and knowledge of the properties of justice exceed the democratic model in coherence of design. More scientist than politician, the philosopher-king is bound and guided by the unchanging principles of truth. Ideally, the philosopher-king's authority comes not from his formal–legal power, but from the legitimacy that flows from his singular goodness (Plato 1992, 293b–6a; 300a–e, 305e).

Socrates makes no bones about his hostility to democracy. And he is too much of a realist to be sanguine about the prospects for government by a true philosopher-king. It was left to Aristotle to articulate more practicable forms of republican government. Aristotle is more open to egalitarian government. Indeed, in the Aristotelian ideal, the good society is one in which citizens are equal in their capacities to govern and be governed and would do each in their turn. Unfortunately, Aristotle sees precious few societies capable of realizing this ideal. More practical is the sort of mixed (aristocratic–democratic) governance espoused by traditional republicans.

However much he might flirt with egalitarianism, Aristotle is fundamentally an elitist. Where a truly great man is present, Aristotle suggests it is in the interests of all to make him king. Such a man cannot abide being governed by his inferiors. He is, Aristotle proclaims, a law unto himself. He is sufficiently magnanimous (or great-souled) that his greatness represents a social good that cannot be qualified or bounded by lesser men (Aristotle 1962, 1284a, 13–15; 1999, 1124a, 1).

Aristotle conceives magnanimity not as a discrete virtue, but as an adornment of the virtues. One is magnanimous when she is peerless in the perfection of the moral virtues (1999, 1124a, 1). From our modern egalitarian vantage point, the great-souled man is anachronistic. Stuffy and condescending, he is in point of fact a bit hard to take. He is also a mass of contradictions. Thus, while he possesses the capacity for greatness in his actions, he does not bestir himself save for the worthiest of causes. He is a social benefactor, but this is because it is proper for superior men to have others in their debt. By the same token, being a recipient of another's beneficence causes him shame. He recognizes his own worth and expects to be honoured for it in a fashion commensurate with his greatness. He therefore despises honour from those unworthy of honouring him, or for causes unworthy of his greatness but will assent to honour from excellent people. However, his pleasure will be tempered by his recognition that although those honouring him are themselves excellent and honour him to the best of their ability, in fact they can offer no honour truly sufficient to his peerless virtue. He takes the time to seek to impress those whose esteem he values with his greatness, but he does not waste his time seeking to impress ordinary men, since to do so would be as vulgar as for a man of great strength to demonstrate that strength to the weak. The magnanimous man is brutally frank with his opinions, having both the courage of his convictions and an indifference to the opinions of others. He considers himself above the fray of ordinary social actions or interactions, but cannot permit himself to be governed by lesser men. He prides himself on his self-sufficiency. He is rational and not emotive, recognizing that it is petty to take small things to heart (1999, 1123a–5a, 16).

The great-souled man epitomizes the Aristotelian ideal of self-sufficiency and rejection of the worldly and pleasurable in favour of the virtuous. His fulfillment, to put this differently, is centred in the soul, not the body (Arnhart 1983, 265). Politically, the magnanimous man was a new-model hero; a reconstruction of the old Homeric aristocratic role model. Stripped (perhaps) of his extraordinary physical capacities, he was endowed with exceptional metaphysical ones. The great-souled man was not just great, he was greatly good.[2] He was also central to the ideal of ancient republican governance. Aristotelian magnanimity epitomized the imperative for authority to be vested in the republic's best men. Cicero sees such greatness in terms of heroic apotheosis. For example, he has Scipio praise the wisdom of the proverb that "the great public servants should be deemed divine by birth as well as in ability" (Cicero 2008a, bk. II, 4). Like the Hesiodic hero on the Isles of the Blessed, in his dream Scipio is advised by the ghost of his grandfather that "for everyone who has saved and served his country and helped it to grow, a

---

2　To define the magnanimous man as greatly good creates something of a conundrum insofar as I understand goodness in the Socratic sense, that virtue is its own reward. On the other hand, the magnanimous man also expects to be recognized and honoured for his greatness. This is the issue that Cicero (1974) seeks to come to terms with in *On Duties* (see Arnhart 1983, 268–71).

sure place is set aside in heaven where he may enjoy a life of eternal bliss" (bk. VI, 13).

Equality in the Abyss of Unlikeness and the Christian Re-birth of Magnanimity

The magnanimous man was also influential in the development of Christian theology through the Middle Ages. For Augustine he represented what was wrong with the ideal of self-sufficiency, symbolizing as it does the falling away from God. By contrast, for Aquinas he was a symbol of God's greatness insofar as his greatness was imbued by God, but his stature among ordinary men was analogous to God's superiority to mankind as a whole. Christianity inserts itself into the narrative as a leading force that, however unintentionally, brings equality to the forefront of modern political ideas.

The general commitment to social and political hierarchy that characterized the traditional republicanism of the ancient world survived into the Christian era, albeit in vastly different form. From the early Christian perspective, the greatness of the pagan great man – Homeric warrior, Socratic philosopher-king, Aristotelian great-souled man, or Roman statesman – was pitiable in his arrogance. Master of the natural order the pagan great man may have been. But his ignorance of the order of grace merely magnified the smallness of his cosmic perspective.[3]

In metaphorically distinguishing Jerusalem from Rome as symbols of the will, Augustine dismisses the pagan city of man as the region of unlikeness (1943, bk. VII, 10).[4] This unlikeness reflects man's alienation

---

3 This is manifest, for example, in the political authority vested in the magnanimous man, which constitutes a postlapsarian deviation from God's intention that man should exercise dominion over only the irrational creatures in the order of nature (Augustine 1943, bk. XIX, 14–15) This political authority is distinct from the Godly authority manifest in guidance or encouragement (*consulere*), which is all that would be socially necessary in a state of innocence (see Markus 1965, esp. 70–2; although see Weithman 1992; Cornish 2010).

4 While Augustine respects the patriotic Roman's love of country, he admonishes him for his misplaced values and for his belief that any earthly city could serve as a substitute for the fulfillment that comes only from God (Roberts 2016, esp. 117–19). By contrast, rather than occupying a purely physical space, the *ekklesia* represents a community of the faithful, called out by God from the sinfulness of the world into association with the baptized (Black 1997, 648–9). The region of unlikeness reflects the separation of man from God after being cast out of the Garden of Eden. Man's quest is therefore one of reunification of the soul with God. The term no doubt comes from Plato's abyss of unlikeness (1992, 273d), which in the *Statesman* he describes as the periodic imperative of the gods to rescue the universe from the abyss as it spins away from the heavenly host.

from God, manifest in a sense of self-sufficiency and misplaced satisfaction in pride of one's achievement (Arnhart 1983, 271–2). Yet such self-satisfaction is antithetical to the universal human desire for eternal peace, realizable only through love of God and obligation to one's fellow man to encourage him in that love (Markus 1965, 69–70). Indeed, only to the extent that these virtues prevail does Augustine feel it is reasonable to speak of a true and just republic (Cornish 2010, 140–1, 144; Roberts 2016, 121–2). Christian civilization is characterized by its fidelity to the serenity of the one true God who, peerless and omnipotent, is a God of creation, not dominion. The prevailing virtues in such a society are compassion, forgiveness, love, and piety (Barron 2007, 50). Magnanimity and pride have no place in the city of God insofar as virtue is born of humility – a recognition of the equality of men in their vast smallness when compared with the greatness that is God's alone (St. Augustine 1887, bk. XIV, 4, 11–13).[5]

Augustine can admire the self-confidence of the magnanimous man, but not his self-satisfaction. Confidence elevates the heart of the magnanimous and this is to the good. But it becomes pernicious when it begins to inform pride. It is destructive when it directs esteem toward the self rather than God. It is deceptive when it provokes men to set themselves apart from other men on the fictive perception of their greatness (bk. XIV, 13). What even the best of the pagan great lacked, then, was the true piety requisite to human perfection, realizable only through the grace of God. Ultimately, Augustine reserves differential status for the next plane of existence. The greatest of men set themselves apart by virtue of their humility, piety, and even their martyrdom. Great men such as these recognize that their greatness is not of their own making, but rather is the gift of God through grace. Differences among men acquire meaning in the spiritual order of grace, not the terrestrial order of nature. Indeed, terrestrial existence serves no meaningful end beyond aiding the soul on its ultimate quest for likeness – to be reunited with God in the host of heaven.

Yet however high-minded the ideal of privileging the order of grace above the order of nature – of eschewing the worldly in favour of the spiritual – the reality is that even good Christians of the Middle Ages were drawn inextricably back to the worldly order. The Christian

---

5 By contrast, the recent sack of Rome constituted the deserts of a pagan theology born of conflict among the gods in a quest for divine domination. After all, Rome itself was named for Romulus who slew his own brother in the quest for temporal dominance (Barron 2007, 48–9).

humanism of the late Middle Ages and early Renaissance sought to reconcile the worldly with the spiritual. Christian humanism was a celebration of the temporal world in proper cosmic perspective. It rejected Augustine's equal nothingness of man in an abyss of unlikeness, and did so as thoroughly as it rejected the self-sufficiency of Aristotle's magnanimous man. From the perspective of Christian humanism, man's prerogative on Earth was no more to prostrate himself in his humility than it was to arrogantly appropriate credit for the greatness that was, in point of fact, but another example of God's munificence.

As towering a figure as Augustine was, it was Aquinas who sought to situate magnanimity in the context of the Christian virtues. For Aquinas, magnanimity was not a reflection of excessive and sinful pride. To the contrary, it represented temperate virtue. The problem with the prevailing Augustinian Christian view of magnanimity lay in conceiving it as spoiled humility. In truth, Aquinas claims, magnanimity and humility are complementary virtues, spoiled respectively by pusillanimity and pride. Humility represents man's recognition of his cosmic inferiority to God. Magnanimity has a countervailing effect. It elevates the soul from the despair born of unlikeness, exhorting it to great things through right reason and the gift of God's grace (Aquinas 1947, II–II, Q. 161, Art. 1, ad. 3, Art. 2, ad. 1–2).

Far from being equal in their nothingness, great men are natural leaders of men. The magnanimous man is fully cognizant of his own worth and expects others to recognize and affirm that worth through honour. Were he to fail to recognize his greatness he would be pusillanimous; his temerity would prevent him from the accomplishments reflective of the redemption of God's gifts. But in his magnanimity, he retains a cosmic perspective. Even as he recognizes his superiority to other men, he exalts God as vastly superior to himself. Magnanimous though he is in the temporal world, spiritually he is virtuous in his humility to God. Given such a cosmic perspective, it cannot be magnanimity that spoils humility. Instead, the culprit is pride. Pride bespeaks a deficiency of humility whereby man is induced to think too highly of his cosmic station. He is prideful in his smug self-satisfaction, mistaking the gifts granted to him by God as a manifestation of his own self-sufficiency, and failing to recognize the relationship between his accomplishments and the power of grace (Aquinas 1947, II–II, Q. 110, Art. 2, ad. 3, Q. 129, Art 6, Q. 133, Art. 2, ad. 4, Q.162, Art, 1, ad. 3).

Aquinas's Christian humanism was important in its legitimation of hierarchy and social privilege at a time when feudalism and hereditary nobility were becoming institutionalized across Europe (Archibald 1949;

George and George 1955; although for a qualification see Herdt 2016).[6] This claim to hierarchy began to be challenged during the Renaissance by those who can be loosely classified as secular humanists.[7] The emergence of secular humanism was not radical. Most secular humanists saw no reason to challenge the cosmic hierarchy that obliged even great men to seek perfection of the Christian virtues. To the extent there was a schism in the ranks of humanists it was between the scholastic adherents to Aristotelian and Thomist principles and resurgent republicans who located virtue in action rather than wisdom.

The neo-republicans of the Renaissance were not conditioned to question the socio-political hierarchy of the temporal space. Theirs was a mandate to universalize – or at least greatly enhance – human dignity and to recognize that human dignity was of man's own making. Secular humanists insisted on the liberty to pursue the celebration of human dignity. But there was no imperative to *equalize* that dignity; or to suggest that human beings were in any meaningful sense morally interchangeable (Kristeller 1939; 1979, ch. 7; Pico della Mirandola 1965; Colish 1971; Pocock 1975, esp. 58–60; Skinner 1978a, ch. 4; Cassirer 2000, esp. 83–4; McCrudden 2008). Indeed, it was not until Machiavelli – himself no great advocate of human equality – that an egalitarian dimension appeared in European secular humanism.

Machiavelli and the Changing Face of Republican Virtue

What makes Machiavelli stand out as the most important secular humanist of this brief narrative is his contention that while human beings are not morally interchangeable, they are to a great extent *immorally* interchangeable. Machiavelli begins from the premise that energy dedicated to the perfection of moral virtues is socially unproductive. Certainly there exist greatly good men whose virtue could be brought to bear for the social good. But they are rare. So rare in fact that to count upon their emergence when they are most needed is tantamount to risking the fate of the Roman Republic. Rome had long relied upon its greatly good

---

6 As with Augustine, Aquinas distinguishes between tyrannical dominion of some men over others and the counterfactual governance that would have existed without man's fall. However, he also accepts the Aristotelian distinction between the great and the ordinary in their capacity for greater intellect and wisdom and in the appropriateness of the great exercising political authority (Weithman 1992, 361).

7 Humanism was an affirmation of man's capacity to enjoy and make his terrestrial existence meaningful, not merely to endure it (Bayertz 1996, 73–5). Such capacity was born of liberation of the will from the determinism imposed in no small measure by Augustinian Christianity (Trinkaus 1949; Rowe 1964).

men, but in the final turbulent generations of the republic precious few such men were to be found.

Machiavelli's good republic is not a product of social architecture or of good moral citizenry. The commonwealth does not rely on the moral goodness of those who make its laws. Instead, the truly good republic is one that divorces civic virtue from morality, adopting the hard-headed distinction between what philosophers might want men to be, and men as they really are (Hirschman 1997, 13–14). Machiavelli agrees with the traditional republican premise that the masses are fickle, tempestuous, corruptible, and vulnerable to manipulation by demagogues (1975, I, 47, 53, 57–8). The problem is that elites are not a whole lot more virtuous than the masses. And they are a lot more dangerous. A "licentious and turbulent populace, when a good man can obtain a hearing, can easily be brought to behave itself," Machiavelli asserts. But "there is no one to talk to a bad prince, nor is there any remedy except the sword" (I. 58).

With the exception of the very rare, truly great man, there is nothing distinctively virtuous about the governing class. Human nature does not discriminate between classes when it comes to caprice and corruption. Or to the extent that it does, Machiavelli claims, warming to his theme to the point of hyperbole, it is among the masses that prudent judgment and stability are more likely to be found. Hence, in ancient Rome, "[n]ot without good reason is the voice of the populace likened to that of God; for public opinion is remarkably accurate in its prognostications, so much so that it seems as if the populace by some hidden power discerned the evil and the good that was to befall it" (I. 58). Rather than the elite saving the masses from themselves, in other words, the opposite comes closer to the truth.

In the vast majority of circumstances, moral virtue is more a function of compulsion than nobility. Machiavelli therefore prescribes strict limits on the length of time that elites hold office lest their love of power overwhelm whatever moral virtues they bring to bear in aid of good government; similarly, he is anxious to decouple such moral virtue as does exist from hereditary privilege.[8]

---

8 Aristocratic privilege is entitlement born of past deeds, or worse, the deeds of past men. Hence, Giovane Buonaccorso's claim that true nobility "lies not in the glory of another man, or in the flitting goods of fortune, but in a man's own virtue," a product of his own "labour and desert" (quoted in Skinner 1978a, 81; this Ciceronian (2008a, II.30–8) theme is repeated among numerous Florentine writers; see, for example, Guicciardini 1994, 115–16; Bonadeo 1969; Pocock 1975, ch. 5; Burckhardt 1990, esp. 231–3; Skinner 2002, 131–4; Najemy 2003, 94). Machiavelli is even more pointed in

The implicit suggestion that elites are substitutable takes Machiavelli and his successors down a very different path from those who preceded them – one that suggests that virtue is determined by the quality of a country's constitution not the character of its greatest men (1975, I. 3, 18, 42, 47). To the extent that Machiavelli depersonalizes politics he opens the door (without actually walking through it) to the development of a nascent egalitarian code.[9] Men could still strive for glory – and indeed that ambition properly constrained remains a good thing. But when the greater good comes to rely less on the character of those who would freely provide it, and more on the compunction imposed by well-constituted laws, the imperative for social privilege becomes more difficult to justify.[10]

The upshot for Machiavelli is that elite corruption moves the republic ever further from whatever moral virtue is associated with its founding principles. It is institutions, as well as the masses committed to the legitimacy of those institutions, that helps slow the drift (1975, III. 1).[11] Goodness, then, is not a product of mass deference; just the opposite, in fact. It is mass efficacy and impudence that keeps elites virtuous (1975, I. 17). Or more precisely in Machiavelli's worldview, prevents their inherent capacity for corruption from ruining the regime (e.g., 1975, I.7–8, 24, III.1; Pangle 1988, 62–63; Honneth 1996, ch.1; Maddox 2002, 541; McCormick 2003, 626–8).

---

castigating the privilege afforded to a landed gentry – "those who live in idleness on the abundant revenues derived from their estates, without having anything to do either with their cultivation or with other forms of labour essential to life" (1975, I.55). For Machiavelli, the gentry "are a pest in any republic and in any province," particularly when they "have castles under their command and subjects who are under their obedience" (I.55).

9 The logic is extant in the work of Francesco Guicciardini who, despite his manifest elitism, comes to the same conclusion: A closed oligarchy cannot be reconciled with liberty. Thus, Pocock interprets: "If authority is to be free it must be public; if it is to be public it must be impersonal; if it is to be impersonal the group conferring it must be over a certain size" (1975, 127).

10 This point is amplified by Trenchard and Gordon, who see the pageantry and honour bestowed upon elites as but an artifact of their offices: "[A]ll this pageantry is not designed for those who wear it. They carry about them the dignity of the commonwealth: The honours which they receive are honours paid to the publick, and they themselves are only the pillars and images upon which national trophies are hung; for when they are divested of these insignia, no more respect and homage is due to them, than what results from their own virtue and merit" (1995, 1. 20).

11 And although we have to move beyond Machiavelli here, the logic is merely an extension of this idea: it is in law that individuals find themselves more equally placed, both with respect to the constraints upon their actions and upon the privileges – rights if you will – associated with citizenship (Pocock 1981, 360–1).

THE PROTESTANT REFORMATION, THE LIBERAL ENLIGHTENMENT, AND THE COMMERCIAL AGE

If, as Machiavelli claims, elites are not a reliable source of moral goodness, the question turns to what the source of that goodness is. Two answers present themselves: God and innate human capacity. The idea that God is the source of moral goodness is not particularly new or insightful. But when coupled with the assumption of innate human moral capacity, the stage is set for the emergence, indeed the hegemony, of a full-blown theory of human equality.

Machiavelli began the process of delegitimizing elitism and church reformers furthered the cause. Obviously Machiavelli is no intellectual forebear of Calvin. But Machiavelli's idea that men have a propensity to corruption and must be constrained in their pursuit of self-interest aligns nicely with Calvin's conception of authority as that which dissuades man from his natural propensity to sin. Machiavelli's work, moreover, is not antithetical to Christian theology. As with Calvin, his oppositional stance toward the church might more rightly be construed as opposition to the specificity of its contemporaneous teachings rather than to Christian morality per se. Even if Machiavelli's "normative scriptures," as Preuss calls them, were more classical than biblical, he shared with Calvinists the contention that the theological drift of the Catholic Church had been poorly navigated over the preceding millennium (Preuss 1979, esp. 174; see also Berki 1971; Colish 1999).[12]

With reformation of the church came an emphasis on the diffusion of political authority on the one hand, and a shift in the source of sovereignty on the other. Protestantism's most fundamental contribution to the rise of egalitarianism was to help nudge the perceived basis of moral knowledge from a complex, hierarchical, and exogenous entity (church or state) toward individuals themselves. Calvinists in particular rejected the paternalistic role of king, lord, and priest and the corresponding infantilization of subject and penitent (Waring 1910, 101; Skinner 1978b, 16–18). Strictly speaking, orthodox Calvinist theology is inegalitarian insofar as there is a marked distinction between the saints (those destined for salvation) and those not granted the gift of grace. But the vexing ambiguity of one's status in that regard tended to limit the practicality of rigid social hierarchy.

---

12 In Machiavelli's words: "If the religious spirit had been kept up by the rulers of the Christian commonwealth as was ordained for us by its founder, Christian states and republics would have been much more united and much more happy than they are" (1975, I. 12).

Similarly paradoxical is Calvin's view on political obedience. In theory, Calvin preached strict adherence to the secular authority of prince and king. Yet Calvinist churches contributed to not merely theological revolutions, but secular ones as well – most prominently the English Civil War and the American Revolution. Reconciling the revolutionary and the obedient was found in the rather significant loophole that one owed obedience only to secular rule that was godly.[13] Similarly, the French Calvinist Theodore Beza in his 1574 *Right of Magistrates* argues that while subjects have an absolute imperative to obey God's commands, this absolutism does not extend to the command of princes who engage in "irreligious" or "iniquitous" behaviour (1969, I). More radically, Beza contends that it is God's will that the government exist as a creature of the people rather than the other way around. As such, those who usurp authority are not legitimate princes, and it is the citizen's responsibility to defend (by arms if necessary) the legitimate institutions of the state "to which, after God, each man owes his whole existence" (1969, V; see also McNeill 1949, esp. 162; Walzer 1969, 58–65; Höpfl 1982, 14–16, 48).

Legitimate institutions were a function of social compact. More specifically, the legitimate authority of the state was born of a covenantal relationship between God and saints.[14] This put the English Calvinists in a contentious position against erstwhile Protestant reformers in the Church of England. Indeed, in sharp contrast to the radicalism of the continental Reformation, the English Reformation under Henry VII was

13 "[I]n that obedience which we hold to be due to the commands of rulers, we must always make the exception, nay, must be particularly careful that it is not incompatible with obedience to Him to whose will the wishes of all kings should be subject, to whose decrees their commands must yield, to whose majesty their sceptres must bow. And, indeed, how preposterous were it, in pleasing men, to incur the offence of Him for whose sake you obey men! The Lord, therefore, is King of kings. When he opens his sacred mouth, he alone is to be heard, instead of all and above all. We are subject to the men who rule over us, but subject only in the Lord. If they command any thing against Him, let us not pay the least regard to it, nor be moved by all the dignity which they possess as magistrates – a dignity to which, no injury is done when it is subordinated to the special and truly supreme power of God" (Calvin 1845, IV. 20, 32).

14 The covenant between God and the saints obliged the elect to the obedient servitude of God as a means to a state of grace. The state of grace was available only to the elect, whose predestination was integral to Calvinism. And while grace required obedience as faith rather than good works, good behaviour was not only a means of paying homage to the glory of God, but was also a useful way of reassuring oneself of one's elect status (Weber 1930, 110–12). To put this differently, while the Catholic ethic saw good works as a cumulative effort toward salvation, with each act serving to credit, or at least cancel a debit against, the ledger of salvation, Calvinism demanded a systemically unified good life in which one's faith informed one's covenantal responsibilities (Weber 1930, 116).

less a theological revolution than an administrative struggle to national-
ize political authority. The Protestant Tudors and Stuarts were content to
extract the political benefits of European Protestant reform while retaining the episcopal hierarchy, symbolism, and pageantry that more radical
Protestant reformers renounced (Bernard 1990, 185–9).

Upon the religious settlement of 1559, therefore, Marian exiles re-
turning to England found little fecundity in their Puritan ideals.[15] The
religious settlement had created a stable ecclesiastical feudalism, as
Walzer describes it (1969, 118–19), in which pageantry reinforced a social order still predicated on rank and distinction, reverence, and deference. To those of the Reformed theology, the self-aggrandizement of the
Anglican bishops smacked of (quite literally) an unholy alliance between
church and state to preserve one another's stature at the expense of
scripturally based theology on the one hand, and the rights of English
citizens on the other (Davies 1934, 160–1; Morrill 1984, 164–5).

The Reformed theology was not overtly political. Challenge to the existing prelate was at the heart of revolutionary Puritanism. The attendant
threat to the political order represented, at least nominally, unintended
collateral damage. Yet distilling the political from the theological was no
mean feat. The medieval socio-religious order inherited by the Church
of England was both organic and pluralistic. Authority was distributed
among prince and baron, pope and clergy, and within the host of heav-
en, with the authority of each contingent upon the authority of the others (Walzer 1969, 152–66; Todd 1987, 180–5). The interconnectedness
of England's historical feudal authority and Christianity's historical
episcopal authority is manifest in King James's famous and oft-quoted
maxim: "no bishop, no king." Indeed, each was legitimated through
what Pocock has called England's traditional "fellowship of experience"

---

15 Puritans were radical Protestants steeped in generally Calvinist, Presbyterian,
Baptist, or Independent Protestant theology who challenged both Roman Catholicism
in England, and what they considered to be the Anglican Catholicism embodied by the
Church of England (Coffey 1998, 963). An essential distinction between the Puritans and
Catholics was that the former believed in a direct, terrestrial relationship with God, whereas
the latter believed that individuals must be guided in life toward preparation for the afterlife. To Catholics the sacraments were a way of characterizing the invisible as a means to
this end. For Puritans, by contrast, such ceremony constructed barriers between God and
individuals, whose faithfulness was more likely to be reinforced through preaching from
learned men than sacrament often performed by the unread and the unable (Padelford
1913, 86, 90–2). Puritans objected to a number of Anglican ceremonial practices, such as
the use of the cross at baptisms, the symbolism of the wedding ring, the idolatry of bowing
at the name of Jesus and at the altar when entering or leaving church, and even the position of the altar (Padelford 1913, 86; Weber 1930, 105; Davies 1934, 164).

(1975, 334), which set effective limits as to how far the Anglican Reformation was willing to stray from its Roman roots. So tidy was the alliance that criticism of the Church of England was tantamount to sedition and of the monarchy to blasphemy (Davies 1934, 161).

If the church-state alliance in England was unified, the relationship between Puritans and secular humanists, whose opposition to the increasing absolutism of the seventeenth-century monarchy represented a contemporaneous challenge to the prevailing social hierarchy, was less clear. Morrill (1984, 157) holds that while there was some overlap in the membership of secular and Reformed opponents of king and Church, both constituted separate sources of revolution, with correspondingly different objectives. Specifically, while secular revolutionaries' complaints about monarchical abuse of authority were particular and their prescription was to restore the monarchy, religious opponents of the socio-theological hierarchy were more broadly revolutionary (160–1; see also Baskerville 1998).

The original battle was fought from the pulpit. In a foretaste of what was to occur to even greater effect in America, the Puritans laid the groundwork for revolution, preaching to a wider congregation than those attracted to the episodic homilies read in the Anglican Church. Far from preaching the obedience and subservience that resonated through the sermons and writings of the Anglican churchmen, the saints sought to disentangle the cords binding the monarchical order to its quasi-Roman Catholic source of spiritual legitimation. By 1622, James's response was to impose significant legal restrictions on the message from the pulpit (including the banning of afternoon sermons) and two years later on regulation of the written word as well (Davies 1934, 169–73; Morrill 1984, 163; Hill 1997, 22–8).[16]

Secular opposition, too, met with official resistance. The dismissal of Parliament after 1629 was a clumsy, ultimately counter-productive means of suppressing anti-absolutist sentiment. The House of Commons' broad, self-defined mandate as "representers" of all English subjects certainly constituted a meaningful source of political opposition to royal absolutism. But parliamentarians were careful to distinguish opposition to centralization of power from opposition to the monarchy per se. Further,

---

16 Restrictions on preaching were common throughout the Tudor period, beginning with Thomas Cromwell's Injunctions of 1536 requiring ministers to reinforce the supremacy of the king at least twice yearly. Further regulation of the pulpit occurred under both Edward and Elizabeth. Similarly, the laity was prohibited from rash or false interpretations of the scriptures, and prohibited "all curious research" into the 39 Articles after their introduction in 1562 (Hill 1997, 19–20).

their overly generous assessment of the problem laid the blame for monarchical intransigence at the feet of the king's advisers rather than the
king himself. Parliament thus held itself up not as defiant of the king's
will but as seeking to protect the king from decisions he made as a result
of poor counsel. Indeed, even at the start of armed conflict in 1642,
many parliamentarians clung to the fiction that they were loyal to a king
who was merely misguided in his actions (Morgan 1988, ch.1, 55–6).

The ham-handedness by which Charles I and Archbishop William
Laud sought to regulate the flow of political and religious information
simply drove activism underground, stimulating separatism, and permitting it the perverse liberty of operating unfettered except by the severest
forms of regulation (Davies 1934, 173–4). With its return in 1640,
Parliament was primed to exact its retribution – if not against the king
himself, then certainly against the Laudian abusers of ecclesiastical authority. By the time of the Grand Remonstrance in 1641, opposition to
the corrupt practices of the Church of England had so crystalized as
to stimulate a radical impetus on the part of many parliamentarians to
sweep aside the episcopal order altogether (Morrill 1984, 166–8).

The Enlightenment

The English Civil War represents the alliance, if only briefly, of secular
and theological commitment to reform the episcopal and political order. Many of the nascent liberal principles that emerged after the Civil
War were Calvinist in form, although Socinian in content. At its most
basic, there is an obvious similarity between the contractarianism of secular reformers and the saints' covenantal relationship with God (Foster
1927, esp. 487; Walzer 1963, 61; Hughey 1984; Morgan 1988, 56, 142–
3; Richards 2002/2003).[17] A latent egalitarianism informs both contract
and covenant. Both begin from the premise of individual contractors'

---

17 The contractual relationship between citizen and sovereign does not owe its entire
genesis to the Calvinist covenant. Historically there was a suggestion of popular consent to
monarchical rule through, for example, the spectacle of royal coronation. Similarly, convention held that ascendancy to the status of God's terrestrial lieutenant rested upon something more substantial than the legacy of what Paine characterizes as a "French bastard
landing with an armed banditti and establishing himself king of England against the consent of the natives" (1986, 78). Instead, the majesty of princely authority was deemed
rooted in ancient compact through which the king conceded to English law and the people accepted him as their monarch. Taken one step farther, most notably by Henry Parker,
it could be argued that the acceptance of English laws implied the ability of the people's
representatives in Parliament to impose parameters constraining royal authority (Morgan
1988, 57–9).

fundamental equality before God. For Calvinists, the equality extends to all predestined for salvation; to humanists such as Locke, equality extended to all of humanity.

More subtly, both compacts ground authority in one order in the legitimacy derived from another. The Reformed theology thus distinguishes the civil covenant from the covenant of grace. Socinian humanists such as Locke make a similar argument, stating that the legitimacy of civil authority is grounded in the natural order. More specifically, civil authority acquires its legitimacy from individuals possessed of natural rights endowed by God (Morgan 1988, 56–7; see also Greaves 1982, 26; Zook 1999, ch.2; Noll 2002, 58–60).

The implications that flow from this are critical. In the order of nature, all individuals stand equal in the eyes of God. Each, after all, is equally possessed of natural rights by virtue of humanity rather than nobility. Such rights acquire no currency as unequal goods. The normative basis for a right to liberty, for example, lies in the innate human capacity for free will. It would be a cruel joke indeed if God endowed men with free will but not the liberty needed to exercise that will. That liberty, moreover, must apply equally to all individuals, insofar as free will must perforce be equally distributed. This equality elevates the status of the individual as a meaningful political actor whose private rights have to be weighed – indeed take precedence – against the public good. Because rights are themselves a derivative of the moral good, they precede any form of social or political hierarchy. Men possess certain moral entitlements, in other words, the very existence of which precludes social arrangements that fail to recognize the equality of those entitlements (Berger 1970, 342).

But there were also fundamental differences between English Reformed theology and the humanism of the English Enlightenment. For example, English Reformed theology places a far greater premium on moral constraint than on personal autonomy. The mandate of the church was moral surveillance, grounded in the imperative to protect man from his own natural depravity,[18] with freedom subordinated to the authority of both church and state. By contrast, the Socinianism of the Enlightenment rejected the assumption of man's innate depravity and, as a consequence, the imperative for moral restraint. The result was a fundamental shift in the mandate of the democratic state – from one

18 Coffey notes a softening of Puritan authoritarianism after the return of the Long Parliament. While some continued to insist on the imperative for magistrates to punish heresy, idolatry, and apostasy, others began to advocate greater religious tolerance and freedom of conscience (1998).

that inhibited liberty in the name of moral order to one in which moral order was grounded in the preservation of liberty.

This distinction is fundamental. In rejecting two premises – that man is insufficient in his moral capacity and that man is naturally depraved – the whole nature of government shifts. If man is morally self-sufficient and can be trusted to exercise his liberty in a morally appropriate way, then historical recognition of the noble as worthy of political privilege and deference was but a horrible political mistake. So it was for Kant, who claims that to kneel down or prostrate oneself before heavenly objects is "contrary to the dignity of humanity ... for then you humble yourself, not before an *ideal* represented to you by your own reason, but before an *idol* of your own making" (1996, 437–8, emphasis in original). Similarly, "[b]owing and scraping before a human being seems in any case to be unworthy of a human being ... [Such that] one who makes himself a worm cannot complain afterwards if people step on him" (1996, 438). In the same vein, Cato maintains that the "opinions" of the great

signify no more to the world, than do the several tastes of men; and all mankind must be made of one complexion, of one size, and of one age, before they can be all made of the same mind. Those patrons therefore of dry dreams, who do mischief to the world to make it better, are the pests and distressers of mankind, and shut themselves out from all pretence to the love of their country: Strange men! They would force all men into an absolute certainty about absolute uncertainties and contradictions; they would ascertain ambiguities, without removing them; and plague and punish men for having but five senses. (Trenchard and Gordon 1995, 2.35)

The moral philosophy of the Enlightenment represented a definitive step in reconciling liberal and republican perspectives on equality. Essential to this reconciliation was identifying the sources of endogenous moral capacity in terms of either moral sentiment or moral reason.

Moral Sentiment

Moral sentiment was a touchstone of the Scottish Enlightenment. Hume suggests that one of the underlying sentiments informing moral action is vanity, or desire for the esteem of others (1751, II.II. 5). We act in morally appropriate ways because we want others to think well of us. This is why, Adam Smith argues, individuals can understand the propriety of their own behaviour only in a social context. One's subjective consciousness of moral self can only occur in the context of others. Society constitutes, as it were, the mirror through which individuals acquire the capacity for moral self-evaluation (Smith 1982, III. 3). Because the judgment of others affects their sense of self, individuals construct a sort of moral reflection by stepping back from themselves and imagining the propriety of their actions as they would appear in the eyes of an impartial observer. The effect is an ethical interdependence, whereby an agent is responsible for his actions to the community as a whole, which implicitly passes moral judgment upon him.

Vanity is a manifestation of an even deeper sentiment: sympathy. Sympathy is the passion of the imagination, the desire for good things for those with whom we sympathize (Hume 1751, II.II. 5; also Smith 1982, I.II. 2.1). Sympathy is not pity or compassion. Instead it is an imaginary emotional transference that allows one to experience the feelings of another such that, in Hume's words, "the minds of men are mirrors to one another" (1751, II. II. 5). This transference is limited to the emotional and does not extend to the physical; we cannot experience the physical pain of another. But it is due to our natural sympathy that we not only root for the protagonists in the movies we watch, we also become emotionally invested in them.[19] It is this sympathy, manifest particularly in the social passions of generosity, humanity, kindness, compassion, mutual friendship, and esteem that permits individuals to live together in society (Smith 1982, I.II. 3, 4.1).

Sympathy need not be a moral virtue; nor does it lead directly to equality. Indeed, Smith argues that in hierarchical societies, the multitude's traditional celebration of the rich and powerful represents a corrupted form of sympathy. So powerful is this sympathy that people come to identify themselves with the great, and to resent anything that might intrude upon their happiness. We should, Smith chides, go so far as to wish the great immortality to insulate them from the disturbance that death would bring to their happy existence.[20] It is this manifestation of sympathy that supports widespread commitment to social distinction and deference. As such, Smith argues, the greatness of the great is more likely to stem from a mass imaginary transfer of emotion than from actual greatness of moral wisdom, civic virtue, or capacity for spiritual guidance.

19 Smith opens the *Theory of Moral Sentiments* with precisely this point. "How selfish soever man may be supposed, there are evidently some principles in his nature, which interest him in the fortune of others, and render their happiness necessary to him, though he derives nothing from it except the pleasure of seeing it" (1982 I.I.1. 1).

20 In modern times, this phenomenon manifests itself in a vacuous identification with celebrity, which is bemusing but not pernicious (although see Nagel 2001).

This being the case, the greats' status in the socio-political hierarchy is not a Socratic functional necessity. Instead, the nobility are great by virtue of nothing more than the perception of their greatness, a perception they typically care not to risk in demonstrating the very virtues that were the ostensible basis of their nobility in the first place (Smith 1982, I.III. 2.2–5, I.III. 3.2–3). From this perspective, deference and privilege are social edifices without moral grounding. Indeed, Smith claims, without social puffery and pageantry, individuals of any sort are not all that different from one another. Certainly they do not differ to the extent that individuals of one type are more worthy of sympathy – or for that matter status or dignity – than individuals of another (see Rothschild 2001; Darwall 2004; Levy and Peart 2004; in the modern context see Berger 1970, 341–2).

While it can be corrupted to preserve a hierarchical political structure, the universal *capacity* for sympathy precludes the imperative for inegalitarian governance in which the putatively noble are the guardians of a common class mired in selfishness and moral ignorance. The great advantage of Smith's position is that it does not rely on the fictive premise that moral goodness demands anyone go beyond his self-interest.[21] Rather, a theory of universal moral sentiment represents the basis of a meritocratic society in which citizens are motivated by a blend of self-interest and concern for the welfare of others. Because "the road to virtue and that to fortune ... are, happily in most cases, very nearly the same," self-interest and virtue are by no means mutually inhospitable. By pursuing their own selfish material interests, individuals are bound to adhere to the propriety – as a means of establishing a reputation for trustworthiness – that permits them to succeed economically (Smith 1982, I.III. 3.5, IV. 1.20).

It is freedom among equals rather than constraint imposed by a moral elite that robs regimes of a common revolutionary impulse. At the same time, the universal nature of moral sentiment means that an egalitarian regime does no damage to the moral goodness of that regime. However, universal moral self-sufficiency does not necessarily preclude the role of theistic or secular forces as guides to moral goodness; moral reason can be aided through external sources of moral reinforcement. However,

21 It is because so few individuals are truly able to transcend self-interest in the name of safeguarding the commonweal that traditional republicans generally adopted the position that regime mortality was inevitable. Smith is not the first to suggest that self-interest is compatible with moral virtue (see, for example, Cicero 1974) but he is among the first to suggest that the combination of self-interest and moral virtue precludes the need for social privilege.

the assumption of Enlightenment moral philosophy is that moral sentiment (or moral reason, as discussed below) is universal and hence not
unique to sages, kings, or priests.

Moral Reason

As with moral sentiment, moral reasoning represents an implicit rejection of Calvinist exclusivity; the moral and civic responsibility of the citi-
zen/saint extends beyond those upon whom God has bestowed his gift
of grace. Moral reasoning therefore can be thought of as common
wisdom, or, more widely, common sense. Such common sense moral
reasoning represents a roadmap for moral self-sufficiency, providing revelation through nature, scripture, or some combination thereof, of the
moral duties and moral entitlements that all individuals assume by virtue
of their humanity.

For Kant, moral reasoning is predicated on the assumption that individuals live better lives if they privilege moral reason ahead of the more
practical, instrumental reason. That is, human fulfillment is realized if
one filters her desires through her moral reason. This deontological understanding of the moral good is what allows human beings to move
from purely subjective self-absorption to *intersubjective* (or social) ethics,
in which the "other" is transformed from object to dignity-bearing subject. As with Smith, Kant admonishes us to view the world from the perspective of others and hence to cherish each individual as an end in
herself and not merely an instrument of one's own enjoyment (Kant
2005, 429; 2006, 200).

In elevating others from objects to subjects (from means to ends), Kant
rejects the historically pervasive socio-political hierarchy that assigns
differential recognition of human dignity and values individuals for their
extrinsic worth or social usefulness. Such hierarchy commodifies individuals in a way that demeans them, rendering them small and insignificant.[22] The alternative he states famously is to regard a human being

as a *person*, that is, as the subject of a morally practical reason, [who] is exalted
above any price; for as a person, he is not to be valued merely as a means to the
ends of others or even to his own ends, but as an end in himself, that is, he

---

22 The logic works both ways in that it is not only the many who suffer a loss of dignity
at the expense of the great. One's self-respect is intimately tied to how an individual treats
another so that to deprive another of recognition of his true intrinsic worth as a person is
ultimately a violation of the depriver's own obligation to himself and ultimately his own
self-respect.

possesses a *dignity* (an absolute inner worth) by which he exacts *respect* for himself from all other rational beings in the world. He can measure himself with every other being of this kind and value himself on a footing of equality with them. (1996, 435; emphasis in original)

Equality for Kant does not mean equal capacity for greatness or for wisdom or for knowledge. Indeed, moral reasoning is distinct from knowledge or wisdom. Humans do not so much *know* the moral good as use their reason to establish its characteristics. Thus: wisdom "is no doubt too much to demand of human beings. Instead moral goodness is inherent in three leading maxims: (1) Think for oneself, (2) Think into the place of the other (in communication with human beings), (3) Always think consistently with oneself" (2006, 200).

Of course, it is one thing to provide logical justification for an egalitarian society on the basis that moral endogeneity renders social hierarchy superfluous and another thing to do something about it. Enlightenment moral philosophy probably would have served no practical end had it not been for significant socio-economic changes. Moral philosophy did not drive social change as much as justify changing social conditions.

The Commercial Age

These changing social conditions were manifest in the emergent commercialism of the eighteenth century and the industrial revolution of the nineteenth. Obviously much of the change was driven by advances in technology. But part of it, reinforcing the general narrative of religion's role in the progression toward equality, was a function of Protestant theology.

It is ironic, insofar as it is often so unevenly held, that commercial wealth became one of the great political equalizers. Unlike land, there is no fixed quantity of commercial wealth, and so wealth is not beholden to the same zero-sum properties as land. As a result, commercial wealth can more easily be broadly distributed. Similarly, commercial wealth is not conducive to monopoly control by an oligarchic elite. To the contrary, it is associated with social mobility. Such mobility, in turn, makes it difficult for an economic elite to hold and acquire the political privilege that so often attaches to a landed aristocracy steeped in immanence and magnanimity.

As he developed the doctrine of justification through faith, Luther became increasingly hostile to the evangelistic counsels of monasticism as a way of drawing Christians away from their worldly responsibilities. For Luther, as with all Protestants, justification was realized through faith. Justification through reclusive, selfless service to God was not merely specious, but actually constituted an abdication of one's true moral duties. Of course, this did not relieve individuals of the imperative for Christian charity. However, Luther maintained that one fulfilled her Christian obligation of charity indirectly; that is, through her labour. Luther thus saw labour as a calling – the means by which individuals worked in the service of their neighbours (Weber 1930, 73–87; Lindberg 1993, 109–110).

By pursuing one's calling, one acquired remuneration and often wealth. Such wealth was a byproduct of a Christian life, but not an end in itself. Indeed, wealth was problematic when conceived as an end. Love of wealth begat love of luxury, which in turn led to indolence, selfishness, and a lack of godliness. Critically though, the source of vice was not wealth. It was the potential *effects* of wealth that were problematic. Such a distinction did not preclude ambitiously pursuing one's calling. By honing the specialized skills at which he was most competent, an individual could be more efficient in the productive process, hence maximizing his contribution to the social good and his concomitant service to God. At the same time, if his hard work in the service of God provided him with material success, not only was it satisfactory to accept such material success, it would actually be an insult to God to refuse His gifts (as long as these gifts were not used for vice). Indeed, one measure of a man was his capacity to acquire material wealth on the one hand and resist sin on the other (Weber 1930, 157–63, 170).

Ironically, given the primacy of predestination in Calvinist thought, Calvinists were quite flexible in their understanding of free will when it came to the calling. One could pursue different callings, simultaneously or sequentially, as long as the motive was to contribute to the greater good and the effects did not harm others (Weber 1930, 162).

In England, the acquisition of material wealth and the freedom to live a life of fulfillment soon outpaced the strict spiritual boundaries imposed by Puritanism (Tawney 1977, 196; Pincus 1998). Indeed, that which was intended originally to serve God and only God soon found its justification in the service of man (and perhaps only man). As commercial enterprise grew, the threat to the soul of offending God through practices such as arbitrage and usury rang increasingly hollow. For many, economic expansion brought with it an insidious "soulless individualism" that sought distance from both church and state (Tawney 1977, 181, 189). Characterizing a growing sentiment of the late seventeenth and early eighteenth centuries, Mandeville's *Fable of the Bees* appeared to drive the definitive conceptual wedge between moral virtue and the greater good. Far from a commonweal reliant on the moral virtue of its citizens, Mandeville sees the greater good in terms of economic self-interest so that, economically speaking, "the worst of all the multitude did something for the common good" (1924, 167–8).

On the face of it, then, the commercial age appears to have been not only antithetical to the values of Protestant theology, but also to the moral virtue demanded by republicanism. Soulless individualism and moral goodness are not generally thought of in tandem. And yet the tension between market and moral virtue remains more apparent than real. Underscoring the operation of the market is a common understanding as to the rules of the game. As Adam Smith notes, the adversarial nature of the market masks an underlying commitment to the very civic virtues that critics of the market claim that free enterprise erodes. Smith was not the first to link moral virtue with the rational self-interest demanded by the marketplace. Samuel Ricard, for example, wrote in 1704 that

Commerce has a special character that distinguishes it from all other professions. It affects the feelings of men so strongly that it makes him who was proud and haughty suddenly turn supple, bending and serviceable. Through commerce man learns to deliberate, to be honest, to acquire manners, to be prudent and reserved in both talk and action. Sensing the necessity to be wise and honest in order to succeed, he flees vice, or at least his demeanor exhibits decency and seriousness so as not to arouse any adverse judgment on the part of present and future acquaintances. (quoted in Hirschman 1982, 1465)

Indeed, free markets cannot work, Arrow points out, without an a priori set of understandings that manifest themselves in trust reflected in a sense of reciprocal obligation (1972, 345).[23] It is for this reason that Montesquieu opines that manners and commerce are intimately connected (1989, bk xx.1) with commerce representing the middle ground between thievery on the one hand and self-sacrifice on the other (1989, bk xx.2).

The progression of egalitarian democracy in the commercial age was all but inevitable. Clearly, success in the free market was born of self-sufficiency, demanding both practical reason (rational utility maximization) and moral endogeneity. If there was one condition that commercial practices demanded it was the freedom to reject conformity as a means

23 This reciprocal obligation is very much a product of the commercial age. The fungible nature of commercial wealth fostered a cooperative ethos that was not possible in more agrarian societies where wealth generated by land ownership axiomatically represented an opportunity cost for the acquisition of wealth by others (see Hirschman 1997, esp. 75).

of realizing one's economic ends (Tawney 1977, 205). All this made egalitarian theories of governance especially attractive. The advantage of a market-centric view of politics was that individuals retained an interest in their liberty and engaged in civic participation not merely as a way of informing the good character of the law, but also as a way of protecting their interests against encroachment by either church or state. The good citizen was motivated to act for the public good because that public good coincided with her own private interests (Burtt 1993, 365). It requires no great leap of political enlightenment to recognize that the broader the base of citizens whose private interests coincided with the public good, the greater the liberty and hence the more secure the regime from rebellion or revolution (Trenchard and Gordon 1995, 2.35–6).

The egalitarian nature of capitalism, of course, lies not in the distribution of assets but in its overt aversion to political privilege. The great capitalist virtue of desert represents sufficient enticement for individuals to contribute to the greater good, as financial reward for hard work, creativity, innate talents, and the like replaces political honour as the motive for civic virtue. At the same time, endogenous rationalism replaces exogenous wisdom as the means by which social organization is optimized, so that Socratic architectonics are accomplished far more efficiently by the dispassionate hand of the market than by the sagacious guidance of pope or prince.

The commercial age necessitated the sharp distinction between the role of the market (which determines the appropriate division of social labour) and the role of the state (which protects the freedom to exercise reason and protect the material rewards which were the desert of that reason). Indeed, for the market to operate effectively, individuals needed to be recognized as both equal and as capable of self-governance. It was this equality, what Cato calls the "soul of liberty" (Trenchard and Gordon 1995, 1.15), that militated against the hierarchy of both church and state which occurred in the wake of the English Civil War.

THE AMERICAN SYNTHESIS: EQUALITY IN THE FIRST LIBERAL REPUBLIC

The American founding represented the culmination of the historical push to unite the egalitarian imperative of the Enlightenment with the moral imperative of republicanism. America was fertile ground to launch a new egalitarian political experiment. Winthrop's famous analogy to a city upon a hill bespoke a latent egalitarian millennialism. But at the same time, eighteenth-century America was ambivalent about the efficacy of constructing a society of equals. Even as they maintained an abiding contempt for those who would seek to distinguish themselves by adopting "certain Airs of Wisdom and superiority," colonial Americans possessed a respect and ambition for social distinction (Wood 1998, 73–5; see also Bailyn 1962; Stout 1977, 526). The America of the mid-eighteenth century was thus culturally conditioned not to question the relationship between hierarchy and good governance too deeply.[24]

The problems facing the new American republic were hardly a revelation. Aristotle had noted centuries previously the difficulties inherent in constructing a government of equals. The problem was even greater for a republic founded upon the nebulous and potentially atomistic celebration of liberty. It was a political truism that if a free people did not put themselves under some form of voluntary restraint, the state would be left with no choice but to impose such restraint. It was for this reason that the English Whigs had relied on aristocracy to constrain the exuberance of the commoners. As Harrington had pointed out in defending the maintenance of an aristocratic upper house as an instrument of moral leadership, the available options for restraint came down to a choice between the aristocracy or the sword (Pocock 1975, 416–20; McDonald 1985, 70–7; Wood 1998, 409–13).[25]

The moral guidance provided by aristocracy obviously was not available in America, which had no analogous noble class ready and able to provide sufficient gravitas to offset popular exuberance. The American solution would have to be found elsewhere. That solution was to substitute laws and religion for great men as a source of moral constraint; legitimacy for deference as a source of political order; and moral

---

24 All of this ambivalence meant that while a social and political hierarchy existed in colonial America, it was of a relatively benign sort, a pale imitation of the aristocratic tradition that proved so difficult to dismantle in Britain. It is therefore one of the great puzzles surrounding the American Revolution that it happened at all. Not only did the Revolution represent a leap into the political unknown, it was not at all obvious that such a revolution could be legitimately justified – at least according to prevailing ideas of good government. As Gordon Wood points out, the revolutionary impulse in America was out of all proportion to the sense of grievance that Americans might have held against Britain. Certainly other peoples had had to put up with far worse and reacted with far less aggression. But the American Revolution was not a response to an intolerable existence. It was a response to the opportunity cost associated with the political status quo; that is, it was an ideological revolution in which the moral entitlement to liberty was coupled with new understandings about the endogeneity of moral virtue in such a way as to make the status quo a bearable, but still anachronistic form of government (Bailyn 1962; Wood 1966).

25 Tocqueville makes the point less directly when he warns of the social effects of excessive individualism. He writes famously: "Aristocracy links everybody, from peasant to king, in one long chain. Democracy breaks the chain and frees each link" (1969, II.II.2).

endogeneity for philosophical wisdom as the basis of a just republic.[26] This precluded a structure of governance in which virtue and good governance percolated downwards. America's God saw to it that – in Paine's evocative language – the king of America was law, and was not embodied by any person or class of persons (1986, 98; Noll 2002). Americans demonstrated their deference to God not through obedience, but through their own autonomous self-governance and through whichever faith resonated with their own moral reasoning. Thus the public good was served through concomitant obligation to one's self-interest and obligation to a God whose manifest intent was the liberty and equal dignity of all men (Morgan 1988, 290; Noll 1985).

The supremacy of good laws as opposed to good men was grounded in the civic humanist conviction that the well-constructed law serves as a repository for the collective wisdom and prudence of society. Indeed, for Emerson, collective wisdom reflects a sort of moral aggregation that marginalizes the social utility of great men (Emerson 2008). Thus, rather than reliance upon the tried and not necessarily true prescription of virtuous moral leadership, the American republic cleaved to its own form of Machiavellian institutionalism – the idea that it is more efficacious to construct better systems of government than to rely on the better motives of virtuous leaders (McDonald 1985, 71).

Yet, foundational to egalitarianism and good governance as it was, even laws constructed by self-governing citizens were viewed with suspicion. Advocates of liberty appreciated the dual nature of law, as both a shield against tyranny and a sword for tyrants. Law was a shield when it restricted the power of the state; it was a sword when it imposed moral virtue from on high. The genius of the American synthesis is that it was the church, and not the state, that assumed the role of providing moral nourishment.

---

26   None of this is to suggest that Americans were of a common mind as to the details. The conflict between federalists and anti-federalists over the nature of the Constitution is testament to that. Revolutionary ideology was a swirling mix of traditional republicanism, civic humanism, Enlightenment moral philosophy, and millennial Protestant theology. Moreover, these ideologies were subject to experiment, innovation, compromise, and distortion to suit circumstances. The fact that we can look back on the American Revolution as the first manifestation of liberal republicanism is not the same thing as saying that American revolutionaries were looking forward to such an elegant theory of governance. To the extent that there was conceptual common ground, it lay in the moral entitlement to some form of liberty. Americans' attachment to liberty (and to a lesser extent equality) grew out of their everyday experience, and hence informed a reasoned sense of normality, as an essentially free people (Bailyn 1962, 345; Wood 1966, 6).

In this sense church and state struck a perfect balance. Americans were sufficiently republican to retain fidelity to an objective moral code, but sufficiently liberal not to enlist the state to articulate and enforce that moral code. Even for those not fully sold on the idea of an innate human capacity for morality, the moral guidance proffered by evangelical Protestant churches was infinitely preferable to the power of a potentially coercive state. Hence, in his farewell address George Washington admonished caution in indulging "the supposition, that morality can be maintained without religion. Whatever may be conceded to the influence of refined education on minds of peculiar structure, reason and experience both forbid us to expect that National morality can prevail in exclusion of the religious principle" (quoted in Noll 2002, 204).

For its part, American evangelical New Light theology relaxed Puritan theological orthodoxy, particularly as it pertained to the natural depravity of man. Evangelists were not the staid preachers of Protestant orthodoxy. Their sermons were not gloomy jeremiads lamenting the sinfulness of man, but exhortations dedicated to illustrating the efficacy, equality, and moral capacity of the common man. Their style dispensed with the ecclesiastical traditions that still adorned conventional Protestantism in favour of the sort of populism and spectacle that resonated more clearly with the masses. Their language eschewed the erudite and intellectual in favour of plain speech, of an appeal to a common moral sense. The subtext of their message, manifest in the unorthodox means of preaching to anonymous crowds rather than the more traditional cloistered congregations, was of nonconformity, of questioning and challenging the prevailing order (Stout 1977, 526–7). If the Puritan Revolution in England was a mass movement engendered through a self-appointed moral aristocracy of the saints, the American experiment was a mass movement engendered through a religious elite that intentionally downplayed its distinctiveness from the masses to which it preached. As Stout summarizes: "Partly through doctrine, but even more through the rhetorical strategy necessitated by that doctrine, the popular style of the revivals challenged the assumption of hierarchy and pointed to a substitute basis for authority and order in an open and voluntary system" (1977, 530; this dynamic persisted well into the nineteenth century, e.g., Hatch 1989, 195–201).

Evangelical preachers instilled in ordinary Americans a consciousness of their own moral and political worth as equal to that of any governor or priest. Their sermons helped to convince Americans of the fallacy of natural dominion – of Britain over America or of great over common. The message reinforced the political empowerment of ordinary citizens. It was a religious message that effectively served as testament to the efficacy of individuals to craft for themselves an existence born of their own liberty. Indeed, that liberty became a moral end unto itself with ordinary people its natural guardians. This proprietary role as keepers of freedom simultaneously elevated the judgment of the people as ultimate arbiters of political, legal, and even theological rightness (Hatch 1989, 6).

Evangelical Protestantism succeeded in America in large part because it recognized the imperative to tread lightly. As the English Puritans had learned all too clearly, it is no mean task to assume the mantle of moral leadership without any institutionalized form of authority. New Light theology was driven by pragmatic, even secular considerations. The market for moral guidance, if we may put it this way, was consumer driven. Producers were left with little choice: "churches had to construct revolutionary forms of Christianity or decline" (Noll 2002, 191).[27]

Perhaps the greatest point of compromise was the general relaxation of the deterministic, Calvinist staple that tied virtue and moral agency to the grace of God. Neither liberalism nor republicanism could accommodate a theory of predestination. Predestination precluded the foundational liberal principle of free will. Indeed, the entire normative thrust of a moral entitlement to liberty was man's inherent capacity to articulate and pursue the good life as he understood it. From the perspectives of liberalism, the idea of predestination and redemption solely through the grace of God threatened to make a mockery of man's rational capacity to think and his moral entitlement to act. Similarly, for republicans,

it was important that virtue *not* be defined exclusively as a product of divine grace, but rather as also a product of self-generated, personally chosen, public self-discipline .... Evangelicals never abandoned a central role for grace, but at

27 This process began well in advance of the American Revolution, especially within the Congregationalist, Presbyterian, Episcopalian, and Methodist churches, which evolved in different theological fashion from those in Britain and Canada. Congregationalists and Presbyterians in Britain, for example, were far more willing to restrain itinerant preaching as a hedge against radical populism and hence social fomentation against the established political order. Similarly, the Anglican Church in both Britain and Canada, it need hardly be said, was strongly resistant to any incipient republicanism that challenged the authority of church or state as it then stood. American Episcopalians, by contrast, operated under no such constraint. Perhaps clearest was the political schism in the Methodist Church. While "pious apoliticism" united some Methodists on both sides of the Atlantic, the more political members of the church tended toward republican radicalism in the United States and monarchical conservatism in Great Britain and Canada (Noll 2002, 64–70; see also Heimert 1966, esp. 21; Clark 1994, ch. 2, 258–9).

least in their enthusiasm as patriotic republicans, most played down the role of grace as an absolutely necessary precondition for public virtue. (Noll 2002, 205; emphasis in original)

If America were to represent God's kingdom on earth, evangelical churches would have to accommodate America rather than the other way around. As such, rather than conceiving man as innately wicked, evangelicals conceived him as a moral agent. This transformation from redeemed saint to secular citizen was facilitated by the abandonment of strict biblicism, thus making it theologically possible for man's moral judgment to be informed not just by scripture, but also by his capacity for (common sense) moral reason.

The theological emphasis on individual self-sufficiency, equality, political, and moral efficacy, and, most of all, liberty was enormously appealing to a society whose very existence in the New World bespoke some antipathy to the paternalism of the Old. The appealing nature of the evangelical message – that God intended all men to be equal, that God intended individuals to use their moral reason to construct a moral parameter to their liberty, that God gave individuals the capacity for self-reliance – helped to legitimate a political order that, to borrow from Arthur Stinchcombe (1965), suffered from the liability of newness.[28]

As a result of the transformation of saint to citizen, so symbiotic did liberal republicanism and evangelical Protestantism become, that by the 1820s, it was not uncommon for evangelicals to imbue the Constitution with divine provenance, and to see America as an Elect nation so that the cause of Christ and the cause of America could be considered one and the same. Indeed, by the middle of the nineteenth century, many religious leaders began to conceive what threatened America as a manifestation of personal moral corruption (Noll 2002, 206, 212, ch. 10, note 52). In much the same way, then, that the Harringtonian House of Lords served as the buckle between liberty and moral order in England,

---

28 Perhaps the clearest articulation of the synthesis of the theological and secular can be found in Emerson: "Trust thyself: every heart vibrates to that iron string. Accept the place the divine providence has found for you, the society of your contemporaries, the connection of events. Great men have always done so, and confided themselves childlike to the genius of their age, betraying their perception that the absolutely trustworthy was seated at their heart, working through their hands, predominating in all their being. And we are now men, and must accept in the highest mind the same transcendent destiny; and not minors and invalids in a protected corner, not cowards fleeing before a revolution, but guides, redeemers, and benefactors, obeying the Almighty effort, and advancing on Chaos and the Dark" (1951a, 33).

evangelical churches helped perform this function in the early United States. Their success in this endeavour is suggested by the massive surge of church membership among evangelicals in the revolutionary era into the early decades of the nineteenth century (Hatch 1989; Noll 2002, ch. 9).

CONCLUSION

In Book VIII of the *Republic* Socrates excoriates the egalitarianism of democratic governance. Democratic societies prize liberty. They do not trifle with ideas like goodness or badness. "The criminal strolls around," Socrates says, "like a hero's ghost, without anyone seeing him or giving him a thought." Such cities are noteworthy for their tolerance. Their citizens embrace leaders who grant them the liberty to lead the pleasurable and hedonistic lives that, in their ignorance, they mistake for fulfilled ones. Such citizens despise great men with the impudence to intrude upon their pleasure. They demand no demonstrable greatness or virtue in their leaders and instead honour a man with high office for nothing more than his willingness to wish them well (Plato 1974, 558a–c).

This antipathy toward socio-political egalitarianism characterized republican and Christian views on good government for centuries.[29] Even for the likes of Aristotle, ambivalent as he is about the efficacy and imperative for elite governance, there was a prevailing understanding that

---

29 Some qualifications are necessary. Cynics such as Antisthenes and Diogenes asserted the inherent equality of men through their disdain for wealth and other social conventions. Hadas (1943) reads Hippocrates and Antiphon, among others, as critics of a general Athenian tradition of chauvinism. In the Roman republican tradition there is a clear sense in Cicero, for example, that the laws of nature preclude one man from seeking to use another for his own ends. And he advances an innate claim to dignity when asking rhetorically: "What kind of discussion can you hold with [a man] if he believes that wronging another man is not an action against nature? His concept of 'man' simply does not include what is essentially human" (1974, III.26). The character, and hence dignity, of man is of two types, Cicero argues. "One of them is universal, deriving from the fact that we all participate in the intelligence and superiority by which we surpass other animals. The other is the character bestowed upon each individual" (1974, I.107). Similarly, we find examples within the Christian tradition that so dominated medieval thought. The universal claim to dignity is manifest, for example, in the concept of imago dei – the Judeo-Christian belief espoused in Genesis that man was created in the image of God. We see in Matthew (25:40), for example: "And the King shall answer and say to them, Truly I say to you, Inasmuch as you have done it to one of the least of these my brothers, you have done it to me" (Novak 1998, 109). More broadly, Christianity is grounded in the belief that Christ's sacrifice restored to humanity the dignity lost through original sin, such that dignity is not a product of human agency but instead of God's love (England 1999/2000, 1908; see also Kraynak 2003).

good governance demanded moral goodness and that moral goodness was not an endogenous capacity. Neither was it evenly distributed. Some men were so greatly good as to preclude governance by lesser men, and where such greatness was extant the best alternative was singular rule.

The relationship between goodness and greatness was also central to medieval Christian theology. Augustine was an exception to the general understanding that good government was the province of great men. Augustine sees the moral space between God and man to be so vast as to render all men equal in their unlikeness. Or rather, if men are to be distinguished from one another, it is through extraordinary capacity (the gift of God's grace) for humility and piety. Such a perspective can only be grounded in a dismissal of worldliness and humanism. Indeed, Christian humanists argued very differently. Aquinas thus reiterates the social importance of extraordinary virtue as the source of man's capacity for temporal greatness, and it is thus magnanimity that justifies exalting the great through honour and high station.

It is only with Machiavelli that the first hints of reconciliation between republican virtue and liberal egalitarianism are brought to the fore. Machiavelli is not ready to abandon the imperative for elite leadership of the republic; nor does he reject true greatness as a source of good governance. But given the rarity of such greatness, he rejects moral virtue as either a requirement or a justification for stable government. Machiavelli is not a champion of equal moral capacity on the part of elites and masses. If anything, he is a champion of equal *immoral* capacity. If immorality (or corruption) is antithetical to good governance, the solution is not to seek out moral excellence. It is to pursue moral universalism through institutions that compel men to virtue. Such institutionalism is not axiomatically egalitarian. However, the implied substitutability of men deemphasizes the imperative for singular greatness.

Christian humanists and Puritans on both sides of the Atlantic, albeit for very different reasons, reoriented the source of moral understanding as it came to be understood in Enlightenment moral philosophy. Rather than grounding moral capacity in virtues found only in the great or the few, the Enlightenment was predicated on endogenous moral capacity. Moral self-sufficiency, through sentiment or reason, was conceived as a universal attribute. The implications were tectonic. If moral capacity was foundational to good governance but common to all individuals, socio-political hierarchy was politically specious, a prop dedicated to supporting nothing weightier than the puffery of an elite class intent on perpetuating the myth of its own nobility.

The dawning realization of universal and equal human moral capacity coincided with the opening of new vistas for human social progress through the acquisition of commercial wealth. The commercial age bull-dozed the venerable social, political, and theological infrastructure that had maintained the differential dignity afforded the few and the many. Truisms of the commercial age drew republican virtue and liberal egali-tarianism ever closer together: markets know only equals; and the ro-bustness of self-interest only buttresses the moral virtue with which it is compatible (Berger 1970, esp. 341).

Ultimately, what Noll calls the Evangelical Enlightenment of nineteenth-century America demanded the synthesis of three values: liberty, moral order, and recognition of the inherent worth (dignity) of each individu-al. The American example represented the triumph of the pragmatic and phenomenological. Experience created a normative conception of the political order that, through the vehicle of evangelism, legitimated the realization of that order through revolution. The consolidation of the new secular order, moreover, demanded the construction of a new set of principles designed to privilege liberty and preclude licentious-ness. At the same time, republican virtue demanded the construction of a regime in which liberty was constrained not through the authority of the wise, but through the legitimacy of the law. Furthermore, the state was relieved of its mandate for moral surveillance. The moral message was not imposed from on high, but tested in the crucible of endogenous moral capacity.

In reconciling liberalism and republicanism, equality represents the great republican compromise. Liberal democratic governance cannot accommodate the sort of differential recognition and affirmation of dig-nity so foundational to traditional republican theories of governance. Yet it was this socio-political hierarchy that republicans deemed neces-sary for the moral goodness that civility demands. The Enlightenment drove the revolutionary idea that far from being an exclusively exoge-nous good, human beings enjoy an innate and universal capacity for moral agency. The gradual emergence of commercialism and industrial-ization put that idea to the test and led to the general acceptance of governance by a society of equals.

The great liberal compromise, if we may call it that, occurs along the other three dimensions that we earlier identified needed to be recon-ciled. For these, it was not historical evolution that facilitated reconcilia-tion but the logical inconsistencies inherent in a purely liberal theory of governance. It is to the remaining dimensions of liberty, obligation, and purpose that the analysis now turns.

3

Liberal Republicanism:
Liberty, Obligation, and Purpose

AS THE PREVIOUS CHAPTER SUGGESTED, the route to a cogent understanding of the universalization of dignity involved an enormous shift in
republicans' commitment to equality. Such a shift was born of necessity;
there was no other way for republican ideals to remain relevant in a
world increasingly shaped by the egalitarian impulse unleashed by the
Enlightenment. In this chapter I explore the accommodations that an
internally consistent theory of liberalism must make to republican principles. The classically liberal understanding of liberty, obligation, and
purpose cannot meaningfully support a liberal republican form of government except by making accommodations to these principles.

LIBERTY

As we saw in the previous chapter, with the Enlightenment, the virtue
supplied by the great in traditional republican theory was no longer understood to be the province of the enlightened few. Instead, liberals of
the Enlightenment understood it to be universally distributed through
the moral self-sufficiency of all individuals. This moral endogeneity in
turn permitted self-governance; that is, it allowed self-sufficient agents to
exercise their liberty, and to do so in such a way that any constraints
upon that liberty were understood to be illegitimate unless justified by
the prevention of intrusion into the rights of others.

In keeping with Berlin's (1991) well-known distinction, liberals have
tended to conceive liberty in the negative sense. Certainly for classical
liberals, liberty represents a set of aggregated, specific freedoms, the universe of which is theoretically constrained only by the physical laws of
nature and whatever obstacles might be placed in one's way by others
(MacCallum 1991; Flew 2001). It represents the sort of liberty to which
all individuals had a natural right. Hobbes defines such liberty as "the

absence of externall Impediments: which Impediments may, oft take away part of a mans power to do what hee would; but cannot hinder him from using the power left him, according as his judgment and reason shall dictate to him" (1976, ch.14, 66).

For classical liberals, a moral entitlement to liberty was the jewel in the crown of natural rights. This commitment to liberty greatly constrained the mandate of the state. Indeed, liberals came to understand the minimalist liberal state's mandate as akin to that of a night watchman. Like the night watchman, the liberal state does not take on the role of mentor or facilitator of the good life. It does not teach individuals to live well – to find their authentic selves. It does not ensure social justice or virtue or moral capacity (Taylor 1991a, 142–3). Instead, from the liberal perspective, the role of the state is to ensure the protection of the natural rights requisite to an individually determined conception of the good life.

In contrast to this emphasis on negative liberty, traditional republicanism advocated something akin to what we now call positive liberty. The positive dimension of liberty represents antecedent conditions, discussed below, necessary to make liberty meaningful – a means to the larger end of authenticity.[1] For liberal republicans, individuals are innately capable of exercising their negative liberty in accordance with the imperatives of virtue. But the conditions that are required for positive liberty are something that must be socially constructed. Indeed, positive liberty can be understood as freedom from the sorts of internal constraints that prevent people from living their best lives. Ultimately, liberal republicanism holds that individuals are truly free only when they are liberated in both a negative and a positive sense.

The Nature of Rights

The first step to understanding the nature of liberty is to understand the nature of the *right* to liberty. Charles Taylor (1991a) argues that the classical, negative conceptualization of individuals' claim of entitlement to liberty starts from an unstable premise. One of the hallmarks of classical liberalism is the principle that individuals have more than just an *interest*

---

1 By an authentic life I mean the good life as it applies to the particular individual. In Brown's words, "When conduct and character come together in a coherent manner, consistent with the sense of self-worth, that person is authentic to himself and in the eyes of others" (2005, 159). Rae's interpretation of Kierkegaard on authenticity is also relevant: "Authenticity describes the highest form of being the individual can achieve" (2010, 78). Emerson appears to define authenticity as the conflation of the good with the particular when he says that "Nothing is at last sacred but the integrity of our own mind" (1951a, 35).

in their liberty, they actually possess a moral entitlement to it. But what is the basis of this claim to entitlement? Is God's intention that man should live and be free sufficient justification to establish the primacy of natural (negative) liberty as the basis for the construction of civil society and the night watchman state that oversees it? God intended that animals too should live, but most of us do not assert their entitlement to life, or for that matter any other rights. We treat animals differently than we treat humans. We keep them in cages for our amusement; use them for laboratory experiments; wear their skin; and consign them to unpaid employment, to name just a few practices that would provoke outrage were they to be practised on human beings.

A common and age-old response is that humans are unique in their inherent capacity to exercise reason (e.g., Cicero 1974, I. 107; Pico della Mirandola 1965). Whether or not this is the case (see, e.g., Hurley and Nudds 2006), it is not altogether clear how this inherent capacity alone can serve as the basis for humans to be uniquely entitled to the full schedule of human rights. What is it about this capacity that distinguishes it from other capacities that are more or less unique to humanity? Taylor notes that most animals cannot scratch themselves in the small of their backs, but doubts that our distinctiveness in this respect is a reasonable basis for any moral privilege. If we do possess a moral claim to human rights, the basis of it must go deeper than mere individual capacity.

What makes humans distinct from other creatures is the moral sense, or *intersubjectivity*, discussed in the previous chapter (Taylor 1985, 192–3; 1989, chs. 1.3–1.4). Human beings are distinct in their claim to rights because they are unique in recognizing and respecting that claim in others. Intersubjectivity entails each person recognizing the innate dignity that attaches to every individual by virtue of her humanity (see also Rawls 1963; Kateb 2011, 6). If rights are to have any meaning at all for Taylor, they have to be understood as but a means to the end of human dignity (see also Kateb 2011, chs. 1–2, esp. 21–7, 36–43; Walsh 2016, 246–56).[2] They must represent tools an individual uses in support of his entitlement to live an objectively good life – that is, a life that is morally good. If rights are to have any meaning at all for classical liberals, they must represent a tool that an individual uses in support of her entitlement to an individually determined good life – that is, a life that is subjectively good.

2 For a fundamentally different perspective on the relationship between rights and dignity see, for example, Feinberg 1980, esp. 151; Macklin 2003; and the discussion in Rosen 2012, 5–6.

For liberal republicans, because moral capacity is innate to all individuals, there is no tension between the subjective and objective dimensions of the good life. A virtuous individual will subjectively choose to live an objectively good life. Where virtuous individuals differ from classical liberals, however, is in the means by which they *develop* moral capacity. At least in the tradition of Locke, liberalism is predicated on the assumption that the moral capacity that makes the right to liberty meaningful already exists in a state of nature. It is this moral capacity that causes Locke to reject Hobbes's social contract and instead hold out for one in which the right to liberty survives leaving a state of nature.[3]

Locke's main point of departure from Hobbes is that he does not conceive of life in a state of nature as the anarchical, Lord-of-the-Flies-type existence that Hobbes describes. Instead, Locke's state of nature is governed by a prevailing moral sense that demands conformity to natural ethical principles. Locke, however, does not justify his assumption that individuals will follow their moral sense in a state of nature, and his assumption that morality will prevail is no more persuasive than Hobbes's assumption that it won't. Indeed, given the chaos of the English Civil War that was the backdrop to Hobbes's *Leviathan* there are reasons to question the basis of human morality in a state of nature, especially if we take Smith's point that moral capacity is born of social reflectivity – by which we can use our social interactions to gauge the cues to our own moral sense.

The argument here, not as arcane as it first appears, is that human moral capacity may be universal and it may be innate. But it is unlikely to be developed outside of civil society. This becomes important if the ethical purchase that attaches to rights is born not of God's intent, but rather of the centrality of rights to the realization of human dignity. Indeed, if Hobbes is correct that rights in a state of nature are used in such a purely subjective way that others are treated merely as objects – obstacles to be removed or overcome – then they enjoy no ethical purchase. Liberty in a state of nature represents a *capacity* but it does not meet the definition of a right as a product of intersubjective recognition and reciprocity. If human beings do not develop a moral order prior to the construction of a civil society, then the evolution from capacity to ethically informed *right* does not take place in a state of nature. One has no distinctly human claim to the sort of natural (Hobbesian) liberty in which one regards the

3 As far as Hobbes is concerned, liberty is no blessing in that while it liberates man to do as he wishes, the lack of constraint in a state of nature affords others equal liberty to visit harm upon him. Because human nature impels men to a ceaseless quest for power over others, individuals can be expected to use their liberty to this purpose.

other as an obstacle to his own ends. Assuming the prerogative of the beast permits no claim to uniquely human entitlement. Without inter-subjective recognition, a right is no different from a preference – a claim with no stronger ethical purchase than one's capability of defending it against the trespass of others.

For freedom to move from a preference shared by all living things to a human right it must make the transition from the solipsistic to the social. Thus Hegel, for example, sees the ethical society in terms of a developed civic consciousness. He conceives man's development in his progression away from a natural state toward a morally evolved condition that subor-dinates natural passions to a reasoned moral consciousness. For Hegel, however, this Kantian ideal is not a natural element of the human condi-tion so that through biological maturation he acquires the capacity for pure moral reasoning. Instead, man's moral evolution is affected by mankind's political evolution. This is reflected in the progressive con-struction of regimes in which man's internal dialectic between natural impulse and moral constraint comes to be reflected in the values that inform the regime. It is this dialectic that informs the relationship be-tween the objective and subjective good. Man's struggle within himself, like society's struggle within itself, ultimately finds resolution in Hegel through a moral synthesis, whereby self-interest and moral existence come to reflect one and the same thing. Our understanding of self-interest is transformed from a moral bad (or at least moral indetermi-nate) to a moral good, in which our natural impulses come to be seen as part of a larger cosmic plan, manifest in the spirit (*Geist*) of human be-ings (Hegel 1977, esp. chs. 4, 6; 2001, ss. 72–81; 105–57).

Hegel's intersubjectivity requires us to recognize the other as a dignity-bearing subject in his own right; one whose claim to the dignified life is no less valid than our own (Fichte 1869) and to mandate recognition of the other as one who carries "weight against one's freedom, and vice versa" (Williams 1997, 117; see also Solomon 1970; Taylor 1979, 14–23; Buchwalter 1992; Williams 1997, 67–71). Liberty is at the heart of dig-nity insofar as a person's dignity requires that she not be subordinated to the will of another. Indeed, for Hegel it is the master/slave relationship that informs the hierarchical structure of, for example, traditional re-publicanism, whereas it is the elimination of this relationship that in-forms the evolved society. Liberty is necessary to fulfill the human condition, that of a social being worthy of dignity and respect who re-quires the esteem of others, or at the very least the recognition that she is not beneath the dignity of others (Howard and Donnelly 1986, 803).

From here we can get a better grasp of Taylor's critique of the negative liberty/natural rights argument. Humans' moral entitlement to rights stems not from unique human capacity, but rather from the centrality of these goods to fulfilling the (unique) human condition in a way that does nothing, for example, to fulfill the canine or equine or porcine conditions (see also Kateb 2011, 9, 17). Further, it is not only the claim to dignity, but also the human capacity to command the intersubjective recognition of others that renders man unique among other forms of animate life in his right to liberty. Liberty exists not as the gift of God, but because other human beings recognize it as integral to what it means to be human. And because animals are incapable of intersubjective recognition of the other's claim to dignity, they are incapable of having rights. Or as Novak quotes a friend as saying, "the problem with animal rights is getting the animals to respect them" (1998, 115).[4]

Positive Liberty

If we claim an entitlement to liberty based on the capacity for reason alone, our job as a society is complete as long as every individual's claim to this right is honoured and protected equally. From this perspective, rationally self-sufficient individuals can realize their authenticity without any affirmative support by state and society. There is an attractiveness to assuming such self-sufficiency. It is tidy. We are free to pursue our happiness without any prevailing metaphysic that extends beyond the injunction against visiting harm upon another's equally valid moral entitlements.

But this position is difficult to sustain in the eyes of the liberal republican. If we are truly to respect liberty as a means to authenticity and ultimately dignity, then freedom must be understood in such a way as to bear directly on the development of that which makes us authentically us; it demands that each individual develop his or her capacities or talents or faculties so as to provide each with the dignity required for happiness. Individuals' lack of self-sufficiency en route to an authentic life broadens our obligations to others. If that which is estimable in human beings is not realizable outside of social context, then one's quest for authenticity – her obligation to herself in other words – demands a symbiotic relationship between self and civil society that extends beyond

---

4 There are any number of ways to state the same point. Rawls (2003, s. 77), for example, privileges human beings over animals by virtue of the fact that the former are unique in constructing an understanding of an authentic life plan for themselves that in turn demands the moral understanding to be able to extend justice toward one another. Taylor (1992, 41–2) suggests that human worth is a function of human potential, which, independently of how it is employed, is the basis of every human being's moral claim to rights.

mere respect for one another's moral entitlement to negative liberty. An individual's obligation to self and others expands beyond mere forbearance from exercising her liberty in such a way that violates the rights of others, toward concern – or an affirmative obligation to others – in their pursuit of an authentic life.

To put this somewhat differently, the problem with assigning hegemony to the negative understanding of liberty is not that such liberty is too all-encompassing, but rather that it is too *narrow*. In failing to identify correctly the basis of the moral entitlement to rights, classical liberalism fails to address, far less protect, what makes rights meaningful in the fulfillment of the human condition (Taylor 1985, esp. 192).[5] Meaningful freedom that privileges the respect for, and hence imperative to develop, estimable qualities is manifestly different from the licentious freedom extant in a state of nature.

The liberal republican argument here must effect a perilous balance. As with any form of republicanism, there is the danger of tyrannical paternalism in this line of thinking, whereby rather than leaving a person's life choices to the individual herself, the state nullifies the liberty that characterizes liberalism in the first place. But the argument need not be taken to such an extreme for it to make sense. A person need not be *compelled* to elevate himself beyond the station to which self-sufficiency alone takes him. He merely should be encouraged, or given the opportunity to understand, or be educated into a realization that the life choices he makes from the perspective of self-sufficiency will be less satisfying – less likely to lead to authenticity and happiness – than the choices he would make by developing his innate capacities and talents.

Liberal republicans hold that unreconstructed, negative liberty is not a panacea. It does not guarantee each individual the prospect of a fulfilling life. Indeed, it can have the opposite effect, serving to enslave a man to his appetites or shackle him to his ignorance and chauvinism, leaving him to the state of indignity more characteristic of the "stupid and unimaginative animal" than a human being capable of fulfilling the human condition (Rousseau 1913, I.8).

From the perspective of the reconstructed liberty inherent in liberal republicanism, meaningful freedom requires the greatest possible breadth of choice, something that comes through understanding the range of options that she has at her disposal. It is achieved by developing

---

5 Taylor's distinction here between liberty as an "exercise concept" and an "opportunity concept" mirrors the Thomist duality of liberty as exercise and specification, as well as, obviously, Berlin's distinction between positive and negative liberty (Taylor 1985, 214; Berlin 1991; Novak 1998, 113).

faculties that permit appreciation and encourage creativity in the arts, in science, in theology, in socio-political ideas and practices. It is born of the sort of knowledge that cannot be acquired through experience alone. Instead, meaningful liberty requires social guidance designed to open the mind to otherwise unknowable alternatives, and instill the confidence to have courage in one's convictions. This meaningful liberty is not exclusively positive. But it is partially informed by the positive freedom that permits meaningful choices – choices that cannot be made through blindly accepting the familiar and rejecting the strange (Taylor 1985, 204–6).

If the reconciliation of liberal and republican theories of liberty is to proceed any farther, it must be demonstrated that individuals are not innately self-sufficient in the pursuit of the good life, and that meaningful, positive freedom is foundational to the construction of a fulfilled and authentic life. There are two bases for refuting the self-sufficiency thesis. The first is that individuals may lack sufficient self-awareness to be able to exercise meaningful choices. The second is that rationality is vulnerable to influences that militate against its effectiveness.

Self-Awareness and Choice

One problem with the conceptual conflation of rational and authentic choices is that individuals may not know themselves as well as they think they do. The deeper meanings to which they should aspire if they are to make their lives more meaningful oftentimes are neither manifest nor innately knowable. To say that individuals know themselves better than another could possibly know them and hence are uniquely situated to determine their choices, is not the same as saying they will make the best choices. We could say that individuals are uniquely situated to understand their own feelings, but this hardly immunizes them from misperceiving those feelings, or from needing help from others from time to time to sort those feelings out. We filter our feelings, as well as our desires, through the lens of our own experiences. This leaves us vulnerable to our own preconceptions, some of which may be suboptimal or even unhealthy. If an individual's preconceptions about the efficacy of a good education, for example, preclude him from pursuing the sort of knowledge that ultimately would provide him with more fulfillment, his choice is suboptimal. If his preconceptions lead him to be suspicious, even hostile, to lifestyles different from what he would choose for himself, his choices may well be suboptimal (Taylor 1991a, 154–8).

A critical problem with the assumption of self-sufficiency is that the life choices we are talking about here are substantial and path-dependent. The sorts of decisions that an individual makes in pursuit of the authentic life cannot be understood as snapshots in time. It cannot be assumed that for every choice an individual makes, she starts with an Archimedean vantage point, that is, with sufficient perspective to see the full range of options laid out before her. Instead, choices that define our lives are part of a step-wise sequence of choices that constitute a life-path. As with all paths, life-paths constrain absolute freedom, vary in width, and afford us different perspectives upon our surroundings. The life-path analogy, moreover, is not an artifact of civil society. Life-paths exist in a state of nature as surely as they do in a civil society. In fact, it is reasonable to assert that not only do life-paths exist in a state of nature, there are fewer of them and the ones that exist offer a more limited perspective.

It is not just choice that sets us upon our life-paths. Circumstance has a lot to do with it, as does the way our families and other ambient agents of socialization bring us up to view and make sense of the world. It is reasonable to argue that a well-structured civil society is superior to a state of nature along each of these dimensions. A well-structured civil society can help individuals make better choices, it can ameliorate circumstances, and it can inform a socialization process so that it provides a broader worldview. Indeed, to the extent that it does any of these, it increases the chances that individuals will choose a broader and more elevated life-path than they would if left solely to their own devices.

From the standpoint of liberty alone, it is therefore critical that the life-path one chooses is born of more than luck, or impulse, or brute self-gratification, or chauvinism reflective of a narrow (minded) range of experiences. Yet these are the stimuli that inform life choices afforded by liberty in its natural state. Freedom may be absolute in one sense, but the narrow and cloistered life-paths that most will follow impose significant restrictions on meaningful choice. It is difficult to conceive how an individual can make optimal choices without guidance on those choices – how can she intuitively choose a meaningful life-path the very existence of which has not been revealed to her? How can she be sure that her choices reflect her authentic self? Can she be certain that her choices are not instead a product of the sorts of internal barriers to meaningful choice that individuals left to their own devices tend to reinforce rather than overcome? It is guidance under law, Locke argues, using a different metaphor, that "hedges us in from bogs and precipices," and that serves not as a limitation but rather "as the direction to a free and intelligent agent to his proper interest" (1974, VI.57).

In an environment in which there is spiritual or academic or legal or artistic guidance, in which people are not only exposed to different worldviews but are forced to defend their own through the process of civic dialogue, in which their minds are enriched through the creative and literary arts, and in which their talents are uncovered and appreciated, their capacities for choice are at the same time conceptually more restricted but practically less constrained. In this sense, the magnitude of freedom enjoyed by an individual is increased when he is liberated from internal constraints through which he filters his rational decisions.[6] His freedom is increased if, for example, he is obliged through some form of civic interaction to recognize his potential. Or if he gains from that same interaction the courage of his convictions to chart a course for his authentic life in defiance of social convention or some long-held internalized self-regard that stands as an obstacle to his pursuit of that life.

Limiting our perspective on our range of meaningful choices has important and negative implications for the authenticity of those choices. However, the lack of an innate capacity for self-awareness is not the only problem with conflating rationality and authenticity. A second, and possibly even more substantial problem, is that our reason is subject to vulnerability. On the face of it, such a claim undermines the point made in the previous chapter that individuals are morally endogenous agents. Indeed, we posited that moral reason was one of two innate capacities indicative of moral endogeneity. However, to claim that individuals have an endogenous capacity for reason is not the same thing as saying that individuals are self-sufficient in employing that reason to live their best lives. The capacity for moral reason may be sufficient to preclude sociopolitical hierarchy but the argument here is that its vulnerability renders it inadequate to the realization of an authentic life.

Vulnerability of Reason

One way in which reason is vulnerable is through passion. For most philosophers, ancient and modern, reason is associated with self-governance whereas passionate responses to circumstances outside our control constitute an abdication of self-governance. Self-governance is fundamental to both liberty and happiness: liberty in the sense that freedom without the agency to employ it has no value, and happiness in the Stoic sense that true fulfillment demands sufficient detachment from our passions to experience happiness independent of circumstance. Self-governance demands, then, that we employ our reason to distinguish properly between that which truly matters to us and that which only appears to

---

6 As Taylor puts it: "We can't say that someone is free, on a self-realization view, if he is totally unrealized, if for instance he is totally unaware of his potential, if fulfilling it has never arisen as a question for him, or if he is paralysed by the fear of breaking some social norm that he has internalized but that does not authentically reflect him" (1991a, 144).

matter (Walsh 1958; Colish 1985; Scodel 2005; see also Aristotle 1999, X.1–8, esp. 1177a–b). Just as the imperative for reason to govern passion has long been accepted, so too has it been recognized that passion can subordinate reason by directing the will toward actions that we would not take in a dispassionate state. So broadly is this potential recognized that, for example, many modern countries' legal systems allow emotion to serve as a mitigation of criminal sanction.

But the power of passion to appropriate temporary control of the will is hardly enough to assail the argument that rational choices and authentic choices are one and the same. Hume argues that passion is more insidious than a force appropriating temporary control of the will. Indeed, he claims that it is passion, not reason, that governs the will. Passion represents a feeling or perception or sentiment antecedent to judgment. Because it represents the lens through which we perceive things, it sets the parameters (limits the choice-sets, if you will) in which our reason operates. There need be no tension between passion and reason. It is reasonable, for example, to feel emotion appropriate to circumstance, such as sadness at a funeral or joy at a wedding. However, there are other circumstances when passion and reason clash in such a way that we think of the passion as unreasonable, or as representing an inaccurate judgment. Hume suggests that passion is unreasonable when it represents means insufficient to one's chosen ends, or when it is based on suppositions that have no basis in fact (1896, II.III.3).

In other words, passion is unreasonable when it is inauthentic. The problem that arises for those who insist on the sufficiency of reason is that we tend *not* to be self-sufficient in our capacity to evaluate the authenticity of our emotions. Certainly it is possible to misperceive feelings. We may, for example, feel shame or fear or resentment when there is no *reasonable* cause to do so (Taylor 1991a, 154–8). We are then not governed by an invulnerable reason, but instead are deceived by our feelings. Our reason is not overwhelmed by our passion, but distorted by it.[7] Thus, when we speak of the courage of convictions we do so in recognition of the fact that oftentimes human beings lack such courage. Their misplaced fear or guilt about causing offence, or alienating others' esteem, or not fitting in, causes them to reject actions that conform to their more authentic convictions (i.e., Emerson 1951a; Budziszewski

---

7 This sort of misperception is not particular to individuals. Machiavelli warns in *The Discourses* that a "populace, misled by the false appearance of the good, often seeks its own ruin, and, unless it be brought to realize what is bad and what is good for it by someone in whom it has confidence, brings on republics endless dangers and disasters" (1975, I.53).

1999). We thus find ourselves living lives in which we are hostage to our own misperceptions.

It is not just passion that illustrates the vulnerability of reason; vulnerability also manifests itself in what Aristotle calls incontinence or akrasia. Aristotle uses the term to connote both impetuosity and weakness of the will (1999, 1150b, 20) – the gratification of short-term preferences at the expense of more cherished, long-term, authentic objectives (1999, 1151a, 5). Akratic behaviour is not irrational. It simply represents an inability to prioritize our desires optimally so that when our desires conflict we overvalue our immediate preferences and undervalue our broader and more meaningful ones (1151a, 3; 1152a, 3). Akrasia represents vulnerability of reason to the extent that our internal weakness causes us to gratify desires that do not authentically represent that which we should desire and that which we *know* we should desire. It is often accompanied by a sort of buyer's remorse that sets in only after the supersized fast food meal, or the repeated use of the snooze button.

Having demonstrated the importance of innate moral reason in the previous chapter, we now run the risk of taking it too far. It is our own rationality that often cannot get out of its own way, leading us not to authenticity but instead to settling for the suboptimal choices that our own conflicted rationality imposes upon us. It is in recognition of this fact that human beings intentionally seek to protect themselves from themselves by pre-committing, to borrow Schelling's (1984) well-known term, to constraints on their own liberties. The chronic late sleeper, for example, might place her alarm clock across the room to compensate for her propensity to silence it. The partier might give his car keys to a friend (with strict orders not to return them) before ordering his first drink.

Socially speaking, the vulnerability of our reason is what justifies Locke's hedges against the bogs and the precipices. It represents Madison's Ulysses-like justification for the sorts of constitutional rules that immunize certain (what we will later call primary) social values from change through the normal legislative process. Ultimately, it informs Rousseau's distinction between liberty that is natural and impulsive and liberty that is born of civility. It is only civil liberty, Rousseau argues, that provides the sort of constraint under law that provides a person with the ability to master himself, to stimulate his faculties, extend his ideas, ennoble his feelings and uplift his soul; to provide him, in other words, "proprietorship of all he possesses" (1913, I.8).

Vulnerability of reason represents a significant obstacle to the ability of individuals to determine an optimal conception of the good life for themselves. It suggests a distinction between the authentic self and the ends it sometimes pursues. The failure of the negative conception of liberty to distinguish the self from its ends – much less give the self priority over its ends – violates the rationality principle insofar as choice becomes a product of chance, of the experiential flotsam and jetsam that individuals randomly accumulate over the course of their life's journeys, rather than the reasoned decisions made by individuals who have been guided into a position from which they can make their best choices (Sandel 1982, 19).

If we accept that our reason is vulnerable in the ways just discussed, it holds that our moral entitlement to liberty is grounded in something different than a natural right based solely on the uniquely human capacity to reason. Instead, it is grounded in the entitlement we all have to develop our capacities in an estimable way – a way that commands respect from others and fulfills the human imperative for dignity. It does not negate the importance of liberating individuals from illegitimate external constraint. Rather, it sees such liberation as insufficient to exercising true freedom. Nor does it mandate the reimposition of a social or theological hierarchy in the name of exogenous moral wisdom. Instead, a broader, positive conception of liberty is necessary, both to justify a moral entitlement to the rights that every individual can claim in support of his dignity, and to live his life in an authentic, estimable, and dignity-enhancing way.

Unless we are willing to accept that individuals are self-sufficient in their capacities to live their best lives – that they could realize their best lives in a state of nature – the liberal position on liberty is too thin. It assumes no internal limitations on the effective exercise of human liberty. But such a position rests on a very tenuous logical foundation. The argument here is that left to their own devices – without the resources, guidance, and general affirmative obligation of citizens to assist one another in the pursuit of an authentic life – individuals will be insufficiently self-aware to make optimal life choices. This is especially so given that human reason is vulnerable to the intrusion of passion and akrasia. By contrast, the reconciled liberal republican perspective on liberty is that true freedom demands liberation in both a negative and a positive sense. A fundamental misreading of human capacity that assigns too much efficacy to human reason renders the classical liberal theory of (negative) liberty inadequate to its ends.

OBLIGATION

One area where both classical liberals and republicans agree is that the ultimate purpose or objective of life is living a life of fulfillment. We can think of this fulfillment as stemming from the obligation one has to oneself. As we have just noted, the classical liberal conflation of rationality and authenticity mandates a thin theory of obligation to the self, whereby an individual fulfills that obligation by pursuing the objectives she rationally desires. Thus, an individual fulfills her obligation to the self by retaining as much of her natural liberty as she can within the protective confines of a civil society. Individual fulfillment is endogenously discoverable through rationality, and individuals are uniquely situated to evaluate their life choices. They will make the most authentic choices when sufficiently unencumbered by external constraint. By contrast, liberal republicanism mandates a thicker theory of obligation to the self insofar as individuals are unlikely to be self-sufficient in developing the faculties necessary to make optimal life choices. Instead, constrained by their own prejudices, fears, and misperceptions, liberal republicans hold that without the opportunities inherent in social guidance – through education or the arts or science or religion or law – choice-sets will be extremely limited. It is only through the development of their abilities to make meaningful life choices that individuals will be able to fulfill their obligations to themselves.

Practical versus Moral Obligation

In addition to the obligation to the self, both classical liberalism and liberal republicanism articulate theories of obligation to the community. In its thin manifestation, civic obligation may be thought of as *practical* obligation. Practical obligation is the product of a simple cost-benefit analysis motivated by the desire to maintain reciprocal consideration – one fulfills her obligation to another because she wants him to fulfill his obligation to her; avoid the threat of sanction – because she does not want to deal with the civil authorities if her failure to fulfill her obligation constitutes a violation of the law; or protect one's reputation – because she cares what others think about her.

By contrast, in its thick manifestation civic obligation represents *moral* obligation. Moral obligations are a manifestation of goodness or virtue. We can think of moral obligation as an affirmative obligation to justice. A moral obligation is undertaken because it is the right thing to do. It requires no calculation of the utility involved or the prospect of reciprocal benefit. Moral obligation may be motivated by self-interest since the individual who performs it does so in pursuit of his own fulfillment. More often, however, moral obligation is imposed by law. Either way, the benefits are neither quantifiable nor excludable insofar as third parties often benefit indirectly (Smith 1982; Hegel 2001, esp. par. 199–228; Germino 1969, esp. 890–1; Putnam 1995).

Foundational to the classical liberal conception of obligation is voluntary consent (Walsh 1997, 63, 134). Such consent is the foundation on which a social contract rests and from which the laws reflective of the mandate of the night watchman state derive their legitimacy. The nature of these laws is that they are grounded in forbearance. One fulfills her legal obligations passively insofar as she respects the rights of others and the laws designed to protect those rights. There is no teleological mandate here; the minimalist liberal state does not exist to impose moral purpose. Its role is defensive and reactive in that it cannot legitimately advance a conception of the good life. It cannot take an affirmative role in the promotion of goodness or fairness or even rightness except to the extent that such affirmative action directly protects rights or militates against a manifest threat to human rights. A good example of the thinness of obligation inherent in classical liberalism is Nozick's rejection of the redistributive principle on the grounds that individuals are justly entitled to possess that which they obtain legally and cannot legitimately be compelled to divest themselves of a portion of their wealth in the name of a set of social purposes that violate the mandate of the reactive liberal state (1974, ch. 7, esp. 150–3).[8]

This thin theory of obligation is elegant in theory. But it becomes unsustainable in practice. Taken to its extreme, the thinness of obligation demanded by classical liberalism calls into question citizens' obligation even to obey laws to which they do not consent (e.g., Simmons 1979). Indeed, an antecedent problem attaches to the contractarian basis of law itself. If obligation is the product of voluntary consent, there must be a vehicle for that consent to be granted. From the liberal perspective the

8 This prohibition extends to the state's legitimate capacity to take affirmative steps toward a conception of the good that reflects social preferences. A utilitarian calculus that extends the mandate of the state still violates the thin theory of obligation unless those preferences are unanimous and perpetual, or (according to Nozick's compensation principle) are offset by sufficient compensation to render dissenting individuals indifferent to the loss of liberties encroached upon by the state's affirmative mandate. The compensation principle demands that individuals who are pre-emptively constrained from engaging in risky behaviour be compensated for such a violation of their liberty. This compensation must be equal to the additional costs incurred by the person pre-emptively constrained. Nozick uses the example of a prohibition of epileptics to drive their cars on the grounds that they might have a seizure and injure those whom the state has contracted to protect. Because it is an untenable violation of someone's freedom to prevent him from doing something that might cause harm (we can imagine how quickly this could spin out of control – every person who drives *might* injure someone) this prohibition is justifiable only if the person who suffers such constraint is compensated to a degree to which he is indifferent to the constraint. In this example, he would be entitled to be compensated out of a public fund for the cost of hiring taxis, chauffeurs, etc. (78–9, 142–6).

state cannot impose even thin, practical obligations if the state itself is not the product of voluntary consent.

Classical liberal conceptions of obligation typically begin with a Lockean social contract, or something very much like it. But as Hume and Jefferson and others have pointed out over the years, a contract is a static good whereas consent is a dynamic process. New citizens are born or come of age every day, while the social contract – or the constitution that reflects it – is subject only to episodic revision. For such logistical reasons alone, true consent is of necessity fictive. Locke's well-known solution is to take tacit consent as a proxy for true consent. One consents to a social contract by receiving the benefits and assuming the obligations of living in a civil society. The problem is, of course, there is no reasonable counterfactual alternative. What does it mean to withdraw tacit consent? Can one simply walk away from a political society that is not to his tastes? Can he do so if he has no money for passage and no linguistic skills or knowledge of foreign mores? Hume (1994) likens it to being put on a ship in the middle of the ocean. No one is forcing you to stay, but the alternatives are not too attractive.

A more reasonable solution is to *assume* voluntary consent. That is, we can assume consent to obligations to which a reasonable person would rationally commit herself. For example, if we accept the fairly reasonable assumption that all individuals value their negative liberty, it is reasonable to assume that individuals will accept legal constraints if such constraints were the means to *preserve* that liberty. We could not assume acceptance of specific forms of constraint – that would be the stuff of politics. But we could assume acceptance of the *principle* of constraint. From here we can make two additional assumptions. Individuals will accept specific constraints under law as long as such constraints are consistent with the principle of constraint. And individuals will accept the constitution or social contract that reflects the principle of constraint.

This assumption of voluntary consent cannot be said to damage the volunteerist imperative mandated by classical liberals. In fact, without it the contractarian basis of civil society is unsupportable. Its centrality lies in the dearth of better options. True consent is a logistical impossibility. Tacit consent cannot be thought of as consent at all lacking a reasonable alternative to consent. And an absence of consent is inconsistent with liberal democratic forms of government. The only palatable alternative is to assume consent to a thing if it is reasonable to assume that any rational individual would support its aims and principles (see Elster 1979; Holmes 1988).

The assumption of voluntary consent, however, has broader implications. If we assume consent to a social contract and the minimalist state that emerges from it, we assume consent to practical obligations, we assume consent to respect the rights of others in exchange for protection of our own rights, and we accept the practical obligations inherent in laws that are consistent with the mandate of the night watchman state. But do we consent to more than this? The problem for liberals lies in limiting the scope of the assumption. Indeed, if we assume consent to practical obligations on the grounds of universal desirability, we open the door to moral obligations that can be justified on the same grounds (e.g., Hegel 2001, par. 149–52).

At its core, moral obligation reflects the means by which we engage one another for the betterment of all within society. Our moral obligation mandates a social, or intersubjective, dimension that extends beyond the thin, practical theory of obligation that informs classical liberalism. At a minimum, moral obligation demands that we lead a public or civic life. Indeed, we have already noted that human beings lack self-sufficiency in pursuing an authentic or good life. As a result, everyone within society incurs an obligation to ensure that others have the social resources to realize authentic and hence fulfilled lives.[9]

We need not construe our moral obligation to participate in public life as narrowly as did the ancient Romans, for example, who insisted on military service. Nor, Kant notwithstanding, must our motives be pure for us to fulfill our moral obligations. Instead, our moral obligation to contribute to public life is realized through manifold means, through contributions to the arts, the economy, the academy, and the non-profit sector. We fulfill our moral obligation by the grand as well as the mundane: by keeping ourselves informed about current events, by voting, and by our participation in civic and other voluntary associations. An important element of this obligation takes the form of judgment of others' behaviour, attaching moral (albeit not necessarily legal) sanction to behaviour that violates standards deemed to be socially acceptable. And of course, we have a moral obligation to help inform the character of the law in such a way as to promote justice, not just to protect self-interest.

Such a commitment to public life is critical to fostering a sense of common purpose that can be expressed as a commitment to the values and sense of usness for which a republic stands. It represents popular stewardship of the public space. It is civic participation in the construction of laws that provides the law with its character and imbues law with legitimacy. The rules and values that bind us, and help inform our

9 Thus, says Mill: "Human beings owe to each other help to distinguish the better from the worse, and encouragement to choose the former and avoid the latter. They should be for ever stimulating each other to increased exercise of their higher faculties, and increased directions of their feelings and aims toward wise instead of foolish, elevating instead of degrading, objects and contemplations" (1972, 133).

understanding of authentic choices, are constructed and perpetuated through refinement born of debate and dialogue (DeLue 1989, esp. chs. 2–3). The character of the laws represents the fruits of the aggregated virtue of the citizenry, what Taylor (1988/1989, 861) calls the "common repository of the citizens' dignity." Just as individuals owe their self-fulfillment to the guidance of the state, the state owes its capacity for guidance to the community of virtuous citizens who employ their talents and capacities in aid of the greater good (Aristotle 1962, 1276b, 5; 1332a, 9; 1333b, 21).

It is difficult to see how a state predicated solely upon the thin theory of obligation would lead to a more fulfilling or freer life than would a society that mandates a thicker theory of obligation. It is difficult to see how a community held together by the bonds of self-interest alone could engender the sorts of positive feelings of society or nationhood or usness necessary to permit societies to weather crises, social conflict, and even war. This is not to minimize the importance of self-interest as a motive for public action. Indeed, the famous "Adam Smith problem," which seeks to reconcile the Adam Smith of the *Theory of Moral Sentiments* with the Adam Smith of the *Wealth of Nations*, disappears if we allow that moral obligation and self-interest are mutually compatible. But this compatibility does not make self-interest and moral obligation substitutable goods. Whether the motives are pure or instrumental, moral obligation is the glue that binds societies together. It guides individuals into an understanding of the sorts of values that inform their life choices. Moral obligation represents a bulwark, if not an absolute prohibition, against dissolute and unproductive life choices that imperil citizens' ability to pursue authentic lives.

PURPOSE

We have seen that moral obligation cannot be excluded from the logic of classical liberalism on the grounds that it somehow represents a burden to which people have not strictly consented. As shown, no burden can pass that test. Moreover, there is no reasonable justification for the position that while practical obligations may be assumed, moral ones cannot. But I have yet to show that moral obligation is a civic *necessity* rather than a mere ideological preference. In order to do so, we must explore the idea of civic purpose to which moral obligation is so central.

As already noted, a critical distinction between classical liberalism and traditional republicanism turns on an understanding of what is meant by *the good.* Classical liberalism is predicated upon the assumption that there is no *ex ante* conception of the good (for example Dworkin 1978, 127).

The liberal state is therefore non-purposive since it is grounded in no metaphysical moral precepts beyond the idea that rights bring with them a corollary set of duties that mandate reciprocal respect of the rights of others (see Walsh 1997, 33–45). As such, the night watchman state exists to be vigilant and even proactive in anticipating threats to life and liberty and taking the appropriate steps to mitigate them (e.g., Nozick 1974, 78–9).

But herein lies great ambiguity and even inconsistency. It is virtually impossible to construct an exclusively non-teleological mandate for even the minimalist state. Civil societies demand certain a priori restrictions on liberty as a means of preserving the rights of citizens. Everyone can agree that the state cannot be indifferent as to the rate of travel of automobiles on its streets, or the unregulated discharging of firearms in urban settings, or the enforcement of fire codes, and food standards, and licensing of medical personnel, and on and on and on. But there are any number of grey areas. Can the minimalist state be indifferent as to the use of helmets for motorcyclists? Or the unregulated use of harmful substances? Or the ability of a woman to obtain an abortion? Whose freedom do we seek to protect, the cyclist's or the society that must care for him after the brain injury? The junkie's or the citizens who must support his lifestyle while protecting themselves from him? The woman's or the fetus's?

Lacking a teleological conception of the good beyond the preservation of rights, these moral problems and countless like them become impossible for the truly minimalist liberal state to resolve. Since individuals' particularistic and subjective conceptions of the good will differ, the question for liberal minimalists is what sorts of decision-rules can minimalist states employ in prioritizing differing conceptions of the good? Given the state's mandate to preserve rights, how can it prioritize, for example, different manifestations of liberty? Even if these different manifestations do not come into direct conflict with one another, it is incumbent on a state to prioritize its agenda.

I would like to explore three options for reconciling competing conceptions of the good. The first is a calculus of rights in which states prioritize actions according to the degree to which such actions enhance or preserve the relevant right. The second is societal preference aggregation in which the state prioritizes civic preferences according to their extent or intensity. The third is what Rawls (1996, 63) calls reasonable pluralism.

A Calculus of Rights

The logic of the night watchman state is that it exists to protect or enhance rights. This would not be a problem if rights were absolutes. The night watchman state would have no difficulties if all policies could be classified as either right-enhancing or right-depleting. But rights are not absolutes. There are always circumstances that demand limiting or qualifying a right. Similarly, states are rarely faced with circumstances that oblige them to discern between right-enhancement and right-depletion. Enhancing or protecting a right typically is less about binary choice than it is about prioritizing competing means to right-enhancement. Unfortunately, the liberal state's minimalist mandate provides it with few tools to engage in such prioritization. One such tool is a crude calculus that permits the state to prioritize its options by determining the *degree* to which different policies enhance the right in question. The issue then becomes whether such a calculus can escape relying on a metaphysical conception of the good.

Taylor argues that it cannot (1991a). He asks us to examine prioritization of liberty if we are guided by nothing more than a calculus of rights. Taylor posits two types of legal constraints upon his freedom. The first is traffic signals on a major road he uses frequently; the second is a proclamation that restricts his freedom to worship as he pleases. Taylor accepts the construction of traffic signals as a reasonable inconvenience; restrictions on his freedom to worship he deems unacceptable. There is nothing remarkable there. Few would question his level of tolerance for either circumstance.

The problem is that the minimalist state would appear to have no mandate for arriving at Taylor's conclusion. If it calculates only the degree to which freedom is constrained by traffic signals on the one hand and edicts restricting freedom of worship on the other, traffic signals should be considered more restrictive. More people are affected by traffic signals than religious edicts, because everyone is obliged to move around a city, but not everyone is affected by restrictions on how to worship. Indeed, many will not worship at all, and many more already will worship in the methods prescribed by the state. Moreover, whereas most religious services are held only once or twice a week, restrictions on vehicular mobility affect citizens every day. Thus, a simple calculus tells us that traffic lights are more restrictive than state-sanctioned religious edicts.

Obviously this conclusion is nonsensical. Common sense demands that freedom of worship is more meaningful than freedom of vehicular mobility. The problem is that the liberal state is not equipped to exercise common sense. There is no metaphysical principle to which common sense can appeal. Without a prevailing metaphysic there is simply no way for the night watchman state to determine which liberties are to be assigned the most weight.

Preference Aggregation

This argument is not dispositive or definitive. In fact, it is easily deflected since the classical liberal state's mandate also demands responsiveness to societal preferences. While the state itself has no inherent means of discriminating between meaningful and trivial protection or enhancement of rights, it does have the means to *import* such discrimination. As such, one way of exercising discrimination independent of social purpose would be through preference aggregation in which the capacity of citizens to discriminate among liberties relieves the state of such an imperative. Rational individuals can be expected to prize the preservation of freedoms they hold most dear (such as unregulated freedom of worship) and assign less value to marginal liberties (such as unfettered vehicular mobility in an urban environment). Simply by aggregating the preferences of rational citizens, a non-teleological state can arrive at a reasonable prioritization of values.

The problem here is that to reach this outcome, the liberal state may be forced to reject other parts of its mandate. We could imagine, for example, a scenario under which a radical secularizing trend altered aggregated preferences in such a way as to devalue the freedom to worship as one pleased. What had once been a cherished freedom for the majority, and very much remains one for a minority of the citizenry, could be relegated to the status of a trivial liberty as easily disregarded as the freedom to drive free from the constraints of traffic signals. Under such circumstances the minimalist state again would struggle to assign appropriate weight to the freedom to worship.

The mandate of the classical liberal state is to protect or enhance the rights of *all* individuals. It is obliged to do more than simply gratify the aggregated preferences of its citizens. Indeed, the whole basis of rights is to provide recourse to all as a means of preserving that to which they are morally entitled: preservation of their dignity in defiance of aggregated social preferences that might otherwise deprive them of that dignity (Margalit 1996, ch. 2). Such safeguards are not built in to theories of preference aggregation. Thus, to take an even more extreme case than freedom of worship, if we rely on the logic of preference aggregation alone, and deprive it of prevailing moral principles such as the fact that it is simply not okay for one person to own another, preference aggregation cannot exclude slave-holding as acceptable public policy.

Reasonableness: Pluralism

While preference aggregation is more likely to provide a reasonable outcome than a calculus of rights, its potential for illiberal outcomes renders it unequal to task prioritization by the liberal state. Reasonable pluralism represents a more promising alternative. Like preference aggregation, reasonable pluralism provides the societal input that allows the liberal state to prioritize different manifestations of rights. Unlike preference aggregation, however, reasonable pluralism represents a way to avoid bad outcomes while privileging individuals' freedom to pursue their own conceptions of the good. Unfortunately for liberal minimalists, though, reasonable pluralism brings with it the imperative for some sort of a priori institutional and cultural agreement as to what constitutes the good.

Reasonable pluralism is fundamentally an enhanced theory of societal preference aggregation. As such, it begins with the premise that differing conceptions of the good life have the potential to become socially intractable and divisive. Militating against such divisiveness is the assumption of a multidimensional issue space in the legislative process. Because group membership is not static – it changes from issue dimension to issue dimension – in a multidimensional issue space permanent allegiances rarely build up, and the same holds true for permanent intergroup hostility. Indeed, as Madison surmised, the reason why minorities accede to majority rule is that where the boundaries of political contestation are wide, the logic of overlapping group membership suggests that no one class of citizens enjoys a monopoly on political success, and no one group is destined to suffer perpetual defeat (see Latham 1952; Dahl 1961). Policy "losers" accept their losses secure in the reasonable assumption that happier outcomes await across other issue dimensions.

Where reasonable pluralism differs from societal preference aggregation, however, is in its reliance upon reasonableness. Reasonableness represents a way of prioritizing values mediated by something more than mere preference gratification. It constitutes a shared normative code predicated on a generalized sense that social purposes advanced by the state might reasonably be understood as conducive to the good of all individuals. It entails, in DeLue's words, a "doctrine that should inform each person's life, and when citizens live as the doctrine requires they are likely to work together to build a society based on a shared conception of the public good for each of the policy domains of society" (1989, x; also Downing and Thigpen 1993). Reasonableness is what Kant means by a *sensus communis*. For Emerson, reasonableness represents "mankind's bill of rights, or Royal Proclamation of the intellect ascending the throne, announcing its good pleasure that now, once and for all, the world shall be governed by common sense and law of morals" (1891, 491).

Reasonableness informs a social consensus as to the parameters of the good that must underscore all legitimate state action. This is not to say that it represents consensus as to how the good plays out with any degree of precision. Consensus cannot be expected to extend to policy minutiae, for instance, that all can be expected to agree on an appropriate rate of speed on a given stretch of road. It does not even demand consensus on larger issues such as how a right to free speech or to bear arms would work in practice. This sort of precision is unrealizable, not to mention undesirable. Instead, given the inevitability of difference over the details, reasonableness demands tolerance of others' conceptions of the good as bounded by consensus about the parameters of the good.[10]

Social consensus, then, does not demand conformity or blind acceptance of law. But it is required to legitimate state authority. A legitimate state can accommodate dissent, even civil disobedience and mass protest. By the same token, however, where reasonable social consensus does not exist, citizens may be expected to have little respect for the authority of the state. Policy decisions undertaken by a state that lacks general legitimacy will certainly be observed by *winners*. But for those whose preferences are not realized, resentment often grows until the alienated and disenchanted ultimately seek their ends outside the boundaries prescribed by civil society (Dobel 1978; DeLue 1989, 4–5). In turn, a state that cannot rely on general acceptance of its rules and policies is expected to have to rely on coercion and limitations on liberty (DeLue 1989, 6).

Reasonable social consensus is informed by an underlying metaphysic, which Galston (1995, 529) calls the "principled path between intrusion and laissez-faire." It is this social consensus that precludes the classical liberal state from being purposively neutral. Instead, the mandate of any democratic state is to promote tolerance on the one hand, and social consensus on the other. Its role is to exercise prudent judgment to ensure that tolerance does not exceed the boundaries of goodness and that the imperative for goodness not extinguish the liberty respected by tolerance. This being the case, the liberal state cannot be without purpose (Walsh 1997, ch. 2). Its mandate must extend beyond merely preserving rights. For people to be reasonable and tolerant, they must be socialized into reasonableness and tolerance. They must acquire what Galston calls social rationality – a set of tools required for effective economic, social, and political participation in the public life of the liberal society. The construction of a state of reasonable and tolerant people must inform the mandate of the liberal state if it is to be generally accepted as

---

10 The above discussion assumes that all individuals' highest ideals can be subsumed under the umbrella of reasonableness. Whether they can (see for example Murray 2005) or cannot (Walsh 1997, 37) is a contestable point.

legitimate. As such, its laws and institutions must be constructed in such a way as to teach and promote reasonableness and tolerance.

The actions of the liberal state must be fair, be seen to be fair, and represent a consensus as to what is fair. The classical liberal state is purposive because it has to be purposive. It cannot exist in any meaningful sense without a metaphysical social consensus as to the nature of the good.[11] The true purpose of the liberal state – a purpose without which it cannot meaningfully prioritize its values – is the basis for the liberal republican state. The liberal republican state's purpose is informed by the thicker theory of obligation discussed above. This purpose infuses the state with a mandate to enforce moral and not merely practical obligation. It obliges the state to protect not only negative liberties, but to some (socially defined) extent, positive liberties as well. It is for this reason that Galston, in rejecting the logical coherence of the non-teleological (night watchman) state, characterizes what we are calling the liberal republican state as the product of "a community organized in pursuit of a distinctive ensemble of public purposes. It is these purposes that undergird its unity, structure its institutions, guide its policies, and define its public virtues. In the constitutional context, it is these purposes that shape an appropriate understanding of compelling state interests that warrant public interference with group practices" (1995, 524). Without such purpose, there can be no meaningful society. Or as Galston puts it, there can be "no pluribus without the unum" (525; see also Galston 1982; 1991; DeLue 1989).

Ultimately, purpose informs national identity. This is why Rousseau raises this purpose to the status of a civil religion, which "gives [a society] its gods, its own tutelary patrons; [civil religion] has its dogmas, its rites, and its external cult prescribed by law; outside the single nation that follows it, all the world is in its sight infidel, foreign and barbarous; the duties and rights of man extend for it only as far as its own altars" (1913. bk. IV.8). For Bellah, the civil religion represents a generally accepted moral order as well as the mythology and symbolism associated with national identity, without which societies lose their social cohesion (1975). The iconic symbols of the civil religion serve to bind the society, whatever else might divide it, during times of crisis and war.

---

11 It may not literally be able to exist either. As Buchanan points out, without a theory of purpose, a liberal state cannot reasonably deny an ethnic minority the right to collective self-determination through secession (1991, ch.1).

CONCLUSION

The theory of classical liberalism represents an elegant heuristic. Yet, as discussed in this chapter, in practice it quickly becomes untenable. The problem with relying on only a negative theory of liberty, a thin (or practical) theory of obligation, and a non-teleological mandate for the liberal state is that real-world democratic states simply cannot work this way. Instead, modern democracies marry liberal and republican principles pertaining to the three values explored in this chapter. It is these three reconciled values, along with the equality discussed in the previous chapter, that informs the liberal republican theories of justice discussed in the next chapter.

Liberalism and republicanism are incompatible only if we restrict our understanding of liberty to freedom from external constraints. Such a restricted understanding of liberty, however, fails to account for the equally significant internal dimension of freedom. Internal constraints represent limitations on our self-sufficiency in living a good or fulfilled or authentic life. As we saw in the previous chapter, liberal republicanism is predicated on the idea of moral self-sufficiency. This should not be understood to mean, however, that individuals are self-sufficient in overcoming the fears or prejudices or lack of confidence that constitute internal barriers to an authentic life.

Individuals do not enjoy self-sufficiency in the pursuit of an authentic life. If they did, their rational capacity would permit them to overcome the sorts of internal constraints just mentioned. But as we have seen, human reason is vulnerable to distortion through passion as well as akratic indeterminism. Given this vulnerability of reason, individuals must rely on social resources – educational, cultural, social, economic, and political – that help them acquire the tools they need to overcome internal limitations on true liberty. The purpose of this chapter was not to show that positive liberty is more important than negative liberty, because manifestly no liberal theory of governance could accommodate such a position. Rather it was to show that positive and negative liberty are inherently reconcilable as two sides of the same coin, both of which are foundational to a truly free life.

One implication of over-emphasis of individual self-sufficiency in pursuit of the authentic life is that classical liberals rely on an insupportably thin theory of obligation to the self (Taylor 1991a). That is, from the liberal perspective, we owe ourselves the negative freedom to pursue our desires, but if we are not self-sufficient in our pursuit of the authentic life, obligation to the self thickens, demanding that we create a social context that provides the resources through which we achieve liberation from internal constraints.

This distinction between a thin and thick theory of obligation to the self also informs theories of obligation to society. The thin theory of social obligation represents what we have called practical obligation – respecting commitments made to others (including the preservation of their rights) as a means to reciprocal consideration from others. This practical obligation is private since it does not entail a social commitment that is beyond obedience to legitimate laws. And even the imperative to obey the law is justifiable only through the volunteerist assumption that all individuals can be assumed to consent to constraints that ultimately benefit them. In relying on the volunteerist assumption, classical liberals assume that all rational individuals will choose to preserve their liberty, and hence will choose the sorts of constraints inherent in a social contract, a constitution, or the law as long as those constraints are dedicated to the objective of preserving liberty.

The thick theory of social obligation demands more of citizens. It obliges all individuals to contribute to the social resources needed to overcome obstacles to positive liberty. This social obligation represents what we have called intersubjectivity. Its demands include limited redistribution of wealth, public funding of education and the arts, investment in scientific research, and the promotion of common cultural objectives. It extends to civic participation in stewardship of the public square, and it imposes a mandate to be a morally good and responsible person. Such a thick theory of obligation is incompatible with the liberal social contract, which assigns the state only a very narrow mandate – to protect rights extant in a state of nature.

Were the liberal social contract able to stand on its own internal logic, a thin theory of social obligation would be tenable. However, manifestly it cannot. The liberal social contract demands unanimous consent, because, without consent, the individual is not ethically bound to respect the authority of the state. Yet there is no reasonable way to ensure the unanimous consent of a population in which citizens come of age each and every day. Even if there were, moreover, there is no viable alternative to consent. In order to support itself, the liberal social contract can only stand if we assume unanimous consent on the grounds that all rational individuals would be expected to consent to the restraints contained within it.

If it is reasonable to assume that individuals will consent to preserve their negative liberty through a social contract on the grounds that all people wish to be free, it is equally reasonable to assume that individuals will consent to enhancing their positive liberty. As such, it can also be assumed that they have consented to principles that allow society to fulfill its purpose of guiding its citizens toward more fulfilling lives. These principles represent thick obligations – in the sense that they provide no direct reciprocal consideration – toward society in the name of bettering the condition of that society.

Classical liberalism holds that society exists for no other purpose than preserving natural rights in a civic context. As the imperatives for positive liberty and thick obligation suggest, however, such a non-teleological understanding of state purpose is unreasonable. Preserving rights in a meaningful or even sensical way demands a prevailing metaphysic. There must be an underlying teleology (or purpose) that underlies the putatively non-teleological classical liberal state.

This prevailing metaphysic can be called reasonableness. Reasonableness reflects a social consensus as to the nature of the good. This social consensus might be thought of as agreement on the principles that inform the boundaries of the good. It can be understood as a sort of moral constitution that, like any constitution, represents the parameters in which adversarial politics take place. Within these parameters, differing conceptions of the good life do battle. Assuming no inconsistency with the moral constitution represented by social consensus, reasonableness demands that each conception of the good life be met with tolerance by state and civil society alike.

Tolerance represents both a manifestation of negative liberty and a fortification of it. It reflects a willingness to live and let live within the moral parameters established by reasonableness. And it reflects a willingness of citizens to accept political outcomes they find unfavourable or distasteful. Tolerant citizens recognize that they cannot realize every political objective they seek or desire. As long as the political process provides a reasonable prospect of realizing some political objectives, they can be expected to accept political losses.

In a society governed by reasonableness, tolerant citizens will prize the principles reflective of social consensus more highly than they will the policies reflective of their personal conceptions of the good life. That is, there will be a prevailing sense of commonality or "usness" that trumps self-interest on any given issue. Just as economic actors prize the principle of the free market more highly than they value gains from a single economic transaction, so too do reasonable people prize the moral constitution reflective of usness more highly than they value gains along a single political dimension.

Reasonableness thus informs the purpose of the liberal (republican) state in two ways. First, it provides a metaphysical basis for state actors to prioritize their objectives in a way that a reasonable person would find reasonable. It precludes the silliness of a liberal state privileging freedom of vehicular mobility over religious freedom. Second, reasonableness represents a social resource that the liberal state has an incentive to promote. This incentive translates into a social purpose that obliges the liberal (republican) state to provide social resources that create tolerant citizens – citizens not hampered by the narrow-mindedness born of internal constraints. Similarly, the telos of the liberal state extends to fostering a sense of usness by promoting the metaphysical values reflected by the moral, or indeed literal, constitution.

4

A Liberal Republican Code of Justice

AS WITH ANY ETHICAL THEORY, liberal republicanism is obliged to articulate a theory of justice that permits us to differentiate between a good society and a less optimal one. Neither classical liberalism nor traditional republicanism provides an adequate theory of justice in the sense that neither accommodates all of the reconciled dimensions discussed in the two preceding chapters. Classical liberalism understands justice as a neutral position. It demands nothing more than the prohibition of procedural rules that treat any individual or aggregation of individuals in a way that works to the systemic disadvantage of those individuals. Justice from this perspective imposes few constraints on individual autonomy. It can be seen as the absence of systemic procedural bias, as the absence of *in*justice (Ewin 1970; Calder 2007). Traditional republican theories of justice are more conceptually complex. To oversimplify, in the interest of space, they tend to reduce them to the imperative to live a life of goodness or virtue. And while individuals generally have some input into the rules governing a just society, rules conducive to justice take precedence over individual autonomy.

Liberal republicanism draws from both of these prevailing theories of justice. It conforms to Hegel's understanding of justice as the nexus of freedom and duty. As with traditional republicanism, liberal republican justice presupposes an ethically grounded social teleology. As with classical liberalism, justice is born not of an exogenous wisdom exclusive to elites, but rather is the product of an endogenous, intersubjective morality. Liberal republican justice avoids imposing a strict metaphysical imperative in which negative liberty is subordinated to the requirements of a moral order. It does not, in other words, restrict life choices in the name of some preconceived understanding of how one ought properly to live one's life. On the other hand, it avoids the untenable conception of the individual as self-sufficient in her ability to live an authentic life.

That is, it does not inflate the importance of negative liberty to the point of celebrating the radically situated subject for whom the self is wholly constituted by its ends (Sandel 1982, 18–21). Instead, liberal republican justice represents an environment in which people are neither wholly constituted by their social identities in the first instance, nor wholly divorced from them in the second (see Gutmann 1985, 316–17).

This chapter argues that liberal republican justice demands four things. The first is a set of principles that reflect a social consensus about prevailing moral parameters. The second is translating those principles – or *values* – into practical form, which we will call rules. These rules must be generally applied in a way that reflects no systemic biases or bases of discrimination. The third is a hospitable ambient environment, which we can think of as a political culture that reflects tolerance informed by reasonableness. The fourth is a commitment to the preservation of human dignity in a way that recognizes an equal and universal claim to human dignity. Practically this means that while individuals may seek superior status in any number of realms of social interaction, they may not do so in the political realm.

The four elements of liberal republican justice permit us a point of contrast with the culturalist theories of justice which follow in subsequent chapters. Indeed, our understanding of culturalism will be informed by critical differences in each of these elements.

FOUR ELEMENTS OF JUSTICE

The Issue of Values

There is a metaphysical dimension to justice, which entails the general acceptance of a moral code, as well as other values that inform a country's sense of identity. We can think of these values as having primary, secondary, and tertiary dimensions. *Primary values* are the values that define a regime or type of society. As such, liberal republics share a set of primary values that *define them* as liberal republics. Primary values are principles that reflect social consensus as to the nature of the good. They are the basis for a country's understanding of the requirements for a good life.[1]

In liberal republics, primary values are inherent in the four (reconciled) dimensions of liberal republicanism discussed in the two preceding

---

1 Primary values might be more reasonably described as primary *principles*. However, given that secondary and tertiary values are not principles, I have used the term *values* to describe all three.

chapters (equality, liberty, obligation, and purpose). To touch on each briefly, primary values are manifest in the equal claim to dignity endowed to all by virtue of their humanity. Operationally, since rights exist as a means to human dignity, primary values reflect the imperative that all individuals enjoy equal protection of their human rights. Primary values also ensure liberty. In part, this liberty reflects individual sovereignty in the construction of her own, individually derived, conception of the good life. Equally, it demands liberation from the internal constraints that prevent a person from living an authentic life. This claim to positive liberty brings with it moral obligation – an affirmative mandate for both state and society to establish the sorts of rules, institutions, or practices that provide every individual with opportunities to make optimal and authentic life choices. Finally, primary values reflect a general under-standing that laws exist to a common purpose predicated on reasonable-ness and tolerance.

Primary values emerge from some combination of natural law (Budziszewski 1988, esp. ch. 4; 1997), pure reason (Kant 1996), an in-herent moral sense (Smith 1982; Wilson 1993; Hegel 2001), an evolu-tionary understanding of social morality (Dershowitz 2005), and a rational calculus (Locke 1974; Rawls 2003). However we conceive of them, the implications are the same: there are certain values that inform the metaphysical foundations of the good liberal republican society with-out which that society is no longer liberal republican and indeed may no longer be good.

If primary values are general in that they define regime types, *secondary values* are particular in that they inform the character of liberal republics in a way that gives each its own discrete identity. Secondary values serve to bind a nation-state and imbue it with meaning. There is a national particularism associated with secondary values. Different nations inter-pret primary values slightly differently from one another, or put more emphasis on one value over another, and construct mores and customs based on these particularisms. Typically these particularistic values are expressed in secular–sacred icons of the civil religion – flags, anthems, founding myths and legends. They may be a component of explicit cov-enant or compact or can evolve simply as part of a nation's experiential tradition. These values are vital for creating the sense of common pur-pose that sustains liberal republics. Secondary values are those that de-fine a nation's character. They are the foundation of what we can think of as usness, or what it means to be "people like us."

While secondary values inform the national identity, we must use the word "national" advisedly. The nation in question is the nation-state in its legal sense such that each liberal republic has one national identity. To speak of collective identity in a more pluralistic way, in the sense that a single nation-state may comprise many subnational communities, each with its own identity, we move into the province of *tertiary values*: those that help define us as differentiated citizens. Tertiary values are critical in that they serve to distinguish usness from what we might call "sameness." While usness is useful in creating and maintaining national identities, especially in countries without a long and evolved sense of nationhood,[2] there is always the danger that secondary values will conflate usness and sameness. Taken to ugly extremes, sameness can lead to the sentiment that truly to be "people like us," individuals must conform to certain ascriptive characteristics, such as skin colour, ethnicity, or religion.[3]

Privileging sameness need not take on dimensions as unpalatable as those just mentioned. But it still has the potential to be pernicious. Centralization of authority within national governments, especially in large and heterogeneous societies, can have the effect of creating a sense of usness that conforms overwhelmingly to the values and mores of the culturally dominant elements of the society. Such a limited conception of usness is potentially destabilizing insofar as the further one lies from what it means to be "people like us," the less likely she will be to buy into the generalized sense of the good that informs liberal republican justice.[4]

2 Heterogeneous settler societies such as the United States, Canada, Australia, and New Zealand are good examples, as are societies, such as Germany in the nineteenth century, that are formed as amalgamations of previously independent states.

3 This sort of chauvinism is extant even in modern liberal republics. For example, Germany's citizenship laws are based upon *jus sanguinis*, which, especially before citizenship laws were reformed in 2000, made it extremely difficult for those not possessing the German right of blood to gain full citizenship; the extreme nationalism that emerged out of the Poujadist movement in France fuels the Front National's rallying cry of "France for the French." The persistence of Jim Crow laws well into the 1960s (and Jim Crow attitudes well beyond the 1960s) in the United States and mistreatment of Aboriginal populations in what were formerly Britain's self-governing dominions suggests that even the most putatively tolerant liberal republics have a propensity to understand usness in terms of sameness.

4 Regional alienation in both Canada and the United States is fairly well contained, at least as of late. But the 1970 imposition of martial law in Canada in response to domestic terrorism in Quebec and the infinitely more destructive Civil War in the US speak to the dangers of too narrow a conception of usness. Race riots in the United States, prevalent in the 1960s, but extant into post–Rodney King LA, are a further example, as are the "troubles" in Northern Ireland and Basque violence in Spain. In large heterogeneous societies in particular, this pluralization of usness has mandated the construction of regional identities through the federal principle, but as discussed below in the context of multicultural justice, there are even broader ways of institutionalizing tertiary values.

The Issue of Rules

If values are metaphysical, rules are political (Bellamy and Hollis 1995). Values are articulated by institutionalizing rules that reflect those values. Foundational to a liberal republican theory of justice is the freedom of a people to govern itself. As such, rules are important not only in terms of their content, but also in terms of the ways in which they are constructed. As with values, we can distinguish between different sorts of rules. *Constitutional rules* are rules to which a society can be said to pre-commit. That is, they are rules immunized from change through the normal political process. They are the codified (or at least enforceable) rules of the moral constitution born of social consensus discussed in the previous chapter. While there are good reasons for constitutionalizing rules, they must be treated with care. By removing contestation over values from the normal legislative process, constitutional rules restrict negative liberty in the sense that they constrain a people's ability to govern itself (Graglia 1992).

Constitutional rules come in different forms, which we can think of as *formal* or *evolutionary*. Formal constitutional rules are constructed either at the time of a nation's founding or through subsequent constitutional amendments. By contrast, evolutionary constitutional rules are less formal. Some are the product of conventional mores – an experiential tradition that over the course of time institutionalizes certain practices. Other evolutionary constitutional rules find their genesis in jurisprudence, particularly in countries with a tradition of judicial review. In many countries, such as the United States and Canada, judicial review does not have the force of institutionalizing strict constitutional rules. Courts are only one of three branches of government that can assess the constitutionality of state action. On the other hand, it is a long-established pattern in the United States and Canada to defer to the judicial branch as the ultimate arbiter of constitutionality (James, Abelson, and Lusztig 2002).

If constitutional rules represent potential restrictions upon a people's capacity for collective self-government, *legislative rules* enhance self-government. Legislative rules give substance and meaning to values through the political process. A bit of a misnomer, legislative rules refer to legislation or executive orders that provide specificity and context to constitutional rules. As such, legislative rules represent a constant means of refining the principles that govern society, as well as a dynamic process of social input into the value-prioritization discussed in chapter 3.

The construction of legislative rules places a premium on civic participation. Civic participation broadens the boundaries of political contestation. It brings to the fore issues that the framers of constitutional rules may not have anticipated as being socially relevant. It accommodates diversity and social dynamism born of technological innovation, economic or military crisis, or shifting demographics. Indeed, without a people's ability to govern itself through the construction of legislative rules, the primary values of liberal republicanism may become brittle and vulnerable over time.

Civic participation is related to justice through what we have called moral obligation (Aristotle 1999, 1159a–61b). Like any good, moral obligation must be produced. The production process involves political interaction and civic engagement. Civic participation conducive to moral obligation represents the buckle that joins the metaphysical to the political. Moral obligation is attitudinal and relational: it reflects the sense of usness that binds an individual to her community and it represents the means by which citizens relate to one another through a series of informal social norms and values informed by an expectation of reciprocity and trustworthiness (Putnam 1995, 19; Fukuyama 1999, 16). Reciprocity among strangers is rarely expected to be direct. One is not helpful to strangers in the expectation that these same strangers will return the favour. Instead, moral obligation provokes an expectation of generalized reciprocity, or what is commonly called social capital – a sense of trust in the fact that others will one day reciprocate should circumstances demand it (Newton 1997, 576).

Yet another benefit of civic participation is that contestation over legislative rules contributes to a collective understanding of what justice demands and what it precludes. The rules that bind us are perpetuated through reasonableness and refinement born of dialogue. Our understanding of just rules and prioritization of values is examined, and sometimes re-evaluated, through the process of debate. Because our subjective sense of justice is by definition filtered through the lens of our own experiences, biases, and self-interest, we protect ourselves and society from this subjective bias by pitting our own sense of the appropriate against those of others. In this way we avoid the trap of confusing "our own judgment with human reason in general and thus escape the illusion that arises from the ease of mistaking subjective and private conditions for objective ones" (Kant 1987, s. 40, 294; see also Taylor 1985; Hirschman 1994; Ajzenstat and Smith 1995, 8; Waldron 1999b, chs. 4–5; Murray 2005, 24–8).

Finally, civic participation contributes to a changing sense of usness. The means by which a people defines itself is dynamic. Generally speaking, the history of liberal republics has been one of an expanding conception of usness that seeks to erode the remaining pockets of chauvinism and bigotry that can be, if not wholly eliminated, at least marginalized and delegitimized. A system that can accommodate social dynamism as articulated by a participatory citizenship is more likely to foster social solidarity than one bound too strictly to the prevailing ethics of long-gone generations.

Where systems are not responsive to accommodation of social dynamism, the result is alienation. As social conditions change, the legitimacy of the political order is dependent on a general perception that its rules are just and appropriate to the times (see Buchanan and Tullock 1962). Lacking such perception, the stability and even the existence of the regime is threatened. Alienation thus brings with it not just an opportunity cost for civic engagement, but the tangible cost that accompanies social fragmentation. An alienated segment of the population cannot be expected to see the law as legitimate or just and indeed may begin to work actively against it. By contrast, civic participation infuses the law with legitimacy. It fosters civic trust in the form of moral obligation and hence a general sense that law is just. Where civic input from all segments of society is encouraged, or at the very least not precluded, laws reflect prevailing social values and are generally self-enforcing. By contrast, where there is not general acceptance of the legitimacy and justness of law, enforcement costs in terms of both material resources and liberty increase (see Uslaner 2002).

Both constitutional and legislative rules are vital for articulating tertiary values, and help to establish the appropriate balance between usness and sameness. This is a tricky balance to maintain. Too much usness and not enough sameness creates insularity. It balkanizes subaltern communities, and divorces them from the commonality of purpose that usness demands.[5] This is what Putnam calls bonding social capital, whereby cultural groups form strong internal bonds of trust, but fail to build bridges (bridging social capital) to other cultural groups (Putnam 1995, 22–4). Too much sameness and not enough usness, on the other hand, leads to a chauvinistic dominant culture and discrimination against subaltern communities.

To anticipate the discussion of culturalism in succeeding chapters, one way in which formal constitutional rules affect tertiary values is through differential representation for discrete communities. The most common means is federalism, which privileges geographic or *spatial* communities as the source of salient tertiary values. This is the liberal republican prescription for accommodating tertiary values. However,

---

5 I use the term *subaltern community* here in the Gramscian sense to mean what we colloquially (though often inaccurately) call minority community. Moreover, the term is used empirically and not normatively or pejoratively.

differential representation can also be based upon *essentialist* criteria – innate characteristics foundational to a common cultural identity. As discussed in chapter 8, representation of this kind can take a number of forms, including seats set aside for members of a particular essentialist community, subaltern community legislative veto rights, power-sharing, and even sovereign levels of government for essentialist communities (Lijphart 1977; Kymlicka 1995b; Sisk 2002).

Tertiary values also find voice through legislative rules and, often confusingly, through evolutionary constitutional rules as well. This duality makes a tricky situation even trickier. Liberal republican justice demands that appropriate boundaries be set between constitutional and legislative rules, such that the former represent the rules of the game as it were, while the latter reflect the contest itself. However, while formal constitutional rules are generally (although not exclusively) procedural, evolutionary constitutional rules and legislative rules are generally (although not exclusively) substantive. In this sense, legislative and jurisprudential rules represent competitors for a common task. Perhaps the trickiest element of liberal republican justice is determining where the line between evolutionary constitutional rules and legislative rules should be drawn. This determination is explored in more depth in chapter 8.

The Issue of Tolerance

Although contestation over refinement of values and rules is foundational to liberal republican justice, it must be informed by a culture of tolerance and acceptance of dissent. Tolerance privileges principles over policies. In particular, it demands that the reasonable social consensus on the nature of the good is valued more highly than any advantage gained by interpreting or prioritizing values (Sullivan 1982; DeLue 1989; Ferejohn, Rakove, and Riley 2001). Tolerance thus entails resisting the theocratic temptation to banish politically heretical ideas from the public square (Knoppf 1998, 686; see also Downing and Thigpen 1993; Ajzenstat 2007, 70).

Such banishment can be accomplished in any number of ways. One is outright discrimination, resulting in barriers to civic participation being erected against members of subaltern communities. Poll taxes and literacy tests, to take two unpleasant reminders of times not long past in the United States, are good examples. Equally distasteful is speech regulation which deems certain social issues – gay rights in countries such as Canada and Sweden for example – to be politically out of bounds so that even expressing a dissenting viewpoint can land one on the wrong side of the law. Criminalizing apostate views – even nasty and unpalatable ones such as we hear from White supremacists and other outright bigots – provides the state with the authority to deprive any or all citizens of the rights and liberties it is universally mandated to protect (DeLue 1989, 53–5).

A second, generally less discriminatory means of banishment is immunizing contested issues. Such immunization is manifested through heavy-handed constitutional jurisprudence – converting what rightly should be legislative rules into evolutionary constitutional ones. Banishment thus occurs when contested social issues are removed from the legislative arena and instead are rendered all but immune from change by resolving the issue judicially. This immunization of contested issues (the constitutional settlement of the abortion question in both Canada and the United States is an example) represents the triumph of the metaphysical over the political. The result can be alienation and even unenforceability of law. The prototypical example is the short-lived Eighteenth Amendment prohibition on the manufacture, transportation, and importation of liquor.

By contrast, tolerance can be seen as a hedge against tyranny insofar as it broadens the locus of political power. The more citizens whose voices are allowed to be heard in public life, who can mobilize to support causes or beliefs, the broader the distribution of power and hence the protection afforded to liberty (Dahl 1961). The deontological parameters reflected by tolerance ensure the inviolability of rules of engagement that exist to the benefit of all. As noted in the previous chapter, a good analogy is an economic free market, whereby the rules of free enterprise are both highly prized and substantively indeterminate (Buchanan and Tullock 1962, esp. ch. 19). As with the economic free market, legitimacy turns not on citizens' certainty of perpetual gratification, but rather on the prospect that their ambitions might reasonably be satisfied (see Vernon 2001, 39). And as with the economic market, the market for political influence demands that contestants' first loyalty be to the process that makes victory possible, rather than to the substantive victory itself.

Tolerance is a fundamental element of liberal republican justice. It is necessary to ensure that a wide range of ideas are permitted access to the public space. The soundness of metaphysical principles is tested in the crucible of civic contestation that can only occur if a society is sufficiently tolerant that it privileges the arena in which contestation takes place ahead of the benefits of victory along any given issue dimension.

The Issue of Dignity

When discussing dignity we need to think in terms of two things. The first, recognition, already has occupied a good deal of attention in our dealings with equality in chapter 2. The second dimension is esteem, which will be of more central concern in this chapter. Esteem is dignity that results not from *being* but from *actions* (for more on this distinction see Kateb 2011, 11–19). Traditional republicanism does not draw the distinction between dignity-as-being and dignity-as-action. From that perspective, one's dignity is earned through his virtue and affirmed through honour and social privilege. By contrast, liberal republicanism does make a distinction between being and action. As we have already noted, liberal republicanism holds that all individuals are equally entitled to dignity in their beings by virtue of their humanity.

However, to ground dignity in being does not preclude the idea that some actions are more dignified than others in generating esteem. Let us think of two types of action: estimable and blameworthy. Estimable action enhances the dignity of at least two individuals – the person who enhances (or *affirms*) the dignity of another, and the person (or *recipient*) whose dignity is affirmed. Blameworthy action is the opposite in that it degrades the dignity of both persons.

The degree to which action is estimable is to some extent in the eye of the beholder. As such, two additional issues are relevant. The first is motive. What motivates estimable behaviour? What moves an affirmer to affirm the dignity of a recipient? Motive is important insofar as it provides insight into the degree to which actions that appear estimable actually *are* estimable. That is, apparently estimable behaviour undertaken out of base motives may well affect the dignity that attaches to both affirmer and recipient. This leads to the second issue, means. What does it mean for an affirmer to affirm the dignity of a recipient?

Motive must be understood as a function of audience. The audience to which an affirmer speaks, in other words, is critical to determining motive. Audience can be internal or it can be external. Where audience is internal, the affirmer of another's dignity is moted by her own self-esteem. She serves as the judge of her behaviour. When she determines that behaviour to be estimable, she feels the satisfaction and self-esteem that comes with living up to her own endogenously derived moral standards. By contrast, blameworthy behaviour generates guilt at failing to meet the standards of morality she sets for herself.

Where audience is external, the affirmer is motivated by the moral judgment of others. This motive might be born of a lack of confidence in his own moral judgment. Alternatively, it may be a function of the greater value he assigns to pride (the esteem of others) than to the esteem of self. To affirmers motivated by external audience, the penalty for inestimable behaviour is shame.[6]

---

6 The distinction between self-esteem and the esteem of others has a long history. It mirrors the difference between a culture of guilt and a culture of shame that divided ancient Greek conceptions of virtue. Hence Socrates's quibble in Plato's *Republic* with the

Just as there are different motivations for affirming dignity, so too are there different ways to affirm it. Some see tough love as the most effective way. Parenting is a good analogy here. The parent who imposes strict conduct in raising her children rarely does so out of some base motive, such as gratification of an unfulfilled desire for authoritarian control. She does it out of a sense of moral purpose: to raise better children, those more likely to make good life choices in the quest for the authentic life. She believes that children who are not overindulged are more likely to be self-reliant. They are socialized at an early age that there are constraints upon their liberties and that living under such constraints – not gratifying every whim just because you can – is the right or good or proper way to live one's life. Of course, it is difficult to raise children this way. They may come to appreciate such an upbringing later on, but at the time tough love means not being able to have or do in the same way as other kids. A parent must accept this fact, along with perhaps her own nagging fears that perhaps she is being as heartless as accused.

Conversely, the parent who rejects tough love in favour of maximizing his children's opportunities to make mistakes from which they can learn operates from the same motive. The parent who indulges his child may do it out of base motivation, to win affection, for example. But he is more likely to do it for the same sense of moral purpose as the tough-love parent. He believes that when a child is socialized in an environment of generosity a child learns to be a generous and praiseworthy citizen. He learns to avoid meanness and selfishness. The parent need not accept an anything goes attitude, but his priority is to provide his children with the material and experiential resources to satisfy their curiosity, indulge their interests and creativity, and pursue their dreams as they come to define them (Clarke and Dawson 1998, esp. chs. 8–10; Jackson 2011).

Which of these means – tough love or indulgence – is more consistent with liberal republican principles? Assuming purity of motive, the argument here is that both are equally consistent with liberal republican principles. This is an important point since it demonstrates that liberal republicanism can accommodate a wide range of both motives and means. On the other hand, when speaking of the stability of liberal republican regimes, it is important to recognize that a lack of cohesiveness with respect to justice has the potential to divide. Indeed, it is the lack of cohesiveness of the liberal republican idea of justice that helps to

---

fruits of Homeric virtue which turned exclusively on recognition by others. Similarly, we see the distinction manifest in the difference between Kant's moral endogeneity predicated upon moral reason and Smith's predicated upon sentiment – vanity in particular. The Kantian moralist speaks to an internal audience, while his Smithian counterpart is at least partially guided by the testimony of an external audience.

explain the headway made by culturalist theories of justice discussed in subsequent chapters.

Two paradigmatic examples help illustrate the dichotomous nature of liberal republican theories of justice. Both rely on the idea that citizens are autonomous agents with an endogenous capacity for rational and moral choices, and that they possess a moral obligation to affirm the dignity of others. Both are liberal republican insofar as neither can be thought of as privileging the gratification of the self over the welfare of the state, nor of subordinating the interests of the self to the greater good. The first we can think of as dignity through self-reliance; the second we can think of as dignity through fairness. While cognizant of the hazards inherent in assigning narrow philosophical labels, it is useful to examine two paradigmatic thinkers: Ralph Waldo Emerson, perhaps the pre-eminent theorist of dignity through self-reliance, and John Rawls, an exemplar of dignity through fairness.

THE TWO FACES OF LIBERAL REPUBLICAN JUSTICE

What makes dignity of particular interest is that it represents a source of cleavage within liberal republican societies. Indeed, to the extent that political contestation in liberal republican societies turns on justice, it is most likely to occur when dignity-as-esteem is affirmed. The Emersonian position reflects the more politically conservative dimension of liberal republicanism. Rawls, by contrast, informs the position of the more politically progressive. The duality reflected by Emerson's and Rawls's respective positions on dignity does not constitute a fatal flaw to the stability of liberal republics. Rather, it is discussed here to demonstrate how broadly the liberal republican theory of justice can be applied.

Self-Reliance

Dignity as self-reliance is a natural outgrowth of the Evangelical Enlightenment in America. Indeed, the roots of American transcendentalism as manifest in the works of Emerson, Thoreau, Melville, and others are to be found in the unique synthesis of liberalism, republicanism, and evangelical Protestantism that elevated the status of the individual with the rights, the responsibility, and the moral capacity to be a good and, at the same time, a self-interested citizen. Reliance on one's endogenous capacities to engage in choiceworthy pursuits was the basis of this transcendentalist synthesis. It is important, however, not to confuse self-reliance with individual self-sufficiency in pursuit of dignity. Certainly there are times when Emerson conflates the two, going out of his way to isolate the individual from any hint of personal interdependence.[7] But although Emerson celebrates the endogenous capacity of individuals to seek and discover the moral truth for themselves, his individualism makes sense only within the context of a social environment – a fact he himself usually recognizes. Emerson is, then, to establish his liberal republican bona fides, an individualist who recognizes that individual dignity demands a social environment in which to flourish.

The tension that exists between self-reliance and civil society is akin to the Hegelian dialectic between nature and civility, in which the absence of the one leaves the other incomplete. To Emerson civil society is both attractive and repugnant. It ennobles individuals by elevating them from their animalistic natural state and showing them what they can become through their own efforts and determination. At the same time, it has the potential to dull individuals' minds and anesthetize their spirits. It risks demeaning by retarding personal potential. Emerson thus at once glorifies society for what it can become, and vilifies it for what it actually is.

The same frustrating distinction applies to individuals as well. While each possesses the capacity to transcend the ordinary and mundane and achieve the estimable, most are mindless conformists. Emerson understands most men to be very much as Kant describes pre-Enlightened individuals: as those content to be led by the paternalistic norms of others. All ages, Emerson complains, are characterized by "imbecility in the vast majority of men ... victims of gravity, custom, and fear ... the multitude have no habit of self-reliance or original action" (2007, 30; see also Wellek 1943; Schwartz 1985; Newfield 1991; Lopez 1996, e.g., 4; Kateb 2002, ch. 4).

Self-reliance is requisite to navigating the perilous seas of civil society. Society is a resource with which individuals can propel themselves further than they could if left simply to their own devices. But it has no capacity to bestow esteem, so as to endow meaningful esteem passively or without effort and commitment. No one can make a person who she is not. The best that others can do is to show her who she can become.[8] In

7 In "Manners," for example, he admonishes even lovers to "guard their strangeness" (1951c, 359). In "Experience" he declares that "An unnavigable sea washes with silent waves between us and the things we aim at and converse with" (1951d, 295).

8 "We are equally served by receiving and by imparting. Men who know the same things are not long the best company for each other. But bring to each an intelligent person of another experience, and it is as if you let off water from a lake by cutting a lower basin. It seems a mechanical advantage, and great benefit it is to each speaker, as he can now paint out his thought to himself. We pass very fast, in our personal moods, from dignity to dependence. And if any appear never to assume the chair, but always to stand and serve, it is because we do not see the company in a sufficiently long period for the whole

navigating treacherous civic waters she must permit herself to be guided toward recognizing her own capacities and to reliance on herself. This guidance is a means to self-liberation; it is navigating away from restrictions on one's capacities born of the habit of the mind or timidity of the soul (Schwartz 1985, 106; Robinson 1993, 90–1).

Estimable citizens are those who accept the responsibility for guiding their fellows.[9] But such amenity must be exercised with prudent judgment. It cannot be driven by indulgence, which is the antithesis of self-reliance, not a guide but a crutch. The indulgent affirmer is an apologist for failure and an enabler of dignity-defeating conformity and mediocrity. Worse, when he indulges others, he indulges himself. His motives are not true guidance toward transcendence. They are self-serving, born not of conviction, but rather of misplaced audience. The indulgent affirmer is more interested in appearing like a good fellow than actually *being* one. This is why for Emerson estimable behaviour demands an internal audience. It obliges an affirmer to remain true to his principles and where necessary to forego the approval of an external audience. Rather than tremble under the moral gaze of others, the truly dignified individual relies on her own sense of duty and does so without the "assurance of [her] fellows any secondary testimony" (Emerson 1951a, 38).

Emerson's theory of dignity begins from the premise that dignity is not within the gift of one person to another. Instead, citizens have an affirmative obligation to wake within their fellows knowledge of the opportunities that await them, to imbue them with the confidence to seize these opportunities.[10] Emerson himself is an unlikely champion of hu-

---

rotation of parts to come about. As to what we call the masses, and common men – there are no common men. All men are at last of a size; and true art is only possible on the conviction that every talent has its apotheosis somewhere. Fair play and an open field and freshest laurels to all who have won them! But heaven reserves an equal scope for every creature. Each is uneasy until he has produced his private ray unto the concave sphere and beheld his talent also in its last nobility and exaltation" (Emerson 2008, 19–20).

9 The point is illustrated in a quote that Howe draws from Emerson's journals. "I waked at night, and bemoaned myself, because I had not thrown myself into this deplorable question of slavery …. But then in hours of sanity, I recovered myself and said God must govern his own world … without my desertion of my post which has none to guard it but me. I have other slaves to free than those negroes, to wit, imprisoned spirits, imprisoned thoughts far back in the brain of man" (1986, 59).

10 Emerson advises, "Let a man then know his worth, and keep things under his feet. Let him not peep or steal, or skulk up and down with the air of a charity-boy, a bastard, or an interloper, in the world which exists for him. But the man in the street, finding no worth in himself which corresponds to the force which built a tower or sculptured a marble god, feels poor when he looks on these. To him a palace, a statue, or a costly book have an alien and forbidding air, much like a gay equipage, and seem to say like that, 'Who are you, Sir?'

man dignity given his caustic view of the sorts of individuals – which is to say most people – who will not do for themselves. His belief that individuals ultimately are responsible for their own fortunes (quite literally) makes him loath to indulge in charity. Certainly he would reject Rawls's imperative for equitable redistribution of goods and resources as the basis of dignity. Such redistribution is not a moral entitlement that citizens may rightfully claim against the rest of society, or that society should rightfully offer. Tough love is almost always more effective in promoting dignity than is soft indulgence. As such, he proclaims,

Dear to us are those who love us ... they enlarge our life; but dearer are those who reject us as unworthy, for they add another life: they build a heaven before us whereof we had not dreamed, and thereby supply to us new powers out of the recesses of the spirit, and urge us to new and unattempted performances. (Emerson quoted in Kateb 2002, 156)

Far from indulging the socially dependent, Emerson rejects them categorically as belonging to the class of individuals unwilling to help themselves. He asks, "Are they my poor?" Emphatically, he decides they are not.

I tell thee thy foolish philanthropist, that I grudge the dollar, the dime, the cent, I give to such men as do not belong to me and to whom I do not belong. There is a class of persons to whom by all spiritual affinity I am bought and sold; for them I will go to prison, if need be; but your miscellaneous popular charities; the education at college of fools; the building of meeting-houses to the vain end to which many now stand; alms to sots; and the thousandfold Relief Societies; – though I confess with shame I sometimes succumb and give the dollar, it is a wicked dollar which by and by I shall have the manhood to withhold. (1951a, 37)

While Emerson here is being intentionally provocative in seeking to expose the hypocrisy of others, the quotation is illustrative of his lack of patience with social norms that inhibit and minimize, rather than dignify

---

Yet they all are his, suitors for his notice, petitioners to his faculties that they will come out and take possession" (1951a, 44–5). The idea that individuals can be guided into self-reliance is a common theme for Emerson, who recounts the "popular fable of the sot who was picked up dead drunk in the street, carried to the duke's house, washed and dressed and laid in the duke's bed, and, on his waking, treated with all obsequious ceremony like the duke, and assured that he had been insane, which owes its popularity to the fact that it symbolizes so well the state of man, who is in the world a sort of sot, but now and then wakes up, exercises his reason, and finds himself a true prince" (Emerson 1951a, 45).

and elevate, the weak or the timid. From this perspective, to anticipate the discussion of Rawls below, the fallacy of dignity as fairness lies in confusing dignity with charity. The decision to grant (or withhold) charity must be born of the conviction that the act is appropriate to the circumstance. Charity does not dignify the donor if it is undertaken out of a sense of compulsion. Self-indulgent charity is not dignified. Dignity does not attach to charity that is undertaken with an eye towards how that action will be perceived; it cannot be an act of penance or expiation; it must not be done as a means of enhancing one's esteem in the eyes of others; nor can it be undertaken as a means of demonstrating one's merit in the eyes of God.[11]

Often it is easier to acquiesce, to give the wicked dollar, to accommodate ourselves to the preferences of others, than it is to remain true to principles one knows to be right. But that ease comes at the expense of true dignity for the donor (see Budziszewski 1999, 129). At the same time, for the erstwhile recipient of charity, self-reliance is what brings dignity to the fore and relegates charity to the last ditch of necessity. True dignity is realized not through facilitation but through exhorting the able poor – erstwhile denizens of Socrates's cave – to live their lives in more fulfilling fashion than they otherwise might realize was possible.

In sum, for Emerson the estimable citizen is one who transcends the norms of reflexive indulgence imposed by a civil society dedicated to superficiality of appearance rather than the substantive burden of true conviction. It is only when individuals have transcended society's superficial preconceptions about human dignity that they can transcend their own selfishness and realize the estimable citizenship that completes them as individuals (Blau 1977; Newfield 1991, 663–6; McWilliams 2011).

---

11 From a very different perspective, Augustinian Christianity comes to a similar conclusion. Augustine sees charity in the form of euergetism as one of the "splendid vices" whereby citizens use their love of neighbour merely as an instrumental means to the enjoyment of God. No sooner, Ramsey suggests, did Christian charity begin than the charitable "let their eyes waver from their neighbor's benefit; their gaze turned inward by way of turning toward merit in heaven; they continued to be charitable for prudence's sake. Both charity and prudence became 'splendid vices,' still splendid on account of the self-discipline and liberality they induce, vicious on account of the neighbor whose welfare they ignore so successfully" (1947, 186 see also Brown 2015, 88–96; Herdt 2015, 101–3). Similarly, there is an obvious analogy to Kant, whose distinction between practical and pure reason turns on what motivates the action being considered.

Dignity as Fairness

As with Emerson, Rawls seeks to reconcile the imperatives for individual dignity with the social obligation reflective of republican virtue. But while Emerson locates dignity in the individual and sees civil society as a potential source of personal corruption, Rawls reverses the logic. For him civil society is an ameliorative to the individual propensity to selfishness. Emerson's tough-love prescription is no doubt born of personal conviction and is not merely justification for selfishness. However, for those on the liberal republican left the fact remains that Emerson's is a very generous assessment of the options that disadvantaged individuals have at their disposal.

Given the inherent selfishness of individuals, Rawls begins from the premise that the appropriate audience for estimable behaviour is external. The obstacles that need to be transcended are not, as Emerson implicitly suggests, social norms of indulgence. Instead, the greatest impediment to dignity is excessive rational self-interest. Rationality is a tricky concept for Rawls. On the one hand, he wishes to tap into the moral endogeneity associated with Kant's pure reason. That is, he believes that individuals are capable of using their reason to arrive at morally appropriate or estimable or just outcomes. On the other hand, he recognizes that individuals often have little incentive to exercise their moral reason, particularly if it comes at the expense of self-interest. Rawls, then, sets two tasks for himself: to demonstrate the endogenous capacity for moral reason and to supply motive for just action.

To address the first task, Rawls seeks to distill moral reason from self-interest. His well-known mechanism is a thought experiment in which individuals place themselves in a pre-social environment that he calls the original position. In the original position, individuals are rational. However, they are ignorant as to the particular details of their lives. They have no knowledge about their share of the distribution of natural or material assets. From this original position we can derive what Rawls calls the thin theory of the good.

The thin theory of the good reflects a common set of preferences for primary social goods such as opportunities, income, basic rights and liberties, and the social bases of self-respect. Even in the original position, all rational individuals will be expected to know that they desire these goods. Whether they will desire a particular primary good equally or merely equitably depends on the good in question. Primary goods that pertain to rules are expected to be desired equally. This general preference is reflected through one of two principles of justice that will be chosen in the original position. Specifically, the equality principle holds that "each person is to have an equal right to the most extensive scheme of equal basic liberties compatible with a similar scheme of liberties for others."

By contrast, Rawls expects other primary goods – particularly pertaining to wealth and income – to be desired equitably. That is, the imperative for equal distribution of such goods is relaxed as long as distribution is fair. Equitability is reflected in the difference principle: "Social and economic inequalities are to be arranged so that they are both (a) reasonably expected to be to everyone's advantage, and (b) attached to positions and offices open to all" (2003, 53). Collectively, the two principles mandate that "All social values – liberty and opportunity, income and wealth, and the social bases of self-respect – are to be distributed equally unless an unequal distribution of any, or all, of these values is to everyone's advantage" (2003, 54). The equality principle can be relaxed, in other words, only in the context of a Pareto-preferred alternative.

Rawls assumes that the principles of justice will reflect reasonable parameters of risk aversion. Individuals will be willing to assume some risk in constructing social institutions that will privilege certain (as yet unknown) individuals ahead of others (who are equally unknown). However, he expects a general threshold of risk aversion such that rational individuals will disqualify all social arrangements in which the most disadvantaged position is intolerable. In the context of the thin theory of the good, such disqualification is not born of concern with others' dignity so much as the rational imperative from behind a veil of ignorance to make the worst-case scenario tolerable.

Rawls's thin theory of the good is constructed solely through individual self-interest. The goodness is an artifact of substantive and textual ignorance. The thin theory thus provides little more than the broad parameters of justice. It tells us what justice looks like. What it does not tell us is why self-interested individuals would ever conform to the good once liberated from a veil of ignorance. To understand motive, then, we need to move from the thin theory of the good to what Rawls calls a full theory of the good (s. 66).

The full theory of the good demands more than mere individual (or subjective) preference gratification. Instead, it demands intersubjectivity – a conception of the good that extends to both self and other (1975, 538). It reconciles individual rationality with a conception of the good in which the welfare of others becomes central to one's esteem. It suggests that rational individuals derive utility not simply from reaping the rewards of just institutions but also from the process of being just – from the process of affirming the dignity of others.

We have already noted that for Rawls, affirmers of dignity are more motivated by external audience than internal audience. One earns the esteem of an external audience when she publicly affirms the dignity of recipients through the support of just institutions. Such support is particularly estimable if it imposes moral obligations on affirmers to forego private benefit in the name of justice (2003, s. 29). The full theory of the good provides motive for the affirmation of the dignity of others by establishing that there is no tension between self-interest and dignity-affirming justice. Life will be more fulfilling where conceptions of the good are filtered through the regulative lens of justice in such a way that the affirmation of dignity comes to "guide, complement and [even] comprise the good" (Freeman 2007, 70).

If the full theory of the good supplies motive for the affirmation of recipients' dignity, we still have to determine how this will be accomplished. What sorts of just social institutions are necessary to affirm the dignity of others? Beyond equally distributing procedural primary goods through the equality principle, Rawls argues that equitable distribution of economic primary goods represents fair distribution of the bases of self-respect. To conform to the difference principle, equitable distribution means that economic inequalities are just only if they advance the Pareto frontier. That is, justice demands that inequality leaves the disadvantaged better off (in absolute terms) than they would have been in the case of equal distribution of wealth.

What this means in practice is that individuals who benefit from income inequality are obliged to redistribute some of their economic advantage in a way that the disadvantaged derive economic benefit. This redistribution of economic benefit contributes to the dignity of the advantaged and disadvantaged alike. The advantaged benefits from the esteem of an external audience who commends him for his industry or his generosity. The disadvantaged benefits from the enhanced dignity to which enhanced economic well-being generally attaches.

The only question that remains is the appropriate mechanism for redistributing wealth. One option is the free market, which is manifestly redistributive. Since it is not an end in itself, the nature of wealth is that it circulates. The wealthy do not hoard their money, Scrooge McDuck–like, for their own private enjoyment. They spend and invest it with the residual benefits distributed through the creation of jobs and stimulation of commerce. Where markets are allowed to work, nations become wealthier and the wealth created by some is indirectly distributed to (almost) all. As such, a strong case can be made that the "trickle-down" effect satisfies the difference principle, and does so in a way in which the stigma of charity does not attach. Indeed, where one's material resources are a product of her own making, the acquisition of those resources brings with it self-esteem. From this free-market perspective, self-esteem must be earned. It cannot be distributed like some sort of enhancement to one's welfare cheque.

On the other hand, however much wealth might trickle down, it is unlikely – to maintain the aquatic analogy – to provide perfect satura-tion. To the extent that certain citizens (those who cannot participate in the free market, for example) fail to benefit from market-based wealth redistribution, a case can be made that the Pareto criterion has not been met. Indeed, for Rawls and others on the material left, there are inherent advantages to the state appropriating the process of redistribu-tion. In addition to ensuring greater saturation, the state has a mandate that the market does not: to protect the liberty foundational to any con-ception of human dignity. Such a mandate, it can be claimed, demands not only the *fact* of wealth redistribution, but also the *extent* of such redistribution.

CONCLUSION

The liberal republican understanding of justice hangs together quite well. Leaving dignity aside, the other elements of liberal republican jus-tice accommodate the entire spectrum of mainstream politics in liberal republicans. Liberal republicanism of both the left and the right de-mands tolerance, for example. And although there are marginal differ-ences in how such tolerance manifests itself, neither the right nor left embraces the theocratic temptation to privilege outcome over proce-dure. Liberal republicans of the right and left also share common ideas about rules – specifically, there is an abiding sense that without reason-able social consensus, contentious political issues should be resolved through legislative rather than constitutional rules. Finally, while value-prioritization might differ, liberal republicans of both stripes embrace the same values. A unified liberal republican understanding of justice incorporates a set of values that reflects the equal innate worth of all hu-man beings under law; the sovereignty of all individuals to construct for themselves the subjectively determined authentic life; the mandate of the state to facilitate (and equally not to retard) individuals' capacity to lead authentic lives; the imperative for popular sovereignty; and the so-cial mandate to recognize the inherent moral claim to dignity that all individuals possess.

The only significant point of contention in the liberal republican con-ception of justice is dignity as esteem. Emersonians and Rawlsians, if we may call them such, differ on the means to universalize dignity as esteem. Both assert the imperative to universalize dignity. However, they differ in motive and means for citizens to affirm the dignity of others. While the distinction of motive is interesting, greater political importance has attached to the issue of means. Specifically, the liberal republican left and right differ over the optimal means of realizing the equitable distribution of primary economic goods. On the right, liberal republicans have advocated a more market-based, tough-love approach to the affirmation of human dignity as esteem. The left has sought a greater role for the state in ensuring that the dignity of all citizens is affirmed.

The dominant line of cleavage through most twentieth-century liberal republics was materialist. It reflected the Emersonian and Rawlsian perspectives on human dignity, particularly as they pertained to the distribution of wealth. Beginning with the civil rights movement in the United States, however, this materialist division between the liberal republican left and right was joined by a second, post-materialist, dimension. Among its effects, post-materialism contributed to a more comprehensive understanding of the requisites for human dignity. This new dimension has mapped uneasily onto the prevailing line of cleavage. For present purposes, the most pertinent effect of post-materialism has been the ascendance of a new understanding of justice advocated by those who view politics through the lens of culture, and whom I have styled as culturalists. The culturalist understanding of justice is in some ways reconcilable with the prevailing liberal republican understanding of justice and in some ways it is not. Where it is, I have labelled culturalism benign; in such cases culturalism represents a challenge, but not a threat to liberal republicanism. Where it is not reconcilable, I have considered it malignant in the sense that it poses a potential threat.

In order to anticipate the discussion to come in chapter 5, it is useful to lay out a number of underlying differences between liberal republican and culturalist understandings of justice. The first is that the locus of liberal republican justice is the individual and not some larger social or cultural entity (Walsh 2016, 34). It is therefore the *individual* who has the moral claim to dignity and the rights requisite to realize that claim. There are no *cultural* claims. The second is that equal recognition of dignity (what earlier we called dignity as being) means that for legal and ethical purposes, a person is a person is a person. Such undifferentiated personhood takes precedence over any idiosyncratic or ascriptive trait that might define a person. To put this another way, one's personhood is understood to be a product of her humanity and not her socio-cultural identity (Berger 1970, 342–3).[12] The third lies in the understanding of

12 Christian Smith's definition of personhood illustrates the distinction: A person is "a conscious, reflexive, embodied, self-transcending center of subjective experience, durable identity, moral commitment, and social communication who – as the efficient cause of

what it means to be *unjust*. Just as the locus of justice is the individual, so too is the locus of injustice. Liberal republican injustice, as discussed more fully in the next chapter, conforms to the criteria of volition, agent-specificity, and violation of reasonableness – the social consensus as to the parameters of the good.

The liberal republican understanding of justice is broadly encompassing. But it is not infinitely so. While it can be said to encompass the entire mainstream of materialist politics, it is less comprehensive along the emergent post-materialist one that includes the politics of culture. The launching point for chapter 5 is that many who view politics through the lens of culture are uneasy about the liberal republican understanding of justice. Indeed, each of the implications discussed in the preceding paragraph distinguishes liberal republican conceptions of justice from culturalist ones. Given these differences, the issue before us in the following chapters is to determine the extent to which culturalism constitutes a challenge or a threat to the stability of liberal republican regimes.

---

his or her own responsible actions and interactions – exercises complex capacities for agency and intersubjectivity in order to develop and sustain his or her own incommunicable self in loving relationships with other personal selves and with the nonpersonal world" (2010, 61).

5

Multiculturalism and Justice

WHEN WE SPEAK OF THE CULTURALIST CHALLENGE to liberal republicanism, we are speaking of challenges to the principles of justice discussed in the previous chapter. Although I will discuss the concept in far greater detail later, for now we can think of culturalists as those who understand cultural identity to be foundational to personhood. As such, culturalists prioritize cultural identity over individual interests.

Because we will be relying on a number of concepts introduced in the previous chapter, it is helpful to revisit some of these. Specifically, we introduced the idea of primary, secondary, and tertiary values and primary and secondary rules. Table 5.1 summarizes these terms.

Culturalism represents a broad range of positions that will unfold over the next few chapters. Thus, in briefly highlighting the differences between liberal republican and culturalist theories of justice some qualifications will be necessary.[1] For example, most culturalists will accept the primary (regime-defining) and secondary (nation-defining) values of liberal republican societies, but some will not. Even for those who do – let us think of these as the mainstream or *multi*culturalists, who will be the focus of this chapter – primary values are often seen as anachronistic and in need of refinement. The putative social consensus that informs an understanding of constitutional rules is not as reflective of general consensus, in other words, as liberal republicans take it to be. Multiculturalists fundamentally disagree, moreover, with liberal republicans over the relative importance of secondary versus

---

1 We can speak of culturalists in only the most general of ways. Not only is there a good deal of difference between forms of culturalism, the paradigm itself exists meaningfully only as a heuristic. Similarly, unless speaking of specific individuals, it must be recognized that the "culturalists" and "liberal republicans" of whom I speak give voice only to the logic of their respective paradigms and exist simply to give these paradigms agency.

Table 5.1

	Primary	Secondary	Tertiary
Values	Regime-defining values	Values associated with national identity	Values associated with subnational identity
Rules	Formal, jurisprudential, and conventional constitutional rules	Legislative rules	

tertiary (subnational or differentiated) values. Liberal republicans may be expected to privilege secondary values over tertiary ones, whereas multiculturalists reverse the order.

On the issue of rules, the conflict between liberal republicanism and culturalism turns principally on the distinction between evolutionary constitutional rules (those born of jurisprudence) and legislative rules. The conflict is not as cut and dried as suggesting that liberal republicans prefer legislative rules to evolutionary constitutional rules. Such is not the case. However, when it comes to regulating tertiary values, culturalists tend toward consolidating their victories through jurisprudence rather than through legislation. This distinction on rules has implications for tolerance.

With respect to the issue of tolerance, liberal republicans understand the political process to reflect competition over legislative rules. In this sense, the political process is akin to an economic free market. There are no barriers to entry and every agent plays by a common set of constitutional rules. Although the process is adversarial, contestation is restricted to disagreement over legislative rules. Constitutional rules are not subject to challenge any more than the adversarial nature of business challenges the rules of the free market. Similarly, contestation, that is, adversarial interaction among competing groups of aligned interests, only occurs along a single issue dimension. Contestation does not extend across issues, with the same actors finding themselves in perpetual opposition to one another.

Culturalists' views of tolerance differ insofar as they disagree about the nature of players in the adversarial process. For liberal republicans, players are individuals who band together to form voluntary interest associations as a means of advancing their political objectives. For culturalists, however, while such voluntary associations certainly exist for a legitimate purpose, other players cannot reasonably be understood as individuals. Such players are essentialist groups that are inherently organic since they cannot be reduced in any meaningful way to a collection of like-minded individuals. Such groups differ from voluntary associations in that they are united not by common interest but by common *identity*.

The implication is that the adversarial process represents two discrete types of game. One is competition among competing interests. Such competition, culturalists can agree, is best regulated by secondary (legislative) rules. The second type of game pits voluntary associations united by common interests against essentialist groups united by common identity. This type of competition, from the culturalist perspective, is best regulated not by legislative rules but by evolutionary constitutional rules. Indeed, where cultural identity is threatened by common interest, protecting cultural identity is sufficiently important to warrant removing the relevant issue from the regular political process. In such cases there is less tolerance for the rough and tumble of politics.

Things become a bit more complicated when discussing the issue of dignity; different types of culturalists understand the relationship between dignity and justice differently. Some types (multiculturalists and what we will later call *cultural separatists*) advocate a theory of equality in which no one group has a greater claim to human dignity than another. Other types of culturalists (*status-seekers, cultural contestants,* and *versoculturalists,* to introduce terms that acquire currency later) seek to assert their place in a cultural hierarchy of human dignity. It is with respect to the issue of dignity that we see the greatest distinction between liberal republican and culturalist theories of justice. Since the immediate focus of this chapter will be multiculturalism, we will restrict our overview of the issue to that form of culturalism for the time being, reserving a discussion of other culturalist perspectives on dignity for the next chapter.

Liberal republican justice is predicated on the imperative to universalize human dignity. The implication is that each individual has an equal moral claim to dignity and hence an equal claim to the rights requisite to pressing that moral claim. Multiculturalism also demands the universalization of human dignity. However, multiculturalists hold that the locus of justice is not just the individual. It is also to be found in the essentialist community, such as women, to take but one example, which informs a shared cultural identity. The implication is that insofar as different cultural communities have different needs, universalization of dignity must be "differently equal."

The idea of differently equal represents a theory of equality that deviates from the liberal republican imperative that individuals be *formally* equal, or equal before the law. Instead, the multiculturalist theory of equality demands what we can think of as *situational* equality. Situational equality demands that all essentialist communities be equally situated before it is reasonable to speak of formal equality.

Essentialist communities will be equally situated when membership in such groups becomes a perfect non-predictor of social achievement. Thus, when African-Americans are proportionally likely to be wealthy, or women are proportionally likely to be political elites, or acknowledged homosexuals are equally likely to achieve positions of prominence in the corporate sector, we will be said to have achieved situational equality. Because different essentialist groups face different challenges to realizing situational equality, universalization of dignity demands that the members of such groups sometimes be treated differently under law. That is, unlike formal equality, which demands equal treatment but permits differential outcomes, situational equality permits differential treatment in the quest for equal outcomes.

JUSTICE AND HUMAN DIGNITY

While liberal republicanism strives to maximize citizens' potential to lead fulfilling lives, it makes no claim that all citizens will lead equally fulfilled lives. Instead, the good society is one in which an individual is free to live the good life as she understands it, and in which she has access to the range of social, artistic, political, theological, cultural, and educational opportunities that liberate her from internal constraints. In return for this rich social milieu in which she operates, she is morally obliged to contribute to the good of that environment. She is obliged, in other words, to contribute to the common end of justice – an end that allows individuals to lead self-directed, *dignified* lives.

Most multiculturalists would suggest, I think, that these are necessary but insufficient conditions for achieving the ends of justice and human dignity. Missing is the imperative to protect and promote the cultural identities of subaltern communities. Indeed, multiculturalism is grounded in the premise that identity precedes interest and is hence more pertinent to understanding human fulfillment. Interests do matter, of course; but these interests are bounded or conditioned by identity, which we can think of as the means by which individuals perceive and make sense of the world (Taylor 1992, 32–4; Kymlicka 1995a, 76).

From the perspective of multiculturalism, identity assumes political salience when it is shared among members of a community. Communities represent repositories of shared histories, mores, traditions, and values. This repository is what we think of as a culture. Implicit in the idea of a culture is particularism, or the sharing of something common to the in-group that distinguishes it from the out-group. It is this shared something that multiculturalists see as integral to human fulfillment and dignity. So integral is this shared cultural identity to human social development that from the perspective of multiculturalism, protecting and celebrating cultural identity serves the same purpose as human rights. Both are the vehicles through which one can protect or assert her human dignity. Unlike rights, however, cultural identities are not socially reducible, that is, they do not attach to individuals. Cultural identity cannot be parsed such that every member of the cultural group can experience her Chineseness or Italianness, for example, as a self-contained individual. Indeed, for multiculturalists, to speak of an individual divorced from her social context is akin to assigning meaning to a word taken from its linguistic context. The individual continues to exist but that existence risks losing all meaning (Van Dyke 1977; Taylor 1985; 1992; 1995; Young 1990, chs. 1–2; Kymlicka 1995a, chs. 4–5).

The centrality of cultural identity is most obvious when individuals are displaced – voluntarily or otherwise – from the social context that informs those identities. Historically, cultural trauma has manifested itself in anomic pathologies (or social problems associated with rootlessness and lacking a sense of belonging) (Sztompka 2000). Durkheim's classic study of increased suicide rates in Europe in the wake of mass urban migration in the nineteenth and early twentieth century is a case in point (1979). Similarly, Fukuyama finds a contemporaneous spike across a number of industrialized countries in social pathologies such as divorce and illegitimacy rates, substance abuse, and crime in the aftermath of the post-industrial suburban migration that began in the 1960s (1999; see also Jackson 1991). Individuals can exist in an environment in which they are displaced from identity-creating social contexts, but doing so is difficult and often traumatic.

Given the properties of essentialist groups as something more than aggregations of individuals pursuing common interests, differentiated citizenship represents a rejection of the idea that a person is a person is a person. Peoples differ based on their cultures. These differences demand that different people not always be treated precisely the same way under law. While no person is more or less deserving of human dignity than any other (and indeed this is the whole point) differentiated citizenship mandates that in some circumstances, different groups must enjoy substantive and procedural privileges not available to all citizens. Differentiated citizenship, in other words, demands that the liberal republican imperative for formal equality occasionally be relaxed in favour of the situational equality introduced briefly above.

Under situational equality, all essentialist groups can be understood to be in an equal situation. Situational equality is an environment in which members of all groups are equally free (or equally restricted) in their choice-sets along any given issue dimension, an environment in which their cultural backgrounds are no more or less likely to help them in their life chances. Under situational equality, men have no greater propensity than women to pursue lucrative and socially prestigious careers, Blacks are no less likely to encounter obstacles to achievement based on racial stereotypes than are Whites, and gays and lesbians are no more likely to feel the imperative to conceal their sexual preferences than are straights. A society will have achieved situational equality when (proportionally speaking) denizens of bad neighbourhoods are no less likely to be members of the dominant ethnic or racial community than of subaltern ones, and in which the boardroom is controlled by a proportionate number of women who feel free to express their femininity, African-Americans who do not feel the need to disguise that which makes them culturally distinctive from the mainstream, and gays and lesbians who don't have to be asked and have no need to tell.

Situational equality demands that a cultural heritage that informs essentialist communities be preserved. The differentiated citizenship that underlies multiculturalist justice demands the recognition that dignity attaches not only to individuals, but also to identity-providing communities as well. From this perspective, one's culture is as foundational to her as any other part of her being. To risk overdramatizing the point, we would find it beyond comprehension to suggest that the price of a person's ability to succeed in her life pursuits should be the amputation of her arm. Yet one of the great problems of liberal republican conceptions of justice from a multiculturalist perspective is that by treating each person as a person as a person, we effectively amputate the cultural identities of members of subaltern communities as the price they must pay to achieve social and material success. Despite the imperative to distinguish usness from sameness, in other words, modern liberal republics do a poor job of this. The result is a cultural hierarchy that only masquerades as justice and universalization of dignity.

Representation of Tertiary Values

A fundamental distinction between multiculturalism and liberal republicanism lies in the way in which each conceives meaningful subnational communities, and (more important) the sorts of tertiary values that must be reflected in constitutional rules. Given the primacy of individual choice, liberal republicans have traditionally understood the most important tertiary values to be grounded in volition and not ascription. That is, they understand that people choose which subnational communities matter to them; they are not assigned membership in such communities on the basis of innate characteristics. It is to provide maximum mobility and choice that liberal republicans have conceived of tertiary values as reflective of discrete geographic rather than essentialist communities.

By contrast, for multiculturalists, tertiary values represent more than a mere concession to diversity of lifestyle. Rather than being simply a matter of choice or free will, tertiary values constitute recognition of the shared values of essentialist cultural communities, the distinctiveness of which may or may not be spatially informed. And while there is volition involved to the extent that one may or may not choose to *identify* with certain ascriptive characteristics, this choice is predicated on cultural identity and not individual utility. For example, one might or might not choose to define herself in terms of her femininity. However, to the extent that she does, that choice will be based on the way in which she views and makes sense of the world, not on rational utility-maximization.

All this leads to very different prescriptions as to how diversity is accommodated through the rules of the just society. For liberal republicans, there is no a priori understanding of what sorts of essentialist values represent "diversity." Instead, diversity will be a function of social mobilization such that diversity extends to the range of issues subject to political contestation. Issues become contestable only when like-minded citizens mobilize to contest them. From this perspective, if a group's essentialist characteristics are important to members of that group, the group will apply pressure on elected representatives to accommodate the group's core values and ideals. This Madisonian approach to diversity absolves the state of having to pick and choose which sorts of tertiary values are worth accommodating and which sorts are not.

Of course, there are limits to the efficacy of this process. As administrative units become larger they become less sensitive to diversity as smaller groups become numerically marginalized. Moreover, because the distribution of interests may be geographically skewed in such a way that more populous regions acquire disproportionate policy influence, the danger exists that regional majorities will come to overwhelm regional minorities. It is in deference to this fact that governance in liberal republics typically manifests itself in some form of spatial representation. Federalism and geographically informed voting districts are thus the principal means by which the diversity inherent in tertiary values is accommodated.

From the perspective of multiculturalism, spatial representation guarantees little by way of effective representation of essentialist tertiary values. The preferred alternative is to accommodate diversity in essentialist terms. As such, multiculturalism generally mandates some sort of special representation rights, such as voting districts arranged according to essentialist characteristics. Voters might vote, for example, not merely as Texans or Ontarians, but as women or First Nations peoples or African-Americans or francophones. The legislature might consist of members whose seats are set aside for members of particular essentialist communities. And as was proposed in the failed Charlottetown Constitutional Accord in Canada, representation could even extend to the creation of essentialist sovereign levels of government.

Liberal republicans are loath to accept qualifications to spatial representation because it boasts a number of advantages over essentialist alternatives. Perhaps the most important is the ability to exercise choice as to the sorts of communities in which individuals wish to live and be politically represented. This is something that most essentialist alternatives cannot offer. One can choose whether to live in Virginia or California, but (practically speaking) one cannot choose his ethnicity, gender, or sexual orientation. Moreover, one cannot be pigeonholed by membership in a community with which she does not identify. A person born in British Columbia is not forever bound to a particular form of representation based upon her British Columbianess. She could choose to move to Alberta and be represented as a member of that province instead. However, a woman whose cultural identity is not defined in terms of femininity, or an African-American who does not define himself by his skin colour, would have no such mobility. For the purposes of representation, individuals would be ascriptively bound to their respective essentialist communities.

Another disadvantage of essentialist representation is that society is obliged to decide which cultural groups matter and which do not. Obviously not all essentialist communities can be given special representation rights. The sheer number of such communities would be greater than the capacity of any reasonably sized legislative chamber. And this assumes that all citizens could be neatly assigned a single relevant essentialist characteristic. (Are Métis, for example, Aboriginals, French-Canadians, or their own discrete group for the purpose of essentialist representation?) Rather than finding some mechanism by which societies could distinguish the cultural communities *that really matter* from those that by extension do not, the advantage of spatial representation is that the public space can remain culturally neutral. The central authority is absolved of the need to champion certain cultures and instead serve as an impartial arbiter of competing cultural interests. Minority cultures assume a position akin to any other aggregated interest in a pluralist marketplace for policy influence (Kukathas 1992; cf. Kymlicka 1995a, esp. 110–15).

Finally, spatial representation is attractive because its legitimacy is grounded in traditional acceptance. It is the *normal* way of representing people in a democracy, a product of what Pocock has called a fellowship of experience (1975, 334; also Walzer 1981, 13–15). Its venerability informs its legitimacy. Legitimacy, in turn, is foundational to liberal republican government. Without legitimacy, for reasons already noted, liberty becomes vulnerable to tyranny. For such legitimacy to be risked by re-orienting the representational structure, the superiority of the new system would have to be clear and significant.

For multiculturalists, it is the last two points – that spatial representation of tertiary values is culturally neutral and historically legitimate – that are the most problematic. In the first instance, these points are mutually incompatible. Historical practices axiomatically produce cultural effects that are not neutral. In the second, these non-neutral cultural effects serve to privilege the historical (and decidedly illegitimate) advantages that the dominant cultural community enjoys over subaltern ones. The hidden vice here is that the appropriation by the dominant community of the normal or appropriate or legitimate has served at worst to de-legitimize subaltern cultural practices and at best to portray them as quaint cultural anachronisms (Feagin and Cobas 2008, 40). For multiculturalists, the effects of this erroneous misrepresentation of benign cultural neglect leads to a fundamental difference in the way in which dignity can meaningfully be universalized. It contributes to an overly narrow understanding of the tertiary values requisite to a just society.

A Hierarchy of Values

Liberal republicanism espouses a normative hierarchy of values such that primary values trump secondary ones and secondary ones trump tertiary ones. In this sense tertiary values represent subordinate qualifications to secondary values. There is an implicit sense that while certainly there is no harm in feeling pride in one's subnational cultural values, the underlying assumption is that such pride is secondary to his identification with a country's society as a whole. This is why protocol in America demands, for example, that state flags be flown below the Stars and Stripes. Tertiary values are an addendum to the just society, necessary to control for what might otherwise be a majoritarian bias.

Multiculturalists order the hierarchy of values differently. As with liberal republicans, multiculturalists assign priority to primary values. An important qualification, however, is that they differ in how they prioritize these values. Most pertinently for present purposes, while multicultural-ism accepts formal equality among individuals as a primary value, such equality cannot be understood as existing prior to protection of cultural identity. Protecting cultural identity takes priority over all rights, insofar as multiculturalists begin from the premise that it is cultural identity – not rights – that represents the most important means to the universal-ization of human dignity.[2]

The most important distinction between liberal republicanism and multiculturalism with respect to a hierarchy of cultural values turns on the position of secondary and tertiary values. Here I do not wish to claim that multiculturalists marginalize secondary values. Such a claim would be unjust and inaccurate. However, while secondary values gen-erally matter a great deal to multiculturalists, they can also be seen as alien, even imperialistic and threatening to subaltern cultural identities (Horowitz 1985, 137). Multiculturalism rejects the liberal republican as-sumption that tertiary values are addenda to secondary ones; instead they assign priority (or at least equality) to the importance of tertiary values. What this means is that liberal republicans start from the homog-enous and then accommodate heterogeneity, whereas multiculturalists start from the heterogeneous and then accommodate homogeneity.

The progression from the homogenous to the heterogeneous reflects what multiculturalists see as the individualist bias in liberal republican theories of justice. If we start from the premise that a person is a person is a person, any deviation from this premise must be mitigated so that even tertiary values are individualist in form. For example, liberal re-publicanism can accommodate the different rules for different people inherent in federalism only insofar as individuals have the ability to choose which set of different rules to live by. Liberal republican theories of justice assign normative priority to individuals such that our dignity attaches to us as individuals and not as part of a larger organic construct. The locus of justice, the foundation of the entire system of values, rules, tolerance, and dignity, is predicated on the rights of the individual *as* an individual (e.g., Glendon 1991, esp. ch. 3).

2 Kymlicka disagrees with this point, suggesting that individual rights are prior to col-lective ones, that is, internal restrictions imposed by cultural groups cannot abrogate indi-vidual rights (1995a, ch. 3, esp. 37). However, this is a tough argument to sustain. In championing multicultural citizenship, Kymlicka is unclear as to how the dominant community in liberal societies should simultaneously regulate internal cultural practices – female circumcision, for example – without engaging in the sort of cultural intrusion that the promotion of tertiary values was intended to protect in the first instance.

For multiculturalists, the problem with this inherent individualism is that it takes too thin a view of the human self. Liberal republican individualism implies a certain portability. At the extreme, because individuals are pre-social, they can be seen as in, but not entirely of, the society in which they were raised. Individuals thus can be expected to thrive in any well-constructed liberal republic. There is an implied cultural substitutability in the sense that all rational agents can be expected to respond in like ways (or within a narrow parameter) to like circumstances (see Taylor 1985; Lukes 2006, ch. 17). The multiculturalist self, however, is not as self-contained. It is intimately tied to a social context that informs one's identity. For multiculturalists, identity so defines who we are that if one's identity were different, it would make little sense to refer to the factual self (who we are) and the counterfactual self (who we would be if our identities were different) as the same person. Identity provides perspective in pursuit of the authentic life.[3]

INJUSTICE

From the multiculturalist perspective, the flaws inherent within the liberal republican theory of justice are as manifest in the former's notion of *injustice* as they are of justice. Both are construed too narrowly. A good illustration of the perceived narrowness of liberal republican injustice informs the so-called blame model. As articulated by Folger and Cropanzano (2001), the blame model grounds injustice in three criteria: an unfavourable condition relative to a comparable point of reference; willful and discretionary action on the part of an agent or agents in bringing about this unfavourable condition; and the transgression of a generally accepted code of appropriate conduct. Thus, we could assign blame to a person who steals money from another for volitional action that creates an unfavourable condition in defiance of a generally accepted code of appropriate conduct. The multicultural theory of injustice stands in opposition to each of these criteria. To take them slightly out of order, we can think of the multicultural critique in terms of agency, objectivism, and universality. This opposition to the blame model of

---

3 Identity, of course, is not an alien concept for liberal republicanism. The significance of secondary values is that they represent a means by which a people defines itself. Indeed, it is what distinguishes one group of people from another, and so we might say that identity is framed as much in terms of who we are as in who we are not (Huntington 2004a, ch. 2). But the fact that voluntary migration occurs and that these migrants are able to accommodate the values of their new host societies suggests that while national identity may be important to people, at least for many it is not foundational to the authentic life.

injustice provides the best illustration of what a multicultural theory of justice looks like.

Agency

Liberal republican injustice exists only as a product of agency – an actor doing something, or failing to do something – for which blame may be attached. The appropriate remedy is to prevent or deter the agent of injustice from doing whatever is causing injury to someone else. By contrast, from the multicultural perspective, injustice does not require agency and instead may be structural. That is, it may be perpetuated by individuals who are not blameworthy under the criteria of the blame model insofar as unfavourable conditions are created without conscious motive on the part of any agent. This is important since if injustice is not agent-specific, then remedies must be structural rather than agent-specific.

Even where we can pinpoint the agent responsible for inflicting injustice on others, it is often difficult to attach blame and hence prescribe an agent-specific remedy. Unlike Emerson's unjust facilitator of another's incapacity, who if he is truly honest with himself will question his own motives, sometimes individuals act unjustly even when they are unconscious of the fact they are doing so, or indeed when they (incorrectly) believe they are acting justly. Charles Lawrence recounts a college experience in which a White classmate, with no malign intent, informed him with great magnanimity that he didn't even think of Lawrence as a Negro (Lawrence 1987, 318). The comment was not meant to demean Lawrence – just the opposite, in fact. In all probability it was not even meant as a slight to African-Americans in general. Lawrence's friend no doubt felt he was being progressive, that he was seeing the inner person and not the outer shell, that we are all the same under the skin.

A similar sentiment is expressed, albeit ironically, in an episode of *Seinfeld*, where George feigns ignorance as to whether or not a coworker is African-American. Looking beyond the superficial, if embracing the ridiculous, George implies that he sees only the human being and not the colour of that person's skin. Here George is affirming the universalization of dignity that privileges individuals' humanity above all other ascriptive attributes. But at the same time, by failing to recognize his coworker's essentialist characteristics, he inadvertently stigmatizes him. One does not feign ignorance about the positive qualities she sees in others, only the negative ones. ("I like your haircut" is socially acceptable; "I see that you have a pimple on your nose" is not.) Because polite society demands that we not draw attention to others' afflictions, the implicit message is that George's colleague is afflicted with Blackness, but wishing to be perceived as a good and decent fellow, George's sense of justice compels him to overlook this "unfortunate" circumstance.

It is difficult to blame either Lawrence's friend or George for the fact that their actions are in fact antithetical to the affirmation of dignity and indeed reinforce an unfavourable condition. While Lawrence's friend and George were theatrically artless in the expression of their sentiments, the ideal of a difference-blind society is foundational to the liberal republican credo that a person is a person is a person. If there is blame to be assigned to all this difference-blindness, it is should be assigned not to difference-blind individuals, but rather to a social culture – an entity without volitional agency – for failing to imbue itself with a greater sensitivity to issues of justice (Young 1990, 99–102; Benson 2004, 187).

Indeed, some multiculturalists go so far as to assert that assigning individual blame often serves as *camouflage* for the social practices and norms that ultimately contribute to blameworthy behaviour, so that even if individuals actually *do* bear responsibility for their moral impairment, they do not explore the source of that moral impairment (Hoagland 1988, 215–24; Benson 2004). It is easier to condemn someone for visiting violence upon someone of another race, for example, than to understand the sorts of social values that led to such behaviour in the first place. Simply, it is easier to blame one than to blame all. And it is a whole lot less disruptive to rules and prioritization of values, to say nothing of our conceptions of what it means to be tolerant and dignity-affirming. As such, it is preferable for liberal republicans and other perceived standard-bearers of the dominant community to blame individual agents for specific acts as an alternative to engaging in the wholesale reform of a society that affords the dominant community privilege in the first place.

So thoroughly have we internalized the imperative to assign agent-specific culpability to specific behaviour, the logic goes, that sometimes we confuse victimhood and blameworthiness. In so doing, we overlook the structural factors that restrict the range of alternatives, or choice-sets along a particular choice dimension, as perceived by the victim. Take the case of the battered woman who decides that her only recourse in escaping mistreatment is to kill her abusive husband in his sleep. To many, the killer's behaviour represents a clear and objective manifestation of blameworthiness. It is not as if her life was in imminent danger. "Why did she not just walk away?" the bemused observer wonders, implying that any rational moral person would have assessed the range of alternatives and favoured a choice less blameworthy. What our bemused observer fails to recognize, multiculturalists argue implicitly, is that the choice-set as the observer sees it and the choice-set as perceived by the battered woman are not one and the same (Hoagland 1988, esp. 215–17; Schneider 1993). As we will see in our discussion of universality below, different people's choice-sets may be culturally conditioned in such a way as to a) undermine the assumption of endogeneity inherent in liberal republicanism and b) work to the advantage of some, and the disadvantage of other, cultural communities.

Objectivity

Before we get there, though, a second means by which the liberal republican blame model fails in the eyes of multiculturalists lies in the understanding of what constitutes an unfavourable condition. The blame model holds that an unfavourable condition is judged from a comparative point of reference, or baseline. That is, reasonableness informs a generally accepted understanding of what represents just behaviour. Injustice is then evaluated according to the deviation from that baseline, and the appropriate remedies are imposed to compensate those harmed by the deviation and to create incentives for others not to deviate. But from the multiculturalist perspective, conceiving injustice this way is as pathological as insisting on agency. If the imperative for agency leads to scapegoating and/or confusing victim and perpetrator in assigning blame, objectivity insulates both agent and the larger society from blame and by extension from the imperative to remedy injustice. As such, in a society that assigns dignity to individuals as individuals, which values a person as a person as a person, which incorporates colour-blindness into its understanding of justice, neither George nor Lawrence's friend nor indeed society as a whole is guilty of deviating from a generally accepted (read reasonable) moral baseline.

But what if the problem lies with the baseline? What if there is slippage between the reasonable and the just such that harm is inflicted, however unintentionally? The multicultural theory of justice starts by questioning the justice of the baseline (Young 2003). In other words, it begins from the premise that justice needs to rely on more than whatever is generally acceptable to the citizens of a liberal republic, because while their conception of what it means to be just may be culturally appropriate to most, it may not be to all. Indeed, that mainstream conception may well have been born of internalizing unjust standards. Under such circumstances, injustice will only appear unjust if those who evaluate the reasonableness of actions are able to achieve sufficient perspective to permit detachment from the cultural environment in which they find themselves (Eyerman 1981).

If people are understood simply as people, such detachment is not terribly difficult. Moral reason or moral sentiment provides the means by which one can evaluate the justness of a circumstance. That evaluation does not suffer from cultural colourization. However, if people are understood as (at least in part) products of their cultural identities, then such detachment is not possible. Inextricably bound to their cultural identities, individuals will evaluate the justness of a circumstance through the lens of that identity. Indeed, where the cultural dominance of the dominant community is sufficiently powerful, it becomes difficult even for victims of injustice to recognize that fact.

Social consensus as it pertains to an objective standard of justice manifests itself in terms of that which we normally come to expect. The way things are, in other words, tends to be conflated with the way things should be. Sometimes this conflation leads to attitudes and behaviour that are difficult to comprehend from a detached perspective. Pritchard (1972, 306–7) provides a hypothetical illustration. He asks us to imagine an extreme case of two individuals born into slavery. The first slave maintains sufficient detachment to regard himself as the moral equal of the man who enslaves him. To him slavery is an affront to his dignity and an injustice that he meets with the appropriate moral reaction of anger and indignation. By contrast, the second slave internalizes the distinction that makes him the social inferior of his master and accepts the circumstance as normal, even just. He understands his enslavement as appropriate to the treatment generally accorded to persons who occupy his position in the social hierarchy.

There is nothing remarkable about the attitude of the first slave. Both he and the one who enslaves him enjoy sufficient cultural detachment to understand the injustice of the circumstance. Clearly it is not acceptable for one man to own another. No matter how much ambient social pressure exists to tell them that "no, really, it *is* okay to own slaves," they are sufficiently detached to know that it is not okay. But how do we make sense of the actions of the second slave? How do we comprehend any attitude that makes the victim complicit in the injustice perpetrated against him? It is one thing to be robbed forcibly of one's of dignity. But it is quite another to accept such indignity as appropriate to circumstance. Such acceptance is only comprehensible if it is informed by prevailing cultural mores sufficiently strong to overwhelm the capacity for moral reason.

Obviously not all forms of culturally informed injustice are as blatant as slave-holding. But few stop to question prevailing social arrangements the origins of which lie in the murky past of a long experiential tradition.

It does not occur to most of us to question any number of social conventions – the fact that in America, most school curricula are taught in English and not Spanish (or for that matter, Ebonics); or the convention that mothers assume disproportionate responsibility for child care; or the conception of marriage as between two and only two people of different genders; or that business hours and standards have been designed by men for the convenience of men. These conventions are understood to be, or have been understood to be in the not-too-distant past, normal.

If we consider such conventions to be examples of injustice, some might assign blame if there is volition involved: an alliance of the strong has chosen to act unjustly against the weak. In such cases injustice is perpetuated by a (choose your adjectives) bourgeois, patriarchal, heterosexist, fundamentalist, racist, Anglo-centric conspiracy dedicated to illegitimizing the true consciousness of the oppressed in favour of a more elite-palatable false consciousness. But for many multiculturalists, the blame model is *not* applicable here. There need be no willful intent on the part of men to oppress women, straights to oppress gays, etc. Confusing the empirical with the normative might render people insufficiently introspective in their understandings of that which constitutes an objective baseline of just behaviour. But it does not make them blameworthy (Young 2003).

Universality

The liberal republican code of justice is universalistic insofar as it applies (almost) the same way to each individual within society. For multiculturalists, the problem with the universality dimension of the blame model is that it conceives, and hence institutionalizes, primary, secondary, and tertiary values too narrowly. The emphasis on civic participation does provide for a wide range of input into the construction of society's rules. But the output is more rigid: one code of justice that is common to all in like circumstances. Moreover, for all of its emphasis on civic participation in the refinement of values, the liberal republican model still reflects preconceived assumptions about the primacy of individualist values, which in turn has the effect of limiting the range of social arrangements that emerge from it. Liberal republicanism holds, for example, that dignity and hence justice are protected through universally applicable human rights. Rights underscore the (formal) equality-imperative by ensuring that individuals are equal in their freedom to make life choices. Rights exist as a means for a rational actor to make an efficacious claim to preserve her human dignity while at the same time compelling others to respect that dignity (Said 1977; Donnelly 1982).

But how valid is this assumption? Multiculturalists challenge it on the grounds that individuals are not equally situated to take advantage of rights as a means to making the sorts of authentic life choices requisite to universal dignity (Daniels 1990, 275–6). In chapter 3 we linked the efficacy of rationality in making authentic life choices to perspective. We suggested that social resources lead individuals to acquire heightened perspective in recognizing the range of options (and hence quality of choices) available to them. We are all rational creatures, in other words, but the efficacy of that rationality is affected by our perspective. It is only by transcending internal obstacles that limit our perspective that we are able to make authentic choices for ourselves.

Multiculturalists argue that situational inequality represents a manifestation of systemic differences in the capacity to attain perspective, which work to the disadvantage of historically oppressed subaltern communities. Different groups are taught to view and make sense of the world in different ways such that groups differ in their members' effective choice-sets along a given choice dimension. Since situational inequality is not naturally constructed, it must therefore be socially constructed. This social construction, which is often not the volitional action of a blameworthy individual or group of individuals, is a cultural phenomenon (Elster 1983; Simon 1990; Mumby and Putnam 1992; Ashcraft and Pacanowsky 1996). Correll (2001, 1691) argues, for example, that when it comes to career choices, gender socialization plays a significant role and that much of the well-documented wage gap between men and women can be accounted for by women choosing employment in lower-paying sectors of the economy. In other words, even though there are no longer any rules in place that force them into such choices, women *rationally* choose less lucrative careers than do men. Such decisions do not stem from lack of opportunities. That would be a comparatively easy fix. Rather, they come from a (culturally) restricted choice-set acquired early in the socialization process.

Writing in the mid-1990s, Jacobs notes that since 1982 more women than men have been awarded college degrees in the United States, a phenomenon that suggests that women are not victimized by discriminatory rules pertaining to educational access (1995, 81). But women earned different types of degrees and were significantly underrepresented in the quantitative fields that are, generally speaking, more remunerative (Berryman 1983; Catsambis 1994; Jacobs 1995; Correll 2001). This difference is not marginal. Using undergraduate college data from 1984, Jacobs finds that in order to acquire equal gender distribution across majors, 30.4 per cent of women would have had to change their majors (1995, 81). Why do women choose so differently?

Because grade school mathematics is an important gateway to quantitative majors in college, it serves as a good starting point for inquiry. In the United States, boys empirically earn better grades in mathematics than do girls. This might be little more than a manifestation of the many biological differences that exist between men and women. Certainly in North America it is a widely held belief that men are wired in such a way as to make them more quantitatively competent. The boys' better math scores would seem to prove it. But *are* boys really better at mathematics than girls, or does it just *appear* that way? Given prevailing cultural perceptions in North America, Correll is not surprised to find that generally grade-school teachers grade boys more leniently in mathematics and girls more strictly (2001, 1694–8).

A daisy-chain of causation follows. A culturally biased evaluation process creates a biased and likely often inaccurate self-assessment of task competence. This biased self-assessment serves to narrow the choice-set for girls and subsequently young women. Girls who are led to believe they have comparatively little aptitude for mathematics show comparatively little interest in it, whatever their true competence may be. This self-assessment bias, moreover, works both ways. Comparatively speaking, girls have an inaccurately low sense of mathematical task competence whereas boys have an exaggerated one. Baker and Jones find support for this perspective by examining cross-national gender distinction in quantitative fields. They find that in most countries, the gender distinction is less pronounced than in the United States. As such, either it is only North American women who are biologically inferior in their quantitative skills, or (as must obviously be the case) the preference distinction is more cultural than biological (1993).

Spencer, Steele, and Quinn (1999) find in a controlled study that when college students were told in advance that men have superior mathematical aptitude, men significantly outperformed women on standard basic mathematics tests. However, when subjects were provided with no prompt as to gender aptitude, there was no significant gender difference. The study supports Correll's hypothesis that an important part of the choice distinction between young men and women is an artifact of perception and not a matter of fact. It is the perception that they are inferior at mathematics that streams young women toward what are perceived to be more women-friendly career choices. And even if later young women come to disavow differences in task competence for advanced mathematics, it is often too late to acquire the necessary background to do much about it (Correll 2001).

In addition to biased self-assessment, situational inequality also can emerge through fear of reinforcing negative cultural stereotypes about one's group. Claude Steele (1999) and others (Steele and Aronson 1995; Spencer, Steele, and Quinn 1999) have called this phenomenon "stereotype threat," and it similarly restricts the effective choice-sets available to members of subaltern cultural communities. Steele employs stereotype threat to explain the high dropout rate for African-Americans at US colleges, and the comparative performance gap between Black and White students. Through the 1990s, the African-American college dropout rate was a fifth to a quarter higher than it was for Whites. And where individuals completed their degrees, the mean grade point average was two-thirds of a letter grade lower for Blacks than it was for Whites.

No doubt some of this problem is institutional in nature. Systemic discrepancies created by district-specific public school funding have long meant that African-American students have been more likely to suffer from inadequate scholastic preparation for college. But institutional bias does not explain all of the discrepancy. Middle-class African-Americans, who presumably went to well-funded schools, also suffered an achievement gap (Steele 1999, 1). As such, it is reasonable to conclude that at least part of the achievement gap can be explained not economically, but culturally.

There are ugly, but prevailing stereotypes about African-Americans that pertain to academic aptitude and work ethic. The fact that African-Americans are underrepresented at American universities reinforces this stereotype. It also reinforces African-Americans' *consciousness* that this stereotype exists. When consciousness is elevated, moreover, sensitivity also tends to be heightened. For students with sufficiently heightened sensitivity, even innocuous or ambiguous incidents can take on sinister undertones. Steele uses hypothetical examples. Did my White girlfriend dump me for a White guy because she likes him better, or because I am Black? Did my psychology professor assign Herrnstein and Murray's *Bell Curve* because at some subconscious level he buys into the theory of the genetic intellectual inferiority of Blacks? Did the White students I overheard denouncing affirmative action in the cafeteria believe that Blacks do not belong on campus?

The greater the sensitivity, moreover, the greater pressure the individual feels not to conform to the negative stereotype. This pressure – what a student once described to me as the "White backpack" – particularly in an environment in which one already does not feel comfortable, can start to overwhelm (Harrell 2000). For some, this pressure is no doubt positive, a spur to achievement. But a common human response is to retire from environments in which the burden is most prevalent (Moos 2002, 24, 27). Indeed, sociological research indicates that African-American students tend to assign less value to domains in which Blacks

traditionally have not succeeded (Harper and Tuckman 2006, 387).
Such *disidentification* results in shifting the basis of one's self-esteem or
dignity even at the cost of negatively affecting her career and other
life choices.[4]

There are two main causes of situational inequality, only one of which
can be reduced to blameworthy action. These causes are bad rules and
cultural hegemony on the part of the dominant group. By bad rules I
mean laws repugnant to both liberal republican and multicultural conceptions of justice. Laws that explicitly deny formal equality to members
of groups such as African-Americans, women, Aboriginals, gays and lesbians, etc., are unjust by any standard. The obvious remedy is to repeal
or modify such rules. Less obvious is the fact that repealing bad laws does
not solve the problem. Bad laws generate long cultural hangovers. They
inspire cultural inequality long after formal equality has been institutionalized. As the case of the achievement gap between Black and White
students suggests, this hangover perpetuates an effective cultural restriction upon choice-sets and ultimately the optimality of life choices. Here
it is impossible to assign volitional blame. Members of both dominant
and subaltern communities are hostage to the cultural web that causes
the former to reinforce a universal standard of what constitutes an unfavourable circumstance, and the latter to risk suboptimal life choices
based on culturally restricted choice-sets.

Remedy

Equality under law and equality of effective choice are not one and the
same. In the wake of bad laws, formal equality, including equal access
to the sorts of rights designed to enforce one's moral claim to dignity, is
insufficient. It does little more than institutionalize a pre-existing inequality. Compare it to a football game, in which one team is victimized
systemically by unfair officiating so that by halftime the team is trailing by
three touchdowns. Few would find it sufficient to remedy the problem

---

4 As Steele puts it: "Pain is lessened by ceasing to identify with the part of life in which
the pain occurs. This withdrawal of psychic investment may be supported by other members of the stereotype-threatened group – even to the point of its becoming a group norm.
But not caring can mean not being motivated. And this can have real costs. When stereotype threat affects school life, disidentification is a high price to pay for psychic comfort.
Still, it is a price that groups contending with powerful negative stereotypes about their
abilities – women in advanced math, African-Americans in all academic areas – may too
often pay" (Steele 1999, 3).

with a commitment to enforce the rules equally in the second half. That might make for a fair second half, but assuming evenly matched teams it is pretty clear which team is probably going to win. The previously victimized team is unlikely to be sufficiently energized by the sudden introduction of universally fair rules to be able to overcome all previous obstacles to fairness. In fact, they may not be energized much at all if lingering doubts about institutional fairness, efficacy, and even task competence persist. For multiculturalists, then, a system that leaves members of some cultural groups in an unequal situation with members of other groups cannot be said to have satisfied the prerequisites of justice.

For multiculturalists, if institutional change is unequal to the task of achieving situational equality, what is required is cultural change. Such cultural change, however, demands a re-evaluation of how to achieve universalization of dignity that takes into account the relationship between human dignity and social context. As we have already seen, liberal republicanism holds that human dignity is realized through undifferentiated citizenship. The ideal is a society that recognizes and affirms the dignity of individuals as individuals, not as people perceived through the lens of their ascriptive characteristics.

Yet from the perspective of multiculturalism this understanding of "universal" human dignity is in fact not universal at all. It is an understanding of human dignity refracted through the cultural lens of the dominant group within society, which is then (in most cases unconsciously) presented as a culturally neutral, universalistic understanding of human dignity. Liberal republicans and multiculturalists thus differ as to the means by which dignity is universally affirmed. Multiculturalists emphasize the relationship between one's cultural identity and his dignity (Harter 1999; Zirkel 2002). As a consequence, liberal republican means for affirming the dignity of others are unequal to the task. Enhancing Emersonian self-reliance without promoting the capacity of identity-creating groups is akin to raising the status of the word, but not the language. Similarly, Rawls's redistribution of material resources to individuals is insufficient if the recipient is unequally situated in his capacity to use those resources to a productive end. True justice demands greater nuance than adequate compensation for unfavourable circumstances.

By failing to take proper notice of the relationship between an individual's identity and her quest for authenticity, liberal republican universalization of dignity places members of subaltern communities in the culturally untenable position of having to choose between exercising their individual capacity or retaining their group identity – that is, of choosing between material and social success or authenticity.

IDENTITY

The multiculturalist conception of justice is grounded in ameliorating the problems inherent in the blame model. Justice, in other words, demands that human dignity be enhanced in a way that is structural, non-objective, and particularistic. It is for this reason that multiculturalist justice focuses on the imperative to protect and preserve cultural identities.

Generally speaking there are three dimensions to one's identity. The first is idiosyncratic, such that individuals' unique personality traits help define their identities. Similarly, people can define themselves idiosyncratically in terms of their personal goals or objectives. This idiosyncratic dimension of identity certainly demands a social environment. But it is largely insensitive to specific societal context. The idiosyncratic dimension exists pretty much intact in a wide variety of social settings. Indeed, it is this idiosyncratic dimension that informs the universalism of liberal republican theories of justice: whatever else it might demand in terms of concern, justice is predicated on the equal treatment of all (unique) individuals before the law.

The other dimensions of identity, however, are more sensitive to the cultural environment (see Spencer 1985). A second dimension of identity is personally or *subjectively* derived. It is grounded in *identification:* in Taylor's words "how individuals or members of a group see themselves – or, as we say, what they identify themselves as" (1993, 13).[5] Thus, in addition to the idiosyncratic dimension of *who she naturally is*, this subjective dimension reflects *who she feels she should be.* Who an individual feels she should be is the basis of the civic self, the self who sees her place in society in terms of her moral obligations. As such, it might be useful to add the qualification that subjective identification is almost by definition intersubjective insofar as identity (unless one identifies as an asocial being) demands commonality of relevant beliefs, practices, mores, traditions, differentiating characteristics, and/or lifestyles (see Anderson 2006, ch. 1).

The third dimension of identity is objective. It is grounded in the perception of how others see us. We can think of this dimension of an individual's identity as *who she is expected to be*, by society as a whole, as well as by members of the in-group (those with whom she shares essentialist ties). With respect to society as a whole, such expectations have an effect

5 Identification can also be oppositional in the sense that one identifies in a particular way in order to distinguish herself from something antithetical to her subjective sense of identity (Young 1990, ch. 5).

on how successful a person will be materially and socially. That is, he is expected to conform to certain professional and social-cultural practices, and to the extent that he is a free spirit or a radical or is considered eccentric or different or controversial or unpredictable or abnormal, he is likely to experience social and material consequences. Liberal republicans tend to see no distinction between the two ecological dimensions of identity. Who a citizen feels she is and who others expect her to be is one and the same – an agent who conforms to basic socio-professional norms and who by doing so maximizes both his life chances and his contribution to the greater good.

But for multiculturalists, this ecologically based harmony holds only for members of the dominant community, whose identification with mainstream values – being American, for example, or being a successful policeman, or excelling in academic and professional endeavours – does not come into conflict with their identities as people who are White, and men, and straight. This is not surprising given that it was people like themselves who forged and shaped mainstream values in the first place. But for members of subaltern communities, the socially contextual dimensions of identity often do not fit as seamlessly into the sorts of mainstream values that dictate career and personal achievement and hence dignity and self-esteem (Spencer, Swanson, and Cunningham 1991; Porter and Washington 1993; Coomarswamy 2002, 484).

To use the example of racial minorities, and particularly African-Americans, identifying with the values of the dominant group can lead individuals into a negative assessment of domain competence (tasks one is good at) and even group esteem. Pritchard's second slave, assuming he is African-American, is a good example of the latter. Part of his identification with his Blackness is accepting that he is a social subordinate. In the same vein, Kenneth and Mamie Clark's race awareness experiments (1947), which were the basis of Kenneth Clark's expert testimony in *Brown v. Board of Education*, also illustrate the point. The Clarks' doll test studies showed, as did numerous subsequent studies in the United States and other multiracial societies, that where there exists a dominant and subordinate race, children of both races tend to prefer and identify more positively with the dominant race (e.g., Morland 1969; Beuf 1977).[6]

6 The doll test was one of a number of experiments used by the Clarks to measure race perception amongst children. When given the option, young African-American girls not only preferred to play with White dolls over Black ones, they also identified more positively with White dolls, assigning them positive attributes that contrasted favourably with the attributes assigned to Black dolls.

More recent studies find that the critical element in explaining the success of African-American students is public regard. That is, students who perceive that out-group members hold African-Americans in sufficiently high regard that their academic achievements are likely to be socially rewarded, are likely to outperform those who are much less trusting that academic achievement will translate into higher levels of social and economic achievement (e.g., Mickelson 1990). Where public regard is low, individuals are less likely to be motivated to excel because the reward, or lack thereof, is not seen as worth the effort. Public regard, in other words, is the proximate cause of academic efficacy.

However, subsequent studies find distinct cluster variations within African-American adolescents. Chavous et al. (2003) construct a typology of Black identity based on deviation from the mean response to a racial identity survey of Black high school students. The polar positions in their typology are what they call *idealized* and *alienated* identities. Individuals with idealized identities identify with their race, view their race positively, and perceive that out-group members also have high regard for their race. By contrast, those with alienated identities score low across all of these issues.

Looking at samples of African-American high school freshmen and high school seniors, Harper and Tuckman (2006) find that in contrast to the logic informing earlier studies, students with alienated identities significantly *outperform* those with idealized ones, a finding that casts serious doubt on the centrality of public regard as a factor in academic achievement. Instead, for Harper and Tuckman, the extent to which one identifies with her race appears to be the critical variable. Their findings suggest that the racial group with which one most closely identifies plays a role in determining academic achievement. This is a troubling finding given Steinberg, Dornbusch, and Brown's (1992) conclusion that young African-Americans find it difficult to enter into Black peer groups that emphasize academic excellence (Harper and Tuckman 2006, 399). Indeed, so restricted are the options for high-achieving African-Americans that they tend to eschew other African-American students in favour of affiliating with peer groups from other racial backgrounds (Steinberg, Dornbusch, and Brown 1992, 728). As a result, African-American students are disadvantaged insofar as they are more likely to be forced into having to choose between identifying with their race or academic and future success.

This problem extends beyond just racial communities. Women in traditionally male-dominated jobs often find that the most effective way to deal with misogyny and sexual harassment from male coworkers is to eschew their feminine identities and become "one of the boys" (Brewer

1991, 240). In management and the professions, where the sexism may not be as ribald or explicit, some women have found it easier to try and blend in to the organizational culture than to challenge it. They become what are disparagingly known as "corporate transvestites," identifying with and adopting the characteristics of powerful male mentors rather than identifying as members of the subaltern group. Again, the tension between objective identity and subjective identification imposes a burden on a historically subordinate community that members of the dominant community do not carry (Olson and Walker 2004, 247).

Gays and lesbians with career or political aspirations have long felt the need to stay in the closet about their sexual orientation. The US armed forces' concession during the Clinton Administration that homosexuality would be tolerated as long as it was not obvious mirrored a prevailing social sentiment that a homosexual identity was inconsistent with the values of the dominant community (Yang 1997). As a result, gays and lesbians in the workplace have been forced to choose whether or not to reveal their sexual identities. On the one hand, homosexuals who reveal their sexual orientation typically are better psychologically adjusted than those who choose to hide their sexual orientation. Moreover, they often enjoy closer relations with co-workers and greater job satisfaction (Oswald 2007, 930). "Often," however, is not the same as "always." The downside is that openly homosexual workers in certain fields risk employment discrimination including "fag" and "dyke" jokes, exclusion from social events, and even physical assault or termination as a result of their sexual identity.

Such discrimination often culminates in a minority stress syndrome akin to stereotype threat (Waldo 2001, 219). The problem is even more acute in adolescents just coming to terms with their sexual identities.[7] Gay and bisexual adolescents are far more likely to contemplate and commit suicide than their heterosexual peers. Many are better able to cope and identify positively with their sexual orientation. But many do

7 Identity construction is a critical part of the development process that occurs largely during adolescence. It demands the construction of "a unification and cohesiveness in the self" that provides direction, purpose, sense of domain competence and adaptive functioning (Spencer and Markstrom-Adams 1990, 290). Identity construction is a large part of what makes those awkward teenage years awkward, and most adolescents experience a good deal of psychic dislocation. Adolescents from socially subordinate groups become cognizant of, and have to come to terms with, the fact that they are different from adolescents in the dominant cultural group. As such, they not only must achieve an understanding of who they are, but also must reconcile that with the cultural values of the dominant group – values that might very well conflict with those they have been raised with or come to identify with (292).

not, suffering self-hatred that manifests itself in denial or exaggerated displays of heterosexual identification – including ridiculing the gay lifestyle (Van Wormer and McKinney 2003).

Normality

Ultimately the issue boils down to one of *normality*. Situational inequality is a function of the fact that "normal" is defined by the values of the dominant group. As such, the closer one comes to the idealized norm, the greater his potential for social and economic reward. However, when normal is defined in terms of Whiteness, maleness, and straightness – and where members of both dominant and subaltern communities internalize this conception of normal – the obstacles for members of subaltern communities to social and economic reward become higher. Not that it is impossible, but there is a point spread. Members of subordinate communities succeed only by virtue of demonstrable market skills *and* their abilities to overcome the handicaps associated with their deviation from the idealized norm.

Culturally, this point spread puts pressure on subaltern communities. The implicit message from the dominant community is that if you are not White or male or straight, just try to do the best you can to act that way and we will do the best we can to try not to notice. It is for this reason that we see the propensity for homosexuals to closet themselves, women to defeminize themselves, and African-Americans to seek cultural conformity to White America in the public spheres of their respective lives.

Yet this public disidentification with their essentialist characteristics as the cost of doing business creates enormous internal dislocation between the subjective and objective elements of identity. A society in which a woman has to choose between her success and her identity, multiculturalists imply, can hardly be seen as a just society. This is particularly so when men do not have to make any such choice. It is not just that African-Americans seeking to pursue their conceptions of the good life have to risk being called Uncle Tom. The greater risk is tangible identity confusion at a vulnerable time in their lives. African-American adolescents who demonstrate superior academic skills risk being admonished to keep it real. They are often called Oreos or some similar pejorative that implies their essentialist identities go no deeper than the colour of their skin. These are not pressures that Caucasian adolescents face, and indeed there is no analogous pejorative (snowball?) that applies.

The prescription from a multiculturalist perspective is to recognize that a just society conceives individuals as differently equal in the sense that the realization of situational equality demands differential treatment under the law. Before we can meaningfully speak of universalization of dignity, important structural remedies must be put into place. These remedies go by various names – affirmative action, political correctness, special representation rights, separate educational curricula, etc. – but the thrust is the same. Rather than conformity to the (large N) Normal, a just society needs to pluralize the normal. Rather than conceive of one universal Normal, a just society must acknowledge that there are numerous (small n) normals. One can be normal, to take the most obvious example, if one's sexual orientation conforms to that of the majority. But equally it is normal to be Queer or transgendered.

For multiculturalists, just social and institutional arrangements that tend toward situational equality are those that elevate the status of subaltern cultural communities in the eyes of both in-group and out-group members. Typically, as a first step this entails taking steps to promote the efficacy and self-respect of members of subaltern cultures. Certainly it demands more than simply distributing rights and resources (however equitably it might be done). The Rawlsian redistributive paradigm fails in the sense that the goods necessary for efficacy and self-respect cannot be apportioned to individuals per se.[8] To be effective, self-respect must instead be conceived in terms of social and institutional arrangements designed to promote the subaltern cultural identity as a whole, and not merely aid individuals whose personal circumstances are dire. In so doing, however, the good society must be willing to reject, suspend, or otherwise relax its commitment to formal equality under law.

THE ENDS OF MULTICULTURALISM

The prescriptive end of multiculturalism demands reconceptualizing secondary values in terms of what we have already called pluralization of the normal. Pluralizing the normal does not require dismantling the Normal; it does not represent a form of cultural appropriation in the sense of replacing the old with the new. But it rejects a homogenous view of social belonging in which groups that are different from the mainstream are obliged to try to make themselves as Normal as possible.

Young prefers to characterize this pluralization of the normal in terms of what she calls the city-life metaphor (1990, ch. 8). One of the

8 Young therefore asks: "What can it mean to distribute self-respect? Self-respect is not an entity or measurable aggregate, it cannot be parceled out of some stash, and above all it cannot be detached from persons as a separable attribute adhering to an otherwise unchanged substance. Self-respect names not some possession or attribute a person has, but her or his attitude toward her or his entire situation and life prospects" (1990, 26–7).

attractive features of a diverse urban environment for Young is its potential for celebrating difference. This celebration represents a disaggre-
gated conception of the good that tolerates as wide a degree of diversity
as the interests and preferences of component cultural communities demand. In the ideal, city life represents "an openness to unassimilated
otherness" (1990, 227). It constitutes an environment in which social
interaction actively affirms group difference; it is the antithesis, in other
words, of the assimilative melting pot. If we wish to translate it into the
language of liberal republicanism, it represents a form of intersubjectivity, albeit one that mandates transcendence not of individual subjectivity,
but rather of cultural subjectivity. In the city, Young says, "persons and
groups interact within spaces and institutions they all experience themselves as belonging to, but without those interactions dissolving into
unity and commonness" (1990, 237). The urban reference in the city-
life metaphor is not incidental. City life represents in this sense a nullification of the liberal republican reliance on geography-as-diversity, or the
idea that tertiary values are grounded in spatial difference.

The city-life ideal manifests important multicultural virtues, providing
both diversity and critical mass for essentialist communities to form and
flourish. More important perhaps, city life militates against both separatism and chauvinism, as different sorts of people use common spaces and
share cultural experiences. Thus, differentiation comes without the pernicious effects of exclusion; and there is an attractiveness, what Young
calls an eroticism, about the city in that people of different types are
drawn to one another culturally. Chinatown, for example, is not seen as
a vexing source of resistance to cultural unity, but rather as an experience that attracts those who are not Chinese. Equally there is cultural
security, a sense that one's culture is not being judged or threatened.
Insecurity and eroticism are incompatible. As such, the attractiveness of
other cultures is enhanced, perhaps even made possible, by the security
one feels in her own culture (1990, 238–41).

Both the cultural pluralism implicit in multiculturalism and the interest-based pluralism of liberal republicanism are predicated on the efficacy of societal groups to come together to affect the rules that govern us
in a way that informs and preserves the greater good. But multiculturalists reject the premise that civic participation in the construction of
legislative rules should turn exclusively on individual interests and preferences. Missing from the market-based model for political influence is
the pernicious fact that group identities are not privileged in the process. Indeed, to the extent they are included in interest-based pluralism,
groups representing the tertiary values of essentialist communities are

treated as if each was just another actor in the market for policy influence.

In reality, however, from the perspective of multiculturalists, identities are prior to, and constitutive of, interests and hence cannot be divorced from a fair political process (Sandel 1982; Walker 1997). As such, to achieve a just and meaningful outcome when constructing legislative rules, just social and institutional arrangements that level the playing field – that create, in other words, a greater degree of situational equality – must be established a priori. We have already noted what multiculturalists see as just social and institutional arrangements that can be designed to promote situational equality. These include special representation rights, sentencing enhancements for hate crimes, reconceptualizing such social traditions as the standard work week, pluralizing language of school and workplace, the state sponsoring multiculturalism, and redefining marriage.

Perhaps the most controversial multiculturalist prescription is the process by which hiring and college admissions criteria are broadened to take into account applicants' essentialist characteristics. For multiculturalists, this affirmative action represents both a means to situational equality and a portrait of what a truly just society would look like if merit were the true deciding principle for career advancement. The argument is illogical on its face, insofar as affirmative action would seem to undermine the merit principle, not advance it. However, multiculturalists claim that the prevailing "meritocratic" system, imbued as it is with the sort of systemic bias that for so long served to privilege the dominant culture, can make no more promising claim to true meritocracy.[9] Ultimately, affirmative action serves merely to balance one social artifice with another. Or, to put a more positive spin on it, we need to recognize "merit" as a sufficiently multifaceted concept to preclude accurate and unbiased measurement. Getting an objective grasp on merit demands a narrow (Normal) means of quantification that, unsurprisingly, works to the advantage of members of the dominant culture (see Young 1990, esp. ch. 7). As a means of pluralizing the normal, affirmative action provides

9 Fishkin, for example, argues that we must distinguish procedural fairness from background fairness. Procedural fairness demands that the rules be universally and equally applied. Background fairness demands that conditions under which procedural rules are applied are also fair. The application of procedural fairness, as embodied in the merit principle, to background unfairness ensures only that a patina of fairness disguises a systemic and sustained bias against groups who have suffered from background unfairness (1983, ch. 2).

role models to members of subaltern cultures. These role models serve to raise the consciousness, broaden the choice-set, and elevate the perspective (choose your analogy) of groups long denied access to the sorts of employment and educational opportunities long afforded to members of the dominant culture.[10]

For many multiculturalists, regulating language is another necessary means to prevent the systemic marginalization of subaltern cultural communities. For them at least three objectives must be realized through such political correctness. The first is protecting subaltern community cultural identities. We need look no further than the Clarks' doll tests, or the high suicide rate among gay teens, to realize that harm extends further than sticks and stones. Attitudes oppress, and while regulating attitudes is difficult (to the extent it can be done, it must be done prophylactically through early socialization), regulating words, as the symbolic expression of attitudes, constitutes a next-best option.

A second objective sought by proponents of speech regulation is not so much to spare the feelings of the victim of social oppression, but to raise or reinforce his consciousness of such oppression. Oppression takes two reinforcing forms: institutional and cultural. In some ways the former is the less damaging insofar as it is at least a visible form of oppression. Cultural oppression is more subtle – so subtle that neither victim nor oppressor may be conscious of it. Political correctness has the effect of raising the consciousness of both oppressor and victim (Ehrlich and King 1992).

A third benefit of speech regulation from the multiculturalist perspective is to promote efficacy. The road to social justice is a long one. Symbolic victories such as forcing speech concessions onto the dominant cultural community may or may not have a direct practical effect. But they do demonstrate that the struggle is not hopeless. Such victories constitute a symbolic concession on the part of Whites (males, straights) that their cultural history places them on the moral low ground and that a degree of social penance is necessary merely to achieve some semblance of equal moral footing. Symbolic victories mobilize the cultural base of subaltern cultural communities, reinforcing the message that White guilt (male guilt, straight guilt) is a tool that can be exploited to extract more tangible concessions (Spencer 1994, esp. 559–63; Iyer, Leach, and Crosby 2003).

10 Role models affect behaviour not merely through inspiration or mentoring, but also through conveying information – pertaining to task competence and/or employment prospects – that enter into the rational calculus of individuals within the role model's cultural community (Chung 2000, esp. 641).

For liberal republican critics, one of the effects of affirmative action and political correctness in general has been intersubjective fragmentation, which renders reasonable social consensus difficult to achieve. Rather than emphasizing points of commonality, this argument states, many advocates of political correctness seem to want to divide us to no good purpose beyond empowering opportunistic group leaders, erecting obstacles to usness in the name of vilifying sameness (Degutis 2006). Liberal republicans challenge the multiculturalist definition of harmful oppression. Harm, at least the sort that should be prohibited, cannot be expressed in attitudes and thoughts. It can only rarely be manifest in words; and certainly is not to be found in words whose only negative quality is to give offence. Speech regulation is not alien to liberal republicanism. Liberal republican societies have a long history of speech regulation; as a result it is generally illegal to utter threats or willfully incite events with a reasonable prospect for public danger. Civil law protects individuals from defamation and loss of social prestige through laws preventing libel and slander. However, speech regulation does not go so far as to prohibit offensive language on the grounds that this somehow constitutes harm. The multiculturalist rebuttal is that if words can harm individuals, they can harm groups as well (Calvert 1997; Leets, Giles, and Noels 1999).

CONCLUSION

The most intractable difference between the liberal republican and multicultural theories of justice turns on how to universalize dignity. Liberal republicanism is predicated on the assumption that the locus of dignity is the individual. While the individual is not self-sufficient in her quest for a good and authentic life, it is she who assumes responsibility for the direction of that life. To this end, she employs her rights as a means to the dignity to which she is entitled. This individualism informs the blame model of injustice. The blame model is predicated on three issues with which multiculturalists take issue: agency, which precludes the idea that injustice can be structural and not just volitional; objectivity, which holds that there is a generally accepted code of justice that informs our collective sense of just and unjust behaviour; and universality, which holds that core elements of justice such as the affirmation of equality and dignity attach to all members of society in the same fashion.

Multiculturalists locate dignity in both individuals and identity-creating cultural communities. Their problem with the liberal republican theory of justice is that in failing to recognize the nature of the relationship between cultural identity and human dignity, members of subaltern communities are denied the same degree of human dignity as are members of the dominant community. Identity is critical to the multiculturalist conception of authenticity. Multiculturalists take a far broader view of it than do liberal republicans. For the latter, identity is a function of discrete entities coming together to create a larger whole – society takes on the properties, if you will, of a chemical compound. By contrast, multiculturalists view cultural identity as an organism – something that cannot meaningfully be reduced to its component parts.

While certainly we have idiosyncratic traits in our identities, significant dimensions of our identities are ecologically informed. Because our identities are so central to our authenticity, any theory of justice that conceives injustice as narrowly as the blame model does is incomplete. Indeed, the problem with the liberal republican theory of justice is not so much that it factors identity out of the question. Rather, it assumes that there is a common national identity and recognizes that there are qualifications to that identity, but that these tertiary values are geographically informed. Thus it conceives of the character of that diversity as spatial and not essentialist.

By conceiving identity as predominantly a secondary value, liberal republicanism uses the cultural identity of the dominant community as the basis for its prevailing moral and cultural principles. This dominant identity represents the baseline of normality from which we assess appropriate and inappropriate, just and unjust, behaviour. The result is that for members of the dominant community, there is no tension between self-identification and the behaviour that others expect (and hence reward) materially and socially.

As a result, a theory of justice tied exclusively to individualism is an unconscious way of creating a hierarchy of identities in which the cultural identity of the dominant community retains a monopoly on the articulation of common values. All individuals may be recognized as equals under the law, but all identity-creating cultures are not recognized as equal when it comes to understanding the normal. This situational inequality born of misrecognition serves to obviate the apparent universalization of dignity in the liberal republican theory of justice.

6

A Typology of Culturalism

MULTICULTURALISM IS IN SOME WAYS both the most and least interesting form of culturalism. It is the most interesting in the sense that it is the most prevalent manifestation of culturalist values and, indeed, represents the foundational logic for other forms of culturalism. It is the least interesting, though, to the extent that it represents the most benign challenge to liberal republicanism. This chapter moves beyond multiculturalism to explore the four other forms of culturalism briefly introduced at the beginning of the previous chapter. The first three (cultural separatism, status-seeking, and cultural contestation) represent mild to moderate challenges to the secondary values that make up national identity. The last (versoculturalism) represents a potentially more serious threat to the primary, or regime-defining, values of liberal republics.

What distinguishes the forms of culturalism discussed in this chapter from multiculturalism is their decreased commitment to value consensus, or an overarching sense of usness. In contrast to the forms of culturalism discussed in this chapter, multiculturalism retains a strong commitment to an overarching national identity. To be sure, as the previous chapter suggests, the multiculturalist commitment to such secondary values is mitigated by the imperative to maintain a meaningful distinction between usness and sameness. But unlike the forms of culturalism discussed in this chapter, multiculturalism is unwilling to promote or even accommodate value dissensus in the name of culturalist objectives.

I would like to discuss the four forms of culturalism in terms of two clusters. That is, I distinguish cultural separatism and status-seeking from cultural contestation and versoculturalism on the basis of cultural appropriation. The first two manifestations of culturalism do not seek to alter fundamentally the secondary or primary values of liberal republics. By contrast, the latter two forms of culturalism do seek to appropriate secondary and primary values, respectively.

The most efficient way to begin is to introduce briefly an overview of each form of culturalism discussed in this chapter before launching into a fuller discussion of the challenges each poses for liberal republicanism. We will start with cultural separatism. Cultural separatists are those whose alienation from the dominant cultural community is so pronounced that they voluntarily seek to withdraw from cultural union with it, at least temporarily. Cultural separatists have little expectation that secondary values can be made more pluralistic. Instead, sufficiently alienated from the cultural values of the dominant community, they seek insulation rather than inclusion.

Status-seeking, by contrast, is about cultural assertion. It represents the attempt by subaltern communities to assert that their claim to recognition and affirmation of cultural identity is superior to the claims offered by some or all other groups. Status-seekers view the political process in adversarial terms in which cultural communities compete for differential recognition. While such status can be achieved through secondary (legislative) rules, the greater prize is the institutionalization of constitutional status. Their quest is to elevate the line of social cleavage that distinguishes them from the dominant community to the level of a foundational – what Marx calls substructural – social division.

When subaltern cultural communities become sufficiently powerful, they may begin to engage in cultural contestation. Cultural contestants challenge the dominant community's monopoly over the articulation of secondary values. That is, they seek to redefine what it means to be "people like us." Cultural contestants may seek to establish themselves so that they become the new dominant cultural community, replacing one cultural monopoly with another. Or they may seek to create, extending the metaphor slightly, a cultural oligopoly in which two dominant cultures exist in the same public space. Either way, the defining characteristic is the appropriation of secondary values, in whole or in part.

Finally, cultural contestants are distinct from versoculturalists insofar as their contestation affects secondary values, but not primary ones. Versoculturalists are true cultural revolutionaries since they seek to replace prevailing primary values. Versoculturalism, then, is incompatible with liberal republicanism insofar as if it is successful, the defining characteristics of liberal republics would be replaced with fundamentally different values. The challenge posed by versoculturalism therefore rises to the level of a threat.

THE FOUR TYPES OF CULTURALISM

While the preceding overview completes a brief typology of culturalism, it does little to spell out the challenges each form presents to liberal republicanism. To that end, this section fleshes out the logic of each form of culturalism. In doing so, it sets up the discussion in chapters 7 and 8, which explore some real-world implications of these challenges.

Cultural Separatists

As briefly noted, cultural separatism represents voluntary withdrawal from the secondary values that inform national identity and are promoted by the dominant cultural community. Separatism is generally a function of cultural marginalization, representing a defensive reaction to the cultural rigidity of the dominant community. It reflects the desire to create, in both private and public spaces, discrete and exclusive cultural institutions designed to promote awareness, support, and solidarity among members of the relevant subaltern cultural community. It constitutes a means to cultural survival in the face of a predatory, imperialist, and assimilative dynamic, resistant and even hostile to any sort of subaltern cultural intrusion. Indeed, such is the magnitude of resistance that seeking to pluralize secondary values in the short to medium term would constitute an exercise in futility (Freedman 1979). Over the long term, the ideal for cultural separatists is reintegrating that community into the more pluralized mainstream culture envisioned by multiculturalists. However, in extreme cases cultural separatism can also be a prelude to political separatism.

Gender, sexual orientation, race, and religion are all bases for the cultural insularity associated with separatism. However, it is with respect to language that cultural separatism becomes most intractable. Language represents the ultimate cultural barrier. Indeed, the politics of language is insidious and potentially destabilizing. For many subaltern linguistic groups, the prestige language (the language of the dominant cultural community) reinforces the relative power imbalance between the dominant and subaltern cultural community. This is particularly the case when the prestige language is held up as the appropriate or standard or correct or normal language through unilingual schooling. Primary schooling is of particular importance insofar as linguistic identity is generally acquired during these formative years.

Similarly, the political salience of language is recognized and internalized at an early age. Nelson-Barber's (1982) study of the Pima Indians finds that children's phonology approximated that of their teachers through the first three years of their primary education. However, by the fourth grade, despite greater competence in the prestige dialect, children were far more likely to employ their own cultural forms of speech. In the dawning realization that their cultural heritage lacks the prestige of the Normal one, Delpit suggests, even young children come to realize the imperative to choose a culture with which to identify (1998, 19).

The issue is not entirely political; the desire for minority-language schooling may turn on issues of pedagogy. Because children learn most effectively in the language with which they are most comfortable, some cultural separatists advocate the use of non-prestigious language curricula as a means of reaching students who are culturally alienated from the mainstream. This was the logic behind, for example, the Oakland Independent School Board's 1996 mandate to the superintendent of schools to "devise and implement the best possible academic program for imparting instruction to African-American students in their primary language for the combined purposes of maintaining the legitimacy and richness of such language [African-American Vernacular English (AAVE) or Ebonics] ... and to facilitate their acquisition and mastery of English language skills" (Oakland Board of Education 1996).[1] The idea was that for children already alienated from the cultural mainstream, forced integration would lead to greater alienation. Use of AAVE in Oakland Schools may not have been, as many critics perceived it, a desire to make cultural martyrs out of young African-Americans whose employment prospects would be negatively impacted.[2] But its efficacy clearly was tied to the perceived importance of cultural insulation for many African-American students.

There have been more explicitly political attempts at African-American separatism. Perhaps the best known is the Black nationalist movement, which is dedicated to the creation of autonomous African-American political, cultural, and economic associations and institutions. For example, Black nationalists have sought to establish African-American political parties at the state level, and even proposed a national third (National Black) party to contest elections at the federal level during the 1970s.[3]

1   In 1981, the State of California introduced the Standard English Proficiency (SEP) Program, which recognized both the rule-based structure of AAVE and the advantages that Ebonics provided in helping students to gain proficiency in Standard English. Oakland's 1996 resolution made the SEP mandatory in all Oakland public schools.

2   Other critics saw the Ebonics initiative as playing into the hands of those who sought to oppress African-Americans. Of these critics, prominent was an advertisement sponsored by the Atlanta Black Professionals in the *New York Times* of 8 October 1996. The ad featured an African-American man photographed from behind and reminiscent of Martin Luther King. Superimposed was the slogan, "I Has a Dream."

3   These parties included the Freedom Now party in numerous Northeastern states and Michigan; in Alabama we have seen the Afro-American Party, the Lowndes County Freedom Party (or Black Panther Party), and the National Democratic Party of Alabama;

Culturally, African-Americans have sought to emphasize their distinctness through a broad Afrocentric movement. The movement rejects the unconscious and pernicious assimilation of Western values. Instead, it advocates initiatives such as independent schools, the proliferation of Black Studies programs on university campuses, and the creation of distinct cultural celebrations such as Kwanzaa. Afrocentricity emphasizes the cultural ties between African-Americans and Africa itself. It is not merely a marginal movement. Brown and Shaw report that by 1993, 71 per cent of respondents to the National Survey of Black Americans felt that African-American children should be required to learn an African language (2002, 25; see also Nagel 1994; Mazama 2001). Finally, in the economic sphere, there has been a dedicated emphasis on the promotion of African-American businesses, and movements to encourage African-American consumers to patronize Black businesses (Brown and Shaw 2002, 24).

Similarly, many feminists insist on the need for a feminine public space that operates independently of the existing patriarchal one as a means of overcoming the traditional division of labour between the sexes and the systemic discrimination that women suffer in the workplace.[4] The idea of a distinctive public space for women is not unprecedented. The "sisterhoods" of the late nineteenth and early twentieth centuries constituted discrete private spheres for women, which, Freedman argues, served to elevate the consciousness of women in advance of the women's suffrage and liberation movements. Indeed, it was through such private movements that women enjoyed the freedom to pursue social and political relationships that empowered women while shielding them from the overt sexism of the public sphere. Ultimately, these private spheres became the

---

Mississippi produced the Freedom Democratic Party and the Loyal Democrats of Mississippi. Other states in the Deep South also produced African-American parties such as the Party of Christian Democracy (Georgia), the Black Freedom Party (North Carolina), and the United Citizens Party (South Carolina) (Walton and Boone 1974, 87). In addition, African-Americans have organized politically within existing institutions of government, most prominently through the Congressional Black Caucus in the House of Representatives (Gurin, Hatchett and Jackson 1989, 46–7).

4 Frye (1993) defines feminist separatism as "separation of various sorts or modes from men and from institutions, relationships, roles, and activities which are male-defined, male-dominated, and operating for the benefit of males and the maintenance of male privilege – this separation being initiated and maintained, at will, by *women*" (92, emphasis in original).

bases from which distinctive women's political institutions, such as the Women's Christian Temperance Union, were founded.[5]

It was the decline of these sisterhoods in the face of an integrationist movement beginning in the 1920s and grounded in the mistaken belief that suffrage would make women the political equals of men that led to the "disappearance" of feminism between the women's suffrage and liberation movements. As such, one of the lessons of the separatist strategy is that without muscle, in the form of a distinct and dedicated constituency of followers, subaltern groups have little leverage in the quest for equal integration into the dominant culture (Freedman 1974; 1979).

Feminist separatism today is associated largely with lesbian feminism, which, especially during the 1970s and 1980s, took separatism quite literally in the sense of forming rural lesbian communities. The idea was that, like other forms of oppression, heterosexuality was a social construction that could be escaped in such a way as to eliminate its oppressive nature. Rural life was symbolically important insofar as it connoted the opposite of the urban or the man-made. Free from social construction, women would be liberated to fulfill their authentic feminist identities (Valentine 1997).[6]

For liberal republicanism, the problem with cultural separatism is that it is erosive of social obligation and civic duty. It is a form of what traditional republicans conceived as corruption, or factionalization, whereby one's overarching loyalty is to some source of authority or legitimacy other than that represented by the national governing structure as a whole (Dobel 1978). It is for this reason that ascriptively grounded factionalism is often seen as especially pernicious.

A greater challenge associated with cultural separatism is that it can evolve from a defensive position to a more assertive one. The long-term objectives can shift from ultimate cultural integration within the dominant community into a desire to *institutionalize* separation from the dominant culture. In this sense, it comes to look a good deal like the cultural

5 Other examples include the creation of a General Federation of Women's Clubs (which claimed as many as one million members by the early twentieth century), the creation of new women's universities the mandates of which went beyond serving as mere finishing schools for society ladies, and of course the National American Suffrage Movement (Freedman 1979, 513–20; for an alternative perspective on the relationship between private and public feminism see Taylor and Rupp 1993).

6 Joyce Cheney (in Valentine 1997, 68) quotes a member of the Wisconsin Womyn's Land Cooperative: "We view maintaining our lesbian space and protecting these acres from the rape of man and his chemicals as a political act of active resistance. Struggling with each other to work through our patriarchal conditioning, and attempting to work and live together in harmony with each other and nature."

contestation discussed later in which a powerful subaltern community challenges the secondary values of the prevailing dominant group.

Quebec nationalism serves as a good example. In the early 1960s, Quebec's Quiet Revolution represented a cultural coming of age. With secularization in the 1950s and 1960s, younger Quebeckers were awakened to a greater sense of worldliness. Rather than identifying as junior partners in a putatively bicultural Canada, an emergent Quebecois nationalism sought to make French-speaking Quebeckers "maîtres chez nous," masters of their own domain (Seljak 1996; Gauvreau 2005). Quebec became the political locus of "la nation canadienne-française," seeking greater devolution of constitutional authority and asserting greater cultural independence.

So pronounced was this cultural independence that the Canadian flag itself has been seen in nationalist quarters as symbolic of Quebec's cultural oppression.[7] More tangibly, in 1980 Quebec held a referendum on quasi-independent "sovereignty-association" with Canada and, on the failure of that initiative, amended constitutional language that would see Quebec recognized as a "distinct society" within Canada. Ultimately, a 1995 referendum on outright independence from Canada was only barely defeated.

The example of Quebec demonstrates the dynamic nature of cultural separatism – from defensive to assertive nationalism. Cultural separatism is also problematic insofar as it attracts adherents with manifold motivations. It is, for example, a good way for more radical culturalists to drive a cultural wedge between subaltern and dominant culture without advertising the sort of cultural extremism that might make moderates uncomfortable. Less programmatically, some cultural separatists are unclear as to their ultimate objectives. Having recognized a cultural pathology, they are open-minded about the range of options best suited to remedy it. And even when cultural separatists *are* clear on their motives and objectives, the agenda can change with circumstances. An activist who favours cultural separation when her group is small or weak relative to the dominant culture may have a very different preference if the size or power of her movement increases. Over time, particularly if the dominant culture is resistant to pluralization, separatists may evolve into more radical forms of culturalism as disillusionment, resentment, and ultimately alienation set in.

7 The Maple Leaf was removed from the Quebec National Assembly during most of the times that the nationalist Parti Quebecois was in government.

Status-Seeking

Status-seekers are not cultural radicals. Instead, they are motivated by the quest for more effective solutions to cultural marginalization. The reasonably sound logic of multiculturalism, in other words, is marred by prescriptive weakness. The main distinction between multiculturalism and status-seeking is that advocates of the former seek to promote the cultural distinctiveness of all subaltern cultures and incorporate each into a pluralized conception of the values that inform the republic. By contrast, status-seekers, while their ultimate objectives are fairly varied, believe that one or both of the following should occur: the relevant nation's secondary values should be pluralized to accommodate the most salient subaltern cultural values; or the tertiary values of the most salient subaltern communities should be afforded special, even constitutional, status (Knopff and Morton 1992, esp. ch. 4; Brodie 1996; 2002).

Given the implied cultural hierarchy, the key to successful status-seeking is to demonstrate the salient cultural community's distinctive claim to redress. As briefly noted, demonstrating salience obliges status-seeking cultural communities to articulate their cultural distinctiveness from the dominant community as a foundational cleavage, the amelioration of which takes ethical precedence over the reconciliation of other social divisions.

This exclusionism is not as prejudicial as it might seem. Status-seeking starts from the premise that the ideal of equal and universal recognition of all identity-creating subaltern cultures is both logistically and morally problematic. With respect to the logistical problem, identity-creating groups, as conceived by Iris Marion Young, are defined as "a collective of persons differentiated from at least one other group by cultural forms, practices, or way of life" (1990, 44). While the prescription might be manifest in the city-life metaphor, the way to achieve such a prescription is to reconstruct institutions and social arrangements to accommodate the distinctive needs of each subaltern cultural community. The problem is that the definition of identity-creating cultures is at once over-broad and under-specified. It is over-broad in the sense that, to take the example of the United States, roughly four out of five Americans would seem to qualify for membership in an oppressed social group (Kymlicka 1995a, 145). It may be trite to say it, but if everyone is special in the sense that he deserves affirmative cultural consideration, then no one is special.

Under-specification is also problematic insofar as the criteria for cultural group membership are infinitely reducible. Take the feminine as a subaltern culture deserving of institutional and social accommodations on the grounds that women are culturally marginalized. If this is so, we must certainly recognize that African-American women are more marginalized (they are oppressed along two cultural dimensions) than White women, and presumably would need to be granted special accommodation on top of that already available to women as a whole. Lesbian African-American women are manifestly more oppressed than straight African-American women, more so if they are transgendered, and even more so if they are also disabled. Such infinite regression renders multiculturalism logistically problematic.

Quite apart from the logistical problems inherent in equal recognition of identity-creating groups and cultures, there is also a moral dimension. It is untenable to maintain that all such cultures are equally *worthy* of affirmation. Manifestly they are not. Some such cultures are antithetical to a moral and orderly civilization. Even if they represent radicalized or bastardized factions of more benign cultures, cultures that advocate crime (think Mafia culture) or violence (any number of religious cultures) or racial superiority may be identity-creating and even oppressed, but they are hardly worthy of respect or a moral claim to affirmation (Holmes 1993, 179). As such, status-seekers start from the premise that meaningful cultural prescription demands the articulation of filters to determine which groups are, and which are not, worthy of special affirmation through just institutional and social arrangements.

While such filters solve logistical and moral problems, they raise new ones. Perhaps the most important is cultural arbitrariness or paternalism. The former, I think, is the shoal upon which Taylor's advocacy of special cultural recognition for Quebec founders. Indeed, Taylor's own arguments lead him in different directions. In *The Politics of Recognition*, Taylor rejects the capacity of members of one culture to pass judgments on the relative merits of another (1992). No dispassionate judgment is possible because all judgment will be coloured by the cultural lens through which it is passed. If our identities do indeed define us, they cannot be discarded at will when the convenience of cultural objectivity demands it. Moreover, to claim the cultural capacity to transcend subjectivity – to achieve the sort of cultural connoisseurship that permits one culture to judge the merits of another – constitutes "an act of breathtaking condescension" (1992, 70).

But in "Shared and Divergent Values," Taylor appears to change course, arguing that the historical compact between *la nation canadienne-française* and English-speaking Canada creates a normative claim for cultural dualism that privileges the French-Canadian language and culture over the claims of other subaltern communities (1991b). Taylor maintains that this claim demands special constitutional recognition of the idea that Quebec, as the locus of the French-Canadian nation, constitutes something more than *une province comme les autres*. But such a moral claim for cultural dualism is difficult to sustain. Not only is it constructed on historically tenuous ground,[8] it is predicated on the idea that historical cultural accommodation somehow assigns moral purchase to contemporary ones. Indeed, any historical compact that privileges the French-Canadian nation ahead of the myriad extant Aboriginal nations (or vice-versa) must surely be vulnerable to the charge of arbitrariness (Lusztig 2002).

Kymlicka seeks to avoid this sort of arbitrariness by establishing decision rules to govern the extent to which subordinate cultures have a moral claim to special status. Kymlicka couches status in the context of group-differentiated, or collective, rights that ethnic minority cultures might reasonably claim. These include self-government rights, polyethnic rights (or claims on public resources to protect and preserve ethnic minority cultures), and special representation rights (whereby ethnic minorities are overrepresented in legislative or administrative institutions) (1995a, 26–33). Such collective rights are compatible with liberal democracy, he claims, as long as they do not come at the expense of individual rights.

Who should be eligible to claim such rights? Kymlicka distinguishes between two sorts of ethnic minorities: those who immigrated voluntarily to an existing (institutionally complete) society, and those who did not. The former, what he calls *polyethnic minorities*, retain the rights to maintain their cultural practices. However, they have no moral claim to cultural *accommodation* on the part of the dominant culture. Cultural practices, in other words, remain *private*, rather than civil, rights. By contrast, *multinational groups* did not voluntarily immigrate into existing

---

8 The compact theory of Confederation, which holds that Canada's emergence as a self-governing dominion in 1867 represented a compact between English and French Canada, has gained wide currency in Quebec. It enjoys limited historical support, however. The British North America Act, which brought Canada into being as a self-governing dominion, was a product of negotiations among the colonies of New Brunswick, Nova Scotia, Prince Edward Island, and Canada (which became the provinces of Quebec and Ontario). Thus, to the extent that it was a compact at all, it was negotiated among colonies, not (ethnically informed) nations. There is some historical support for a binational compact as reflected in the 1791 Constitutional Act. But this act, which created the provinces of Upper and Lower Canada, pertained only to the colony of Canada, and it is difficult to see how it could be as binding on colonies (and later territories) that entered into Confederation with Canada as opposed to being incorporated into it. (For more on the controversy surrounding the compact theory of Confederation see Vipond 1991, ch. 1; Romney 1999.)

societies, and by virtue of that, *do* have a moral claim to group-differentiated cultural rights within the public space.

Multinational groups represent what are for all intents and purpose
nations housed within territory governed by other nations. Members of
multinational groups are distinct from members of polyethnic groups in
that they did not voluntarily immigrate into existing, institutionally complete, societies. Aboriginal nations in Australia, Canada, and the United
States are obvious examples.[9] In other cases, settlers occupied institutionally incomplete territories with an eye toward reproducing their
heritage cultures (Chicanos, French-Canadians, Puerto Ricans). Other
criteria for classification as a multinational group, Kymlicka maintains,
are occupation of a given territory, the construction of a more or less
institutionally complete society within that territory, and the sharing of a
distinct language and culture (1995a, ch. 2).

The relatively clear criteria articulated by Kymlicka provide a non-
paternalistic means of privileging certain minority cultures. But they
do not provide much protection against arbitrariness. Perhaps the big-
gest problem with these criteria for special multinational group status
is that they exclude groups like African-Americans. African-Americans
are obviously ethnically distinctive. And as Kymlicka acknowledges, the
ancestors of most African-Americans can hardly be called voluntary immigrants. But neither do they qualify as national minorities as Kymlicka
defines the term. They do not occupy an institutionally complete territory, they do not share a distinct language and culture. And on top of
this, "most Blacks do not have and do not want a distinct national identity" (1995a, 25).

But there is a perverse reasoning here which amounts to the idea that
if your culture has been sufficiently discriminated against, you lose your
cultural rights. African-American slaves obviously did not enjoy the option to create distinct ethnic, institutionally complete territorial enclaves.
Similarly, they can hardly be said to have voluntarily alienated their native languages and cultures. And while it is true that most African-
Americans do not favour cultural distinctiveness, many do (Perry and
Delpit 1998; Roberts 2006, ch. 3; Painter 2006). More to the point, if
cultural rights have the significance that culturalists say they do, they are
especially worthy of protection for those to whom cultural distinctiveness
does matter.

9 In reality, almost all liberal republics are multinational by dint either of extant original occupants (Britain, Finland, France, and Spain are prominent European examples),
geopolitical evolution (Belgium, France, Germany, etc.), or conscious cultural union
(Switzerland).

A broader issue of arbitrariness is why we should privilege ethnic cultures over non-ethnic identity-creating cultures. Why are cultural issues of more importance to ethnic minorities, for example, than they are to religious minorities or women or those of alternative sexual orientations? Kymlicka's position boils down to the argument that we have to draw the line somewhere. He acknowledges that cultures can be defined more broadly, and refer to a distinct set of traditions, norms, and mores as practised by any group, essentialist or otherwise. Kymlicka is thus forced to offer what he calls a "stipulative definition" of culture as pertaining exclusively to a nation or a people (1995a, 18–19). He acknowledges that other subordinate groups have been marginalized and excluded, but hopes to show that his theory constitutes an "adequate theory of the rights of cultural minorities," which he claims must be compatible with "the just demands of [other] disadvantaged groups" (1995a, 19). But it is hard to see how that could be when he appropriates the word "culture" (and therefore all of its attendant rights) thereby effectively precluding already marginalized and excluded groups from like moral claims.

From a liberal republican perspective, it is unfair to single out Kymlicka for such stipulative decision rules. The fact that you have to draw the line somewhere is a good way to characterize the problem liberal republicans have with assigning moral claims to essentialist tertiary values in the first place. In fact, the criticisms that liberal republicans might reasonably level at status-seeking have already been raised. Recognizing the cultural superiority of one group over another is also logistically and morally problematic. Once the state steps in and starts selectively recognizing certain preferences, it replaces the dispassion of the civic political process with the inherent bias of cultural adjudicators. It is for this reason that liberal republicans have advocated cultural neutrality – the sort of benign neglect discussed in the previous chapter.

Status-seekers typically seek remedy by reforming formal or evolutionary constitutional rules. The latter is particularly pernicious for liberal republicans. Status-seeking through the courts is problematic for liberal republicanism insofar as it represents an alternative to the sort of civic participation promoted by the pluralist, legislative process. Litigation is not a mass movement; it requires little political mobilization, and instead is an elite-oriented process. Put differently, success is not contingent on group mobilization to persuade electorally responsive legislators. Rather, it turns on the constitutional lawyering skills of attorneys employed by advocacy groups. Status-seeking through litigation robs liberal republican societies of the social-coalition-building requisite to success in constructing and altering legislative rules. Indeed, such social-coalition-building represents a socially integrative process as membership in winning (and losing) coalitions is fluid across policy issues. Opponents on one issue, in other words, find themselves politically allied along a different dimension. The effect is to militate against lasting social divisions that ultimately undermine moral obligation and an enduring sense of usness.

Status-seeking through constitutional remedies similarly affects civic participation negatively to the extent that it encroaches upon a population's sovereignty in governing its own affairs. Because constitutional rules are, intentionally, insulated from popular passions, they represent qualifications to self-government. Status-seeking thus serves as a means of expanding the scope of constitutional rules at the expense of legislative ones. By constitutionalizing certain values (and when achieved through litigation this often comes in defiance of popular consent) the effect is to terminate all meaningful political participation along that policy dimension. The prudence of the population as a whole, in other words, is replaced by an elite whose primary qualifications as the repositories of neo-Socratic wisdom are the ability of its members to get themselves appointed or elected to the bench.

Finally, status-seeking is also problematic because constitutional reform is a winner-take-all proposition. Neither formal constitutional amendment nor constitutional litigation lend themselves to policy compromise. And while splitting the difference is not always possible in the legislative arena either – think of issues such as capital punishment or abortion – legislative solutions to intractable and divisive policy issues have the advantage of being easily remedied if the effects lead to negative externalities, or if social conditions change. Formal constitutional construction and jurisprudential precedent, on the other hand, are intentionally rigid; and while they are not entirely resistant to change, the logistics of repealing formal construction or reversing precedents are such that once adopted, constitutional rules are functionally permanent.

Cultural Contestation

In the introduction to this chapter we defined cultural contestation as the appropriation of secondary values. While such an abbreviated definition is fine for a conceptual overview, it is too crude to provide a meaningful understanding of cultural contestation. Indeed, cultural contestation itself needs unpacking in the sense that it can take two forms – what we can think of as *complete* and *incomplete* appropriation of secondary values. Complete appropriation occurs when the previously dominant culture is supplanted to the extent that the public life of the community reflects a different dominant culture. The French culture in Louisiana or the indigenous Hawaiian culture in that state are good examples of formerly dominant cultures that have been supplanted. Complete appropriation is also achieved through secession, with the case of Texas's secession from Mexico serving as the final act of complete cultural appropriation.

Incomplete appropriation of secondary values also occurs when the secondary values of the previously dominant culture are rejected by a contesting or appropriating culture. However, in the case of incomplete appropriation, the result is not the marginalization of the formerly dominant culture. Instead, the contesting culture articulates a rival, or parallel, set of secondary values. Such incomplete appropriation manifests in deep cultural division as well as a contested, ambiguous, and/or bifurcated national identity. The case of Quebec and Canada is the best example of such incomplete appropriation, although the near breakup of the country in the mid-1990s speaks to the fineness of the distinction between complete and incomplete appropriation.

The stimulus for the appropriation of secondary values can be internal or external to a country. The internal stimulus for the appropriation of secondary values is changing ambient conditions – social, theological, political, economic, or technological – that create a shift in the relative power of culturally distinct groups. In such cases, the transformation of the status quo represents a catalyst for competition among social groups as they jockey for position within the social and economic hierarchy (see Sambanis 1991).[10] In ethnically divided states that are experiencing significant ambient change, the result is typically exacerbated ethnic conflict (Deutsch 1961, esp. 501; Zolberg 1968; Melson and Wolpe 1970; Connor 1973).

Nigeria in the 1960s represents a case in point, as competition among the (previously politically non-salient) Hausa-Fulanis, Igbo, and Yoruba arose in the wake of Nigerian independence and subsequent political and economic modernization. Particularly relevant was the conflict among the (then) less-developed Igbo and the Yoruba, which Melson and Wolpe characterize in terms of relative deprivation manifest as an

---

10 The literature is divided as to the basis of this competition. Some argue that it is based on the primordial endurance of group-based identity, which is resistant to broader socio-political changes; others maintain that ethnicity represents an instrumental means of extracting maximum material benefits for groups (see Geertz 1963; Nagel and Olzak 1982; Newman 1991; Fearon 1999).

increasingly violent competition for political and economic resources (Melson and Wolpe 1970, esp. 1117).

The catalyst for appropriating secondary values is also often external – population migration through mechanisms such as colonialism, refugee migration,[11] or immigration.[12] And while population migration need not, in fact usually does not, result in a significant threat to a country's primary or secondary values, it can in some circumstances. In liberal republics, international migration has typically been accommodated through two key mechanisms: an ideal of acculturation manifested most obviously in the metaphor of the melting pot, and immigration control. It was these mechanisms that permitted early immigrant societies, such as Australia, Canada, and particularly the United States, to accommodate enormous numbers of immigrants without sacrificing their nascent national identities.

Migration may or may not be a *strategy* of cultural appropriation. Certainly we can think of classical colonization as a strategic form of cultural appropriation in which migration was undertaken with an eye toward what was euphemistically thought of as civilizing indigenous peoples. In the modern world, however, there tends not to be much grand strategy behind mass migration.[13] Instead, to the extent that cultural colonization happens, it generally emerges as a byproduct of immigration, or more accurately of an immigration system inadequately managed. Two important conditions for cultural colonization are the admission of a large number of immigrants, legal or illegal, from the same cultural background, and an incomplete commitment to acculturation.

Let us take these in order briefly, before tabling the discussion for the next chapter. Immigrants come to a host society for myriad reasons, generally the most important of which is affinity for the values of the host

11 An example is the movement of Kosovar refugees in Macedonia, which helped destabilize what was already a delicate balance between Macedonian and Albanian cultural identities (Saideman and Ayres 2000, 1129–30; Ackermann 2000, 69–71).

12 One need tread carefully to avoid the nativist knee-jerk response that the very concept of mass migration can trigger. But to vilify that response is not the same thing as saying that there is never any truth to the relationship between mass migration and cultural appropriation. As the old joke about the Indian chief's advice to President Lincoln suggests, it is wise to pay attention to your immigration policy.

13 On the other hand, it would be naive to ignore the fact that some emigrate to create sleeper cells as a means of furthering political objectives (Rudolph 2003; Tancredo 2004). Following in the tradition of the fundamentalist Kharijites, for example, Osama Bin Laden mandated the *hijra*, or migration, for the purpose of constructing an Islamic state (Ali 2010, 184).

nation. But immigrants also arrive for reasons that have little to do with the values of the host society and almost everything to do with emigrating from a less desirable environment. For these newcomers, the values of the host society are often beside the point, and to the extent to which they are relevant, they are often alien and threatening. Because it is a natural human impulse to reject the alien in favour of the familiar, for immigrants whose cultural kin are also arriving in large numbers, there may be significant incentives to retain the values of the heritage culture at the expense of those of the host culture. This is especially so where, as is often the case, a nativist element to the host culture exists that marginalizes newcomers.

The second important condition for this sort of cultural colonization is the host society's incomplete commitment to acculturation. Acculturation demands that the primary and secondary values of the host society be internalized. It takes two main forms: assimilation and integration. Assimilation has long been liberal republicans' preferred means of accommodating immigrants. It occurs when immigrants and their successors abandon heritage cultural values, particularly as they pertain to language, in favour of the values of the host society. Early literature on assimilation starts from the premise that host and heritage values represent a zero-sum game, such that attachment to one represents a corresponding lack of attachment to the other (Stonequist 1935).

The problem is that there is little evidence to support the zero-sum relationship between retaining heritage values and acquiring host values. In recognition of this, integration occurs when immigrants and their successors retain heritage cultures, which often include language retention, but also become thoroughly integrated into the host country's culture (Berry et al. 1989; Sayegh and Lasry 1993). One of the hallmarks of integration, and what distinguishes it from cultural appropriation, is that heritage values represent private or associational values, those that do not intrude on the constitutional or legislative rules of the host society.

Where acculturation does not occur in the face of large-scale immigration, the prospect of cultural appropriation becomes possible, although certainly not inevitable. Where it does occur, it takes one of three forms. In the first, the appropriating culture is sufficiently powerful to sweep aside the host culture. This sort of cultural tsunami has hit before, as the plight of any number of erstwhile host cultures in the United States (Aboriginal, French, Mexican, Pacific Islander, etc.) can attest. If such total appropriation were to occur in liberal republican societies, tsunami would be the wrong metaphor. Liberal republics are sufficiently powerful – particularly through international alliances – that cultural appropriation could not happen all at once. Instead, such an event would have to play out over a significant period of time, and presumably liberal republican societies would take necessary measures well in advance of it.

The second and most malignant possible outcome of poor acculturation in the face of large-scale immigration is civil war. Such an outcome would almost always entail the simultaneous appropriation of secondary *and* primary values and would require significant immigration from societies particularly resistant to acculturation. This resistance would reflect incompatible primary values between the host and heritage communities. It also would demand inadequate commitment to acculturation; inadequate in the sense that the relevant community is afforded too little or much cultural sensitivity.

The third would be irredentism and secession. However, such an outcome would require a significant geographic concentration of immigrant groups to be feasible. As such, it would require something like what happened in Texas, where American immigration was sufficiently concentrated that American secondary values overwhelmed Mexican ones in a discrete region of the country. If other conditions had been present, it might be reasonable to talk of the same thing happening in reverse in the US Southwest. However, for reasons discussed in the next chapter, this would not appear to be a significant concern.

While complete cultural appropriation constitutes a challenge, the advantage is that it rarely sneaks up, and almost certainly could not, in liberal republics. The process unfolds over a number of years in step-wise progression. One of these steps is the subaltern culture's incomplete appropriation of secondary values. Here the result is a deeply divided bicultural society. Such an outcome is not the end of the world, since liberal republics can survive such division, although the experience of Quebec and Canada reinforces the idea that an insufficiently developed sense of usness can threaten the integrity of deeply cleaved societies. But to say that liberal republics can survive a suboptimal circumstance is not the same thing as saying they should court one. Ultimately, cultural contestation is a challenge born of chauvinism and/or acculturalist failure – a pathology stemming from either too much or too little sensitivity to the tertiary values of powerful subaltern communities.

Versoculturalism

As noted, versoculturalism is about appropriating primary values. This type of cultural appropriation is far more dramatic than the appropriation of secondary values. It represents a true regime-changing revolution. While it can take the form of an evolutionary or quiet revolution, successful versoculturalism is more likely to be accompanied by violence. In pre-Enlightenment times, versocultural revolutions were generally theological, with the Protestant Reformation serving as the prime example. Later, the first major versoculturalist threat to liberal republicanism was expressed in Marx's *Communist Manifesto.* Appropriating primary values requires an alternative set of universalist values that define a different regime type. Therefore there is generally a global dimension to the appropriation of primary values that amounts to what Huntington has called a clash of civilizations and which, if truly a threat to liberal republicanism, represents a qualification to the idea that we have reached the end of history.

Implicit in the primary values of liberal republicanism is the cosmopolitan idea that there exists a common set of values that define a good society and which therefore every good society must privilege. Because these values are universal and transcendent, they are insensitive to ambient conditions. Constitutional articulation of primary values in one society will therefore look very much like such articulation in another. Citizens have the same obligations toward one another, the same requisites to live the good life as each understands it, the same moral and rational endogeneity, and the same relationship with state and market in one country as they would have in another. In other words, one good society looks very much like another good society. Just as a person is a person is a person, so too is a good society a good society.

Liberal republican cosmopolitanism enjoys high normative salience insofar as it is predicated upon two assumptions: that cosmopolitanism gives every rational individual what she would naturally want if she could have it; and that it is culturally neutral in the sense that it privileges no one set of secondary values and merely establishes the means for citizens to determine for themselves what sorts of lives they wish to live.

Versoculturalists challenge both assumptions. It is by no means axiomatic, for example, that every rational individual would naturally desire the individualistic primary values of liberal republicanism. That is an assumption grounded in a particular cultural worldview to which not all people subscribe. Moreover, even if primary values truly are universally desired, it is not clear that liberal republican cosmopolitanism has done an adequate job of distinguishing between the exportation of primary values and the exportation of secondary ones. It is difficult, in other words, to challenge the premise that cosmopolitan primary values tend to look very much like American secondary values. This cultural imperialism flows from the United States' dominance of mass media, which tend to promote (to varying degrees) materialism, secularism, English as a prestige language, and the cultural glorification of the American dream. The spread of cosmopolitan values, despite its apparent cultural neutrality, serves to displace indigenous secondary values in such a way as to change what it means to be Mexican, or Japanese, or Moroccan, etc. (Kant 1795; Schiller 1976; McCarthy 1999).

It is in response to liberal republican cosmopolitanism that we see the emergence of a cultural backlash that seeks to replace liberal republican primary values with new ones. This neo-universalism has acquired a large and transnational salience, dividing the liberal republican (and increasingly post-Christian) West and a resurgent fundamentalism in most of the major world religions. This resurgence represents an explicit cultural rejection of liberal republican values in a way that is anti-secular, anti-relativist, anti-individualist, and anti-commercialist (Huntington 1996, 100; Milton-Edwards 2005, 1–8; Thomas 2010). As discussed in chapter 7, of the neo-universalist challengers to the hegemony of liberal republican primary values, sharia law is the most prominent.[14]

The increasing secularism of liberal cosmopolitanism is part of the eschatological conception of human progress which equates secularism with rationalism and modernity. As Lipset and other modernization theorists have pointed out, one thing that distinguishes the liberal republican developed world from the developing world is that the former has transcended the salience of ascriptive political cleavages in favour of materialist ones. Issues such as social caste, ethnicity, race, and religion are deemed to assume less political significance as countries modernize economically. As we have already seen, modern economies support liberal republican polities because they are grounded in requisites such as fair competition (which requires equality under law), freedom to allocate resources as one chooses, and (property) rights that must be protected for the economy to function. Recursively, in their political manifestation, the values of the modern economy are reflected in the political primary values of liberal republicanism (see Almond 1955; Lipset 1959; 1981; Dahl 1961).

But the progression of history toward an economically modern, liberal republican end may not be so simple. Resurgent Islamic fundamentalism appears to be a product of the very economic modernity that has

---

14 Neo-universalism is a bit of a misnomer when applied to any religious tradition, of course, insofar as all major world religions predate liberal cosmopolitanism. Certainly Islam has been self-consciously expansionist for centuries. The "neo" dimension therefore applies to a resurgence of fundamentalism that has occurred within world religions over the past half-century.

helped fuel liberal republican cosmopolitanism. Modernization creates disruption. As populations migrate toward urban centres, there is short-term anomic dislocation that ultimately resolves itself through the natural reconstruction of community values (Tönnies 1974; Durkheim 1979; Piore and Sabel 1984; Fukuyama 1992). In the Islamic world, religious fundamentalism has served in large part as the antidote to that dislocation (Fuller 1991; Euben 1999, ch. 2; Esposito 2003). Islamic fundamentalism is thus not a relic hanging on by its fingernails in the face of the modern-rationalist onslaught. Instead it draws strength from such modernization (Göle 2000). It is culturally progressive, not a cultural anachronism. As Huntington puts it, "the young are religious, their parents are secular" (1996, 101).

And there are a lot of young. As of 2002, 50 to 65 per cent of the Middle Eastern population was under the age of twenty-four (Fuller 2003). And while it is important to note that birth rates in Islamic countries have declined fairly steeply in recent years, they are still well ahead of those in the West. Islamic countries[15] over the past thirty-five years witnessed a drop in average total fertility rate (TFR) from 6.28 in 1975–80 to 3.11 in 2005–10, with a composite average rate at around 4.66. The comparable average rates for Western European and North American countries[16] are 1.87 and 1.67, with a composite mean of roughly 1.68. More salient is the differential in real population replacement rate, which creates a bit more balance between Islamic and Western nations.[17] But even factoring in differential replacement rates, the average TFR for Muslim countries is still comfortably above the real replacement rate while in Western countries TFR is uncomfortably below it. As early modernizing states, most liberal republics feature aging populations and high social wages; as late modernizing states, many Islamic nations feature youthful populations and socio-ideological commitment.[18]

---

15   Countries that today have a minimum population of 25 million and are at least 80 per cent Muslim. All figures are calculated from data supplied by the United Nations (2011) unless otherwise cited.

16   Countries that today have a minimum population of 25 million.

17   The real population replacement rate takes into account the sex ratio at birth and the probability of living until the mean age of fertility (Espenshade, Guzman, and Westoff 2003, 577). Espenshade and his colleagues find that the real population replacement rate for developed countries is a fairly stable 2.09, whereas there is considerably more variation, with some rates as high as 2.75, in the developing world. The global average is around 2.34 (580).

18   As Mark Steyn calculates the equation: "Age + Welfare = Disaster for you; Youth + Will = Disaster for anyone who gets in your way" (2006, xix).

Exacerbating a potential crisis of demographics is conviction. If we take the United States as the quintessence of liberal republican cosmopolitanism, it is clear that the Islamic world decisively has rejected these values. A 2005 Zogby Poll, for example, showed that unfavourable attitudes toward the United States were held by 63 per cent of Jordanians, 64 per cent of Moroccans, 66 per cent of Lebanese, 73 per cent of citizens from the United Arab Emirates, 85 per cent of Egyptians, and 89 per cent of Saudi Arabians (Shore 2006, 5). Moreover, there is an imperialist dimension to Islamic neo-universalism. One study of young Turkish-German Muslims, for example, showed that roughly one-third believed that Islam must be made the state religion of every country in the world and were prepared to use violence in support of Muslim objectives (Shore 2006, 5). Islamic imperialism in Europe is fueled by a deep and growing sense of distrust between Muslims and Christians. It is enhanced by technological innovations, particularly the internet, which has made readily available the same sorts of Islamic cultural exports that in previous generations were the exclusive province of the developed West (Shore 2006, ch. 1). Al-Jazeera, it might fairly be said, is the Radio Free Europe of the current age.

Islamic fundamentalism remains a comparatively localized phenomenon (that is, one restricted largely to Muslim states) that still cannot make a credible claim to speak for Islam as a whole. It lacks focus and leadership. But many of the same things could be said of the early decades of the Protestant Reformation as well. And while this fact in no way guarantees the successful transition from parochial theological values to global political ones, it does bespeak the need for a certain caution before declaring the end of history.

CONCLUSION: THE CULTURALIST CHALLENGE

The four types of culturalism presented in this chapter pose potential problems for liberal republicans in ways that can be summarized here and amplified in succeeding chapters. Cultural appropriation represents the most obvious threat, particularly as it pertains to primary values. This is something we will deal with in chapter 7. The appropriation of primary values demands the existence of an alternative set of primary values. Such is the challenge presented by neo-universalism. The global challenge to liberal republican cosmopolitanism threatens to create an international environment that liberal republics, of which the US is the standard-bearer, might find increasingly difficult to control. The decline of cultural hegemony, to put this differently, has had the effect of undermining American political hegemony.

There are two important manifestations of this. The first is that neo-universalism, the Islamic resurgence in particular, represents a threat to the sovereignty of nation-states and by extension their salience. Political hegemons typically achieve their global objectives through a complex set of positive and negative incentive structures that entice/coerce foreign governments to follow their political, economic, and even cultural lead. Political hegemony, however, operates at the interstate level. Hegemons do not effectively meet the challenges presented by non-state actors. The uneven success of the War on Terror speaks to this point. Neo-universalists cannot be brought to heel by threats of warfare against territories they do not officially govern. And while it is to be expected that neo-universalists, ISIS being a good example, will come to control certain nation-states, these states in many ways will remain the agents of resurgent Islam and not sovereign principals in their own right. As such, their leaders will be less susceptible to soft-power co-optation techniques that hegemons can use against more pragmatically driven states. This creates a far different dynamic than the Cold War, the termination of which appeared to portend the end of history. In spite of rhetorical pretense, communism was a state-sponsored form of universalism that failed because of its inability to maintain mass allegiance.

The second important manifestation of neo-universalism for the political hegemony of the United States is that formerly staunch allies are becoming somewhat unreliable in the conduct of international affairs. The United States had to work awfully hard, with only limited success, to construct a coalition of allies to support its invasion of Iraq. And whatever one's position might be on the efficacy or morality of that invasion, the fact remains that true hegemons do not have to go cap-in-hand to the United Nations in the vain hope of receiving international sanction.

Of course, there are all sorts of explanations as to why America's leadership seems to be slipping. Hegemons do decline in power and influence; the diminution of the Soviet threat has militated against the imperative of Cold War allies generally to support US foreign policy, and it is natural that in a unipolar environment, states will engage in balancing as opposed to bandwagoning behaviour (see Paul 2005). However, it cannot be ignored that one reason why the erstwhile allies of American hegemony have been so reticent to support US foreign policy in the War on Terror has been that domestic politics, in an extension of Putnam's two-level games (1988), has greatly constrained the win-sets from which state-level actors can select policy options. Europe features rapidly expanding and weakly assimilated Muslim populations, and the danger of political unrest and increased radicalization factored into European international decision-making (Gordon 2002, 16–17; Shore 2006, ch. 1).

Where universal philosophies collide, the battlefield is the hearts and minds of citizens, both foreign and indigenous. If successful, the battle for hearts and minds results in cultural appropriation, or displacing one set of values with another. This is what makes high levels of immigration potentially problematic. The dangers that liberal republics face with respect to mass migration are three-fold.

First, as discussed in the next chapter, the crisis of demographics facing liberal republics means that modern states with barely sustainable welfare systems (think Social Security in the United States, or health care in numerous countries) must contend with a decline in their indigenous populations. The danger that looms is the coincidental phenomenon of aging populations that constitutes an ever-larger drain on the resources of the welfare state, and declining populations in which an ever-larger burden is placed upon younger generations to support the welfare state. Because welfare states tend to be politically intractable, rather than rolling welfare provisions back to the point that people who contributed to them for all of their working lives suddenly find themselves deprived of their benefits at a time when they most need them, governments have begun to address both problems simultaneously through immigration.

Second, because the countries that share primary values with liberal republics face looming population crises of their own, they represent unpromising sources of new blood. If immigration is to solve the first problem, new citizens will have to be imported from countries whose commitment to liberal republican values might be tenuous (Huntington 2004a, 180).

Finally, and to qualify the second point, mass immigration can be accommodated, but such accommodation demands, or at least has always relied on, acculturation. Such acculturation can occur in two ways. *Integration* is inclusive of new citizens and sensitive to their cultural heritages. However, it also demands that they accept the primary and secondary values of the host community. *Assimilation* is inclusive of new citizens by emphasizing cultural commonalities and marginalizing differences. It ties complete citizenship to immigrants internalizing the primary and secondary values of the host community. Both types of acculturation can be problematic. Where integration fails, it is through insufficient attention to ensuring conformity to primary and secondary values. Excessive cultural sensitivity, in other words, precludes effective acculturation. Where assimilation fails, it might be argued, it is through insufficient cultural sensitivity in the quest for conformity.

In many liberal republics, there has been a tendency to err on the side of excessive, not insufficient, cultural sensitivity. The problem is that while cultural sensitivity is a positive thing, excessive cultural sensitivity constitutes a permissive condition for all forms of culturalism. Indeed, while fraught with its own pathologies of excess, assimilation represents a breakwater against the viral spread of the more radical forms culturalism in liberal republics. However, assimilation and anything that smacks of it has fallen out of favour among political and intellectual elites; it has become increasingly marginalized as the knee-jerk response of the nativist bigot. As culturalism has established itself, the moral entitlement to retain the heritage culture has become so powerful that it has taken on the status of an informal human right, a primary value that at once redefines and threatens to undermine the cultural values of liberal republics.

There is a certain irony here. It was immigration and attendant cultural diversity that reinforced the secondary values – the sense of usness – that defined the United States between Reconstruction and the mid-twentieth century. America drew strength from successive waves of immigrants, but took steps to ensure that American values were not overwhelmed. The trick was to construct a national compound that could withstand whatever inherent divisions the melding of distinct cultures might bring to the fore. But today the normative distinction is reversed. It is the national compound that is seen by opponents of assimilation as the potentially destructive force. By the 1960s, culturalism had emerged as the bulwark against the triumph of narrow and exclusive secondary values against the fragile existence (as it then was) of essentialist tertiary values. The culturalism of the 1960s represented an instrumental good: a means to a stronger national identity informed by inclusion and social justice. Such indeed is the (non-threatening) mandate of present *multi*culturalism.

For many advocates of cultural separatism and status-seeking, however, diversity has come to represent more of an intrinsic good. When cultural diversity is cast as an intrinsic good, we see the potential for eroding the moral obligation and civic virtue requisite to usness. In other words, we see factionalization, akin to the traditional republican conception of corruption (see Dobel 1978). If we unpack this a bit we can see that on the one hand, the indigenous threat represented by cultural separatism is facially remote. The American republic doubtless can withstand agrarian colonies of dissociative lesbians. But potentially more problematic is the relationship between cultural separatism and cultural appropriation. Cultural separatism, as we see in Europe (with Britain and the Netherlands serving as the best examples), can serve as a way station for more radicalized divisions between cultural groups. Indeed, there is often a dark and ugly side of separatism manifest in violence and hate. A good example is White supremacist and militia groups in America. And while it is a bit rich to blame culturalism for a bigoted nativist backlash, the fact remains that such a backlash *is* a reasonable expectation when the bonds of civic obligation are eroded (Hoover and Johnson 2003/2004).

Status-seeking, or the quest for differential recognition, sets up similarly as an apparently mild threat. Status is not an alien good in either the republican or liberal traditions. Republican virtue in the ancient world was conceived, after all, in terms of honour – or the ambitious pursuit of status and recognition. Classical liberalism is predicated on the driving force of self-interest whereby individuals seek to exceed others in social status bestowed by material resources. But culturalist status-seeking is problematic in the sense that it has the potential to promote factionalization. The greatest problem with status-seeking is not its existence, but how it manifests itself. The preferred means by which groups seek status – through reforming formal or evolutionary constitutional rules – has implications for social cohesion. The next two chapters amplify the potential challenges introduced in this chapter posed by both cultural appropriation through immigration, as discussed in chapter 7, and factionalization that is the result of status-seeking, as discussed in chapter 8.

7

Welfare, Immigration,
and Cultural Appropriation

THE EMERGENCE OF CULTURALISM IN LIBERAL republics is a late-twentieth-century phenomenon, the decades preceding not being noteworthy for their linguistic or discursive sensitivity. Particularly in America, the outright bigotry of the nineteenth and early twentieth century speaks to an underdeveloped commitment to the cultural sensitivity that culturalists see as foundational to a meaningful theory of justice. Chapter 5 examined culturalism in a fairly static context, representing multiculturalism as a benign form of culturalism that may well deepen the general commitment to liberal republican justice. Chapter 6 set the stage for a more dynamic evaluation of culturalism as it pertains to the book's central focus – the robustness of liberal republican regimes. The current chapter continues that mandate. It has two purposes: to examine where we have been with culturalism, and to demonstrate where we are going.

WHERE WE HAVE BEEN

Unlike liberal republicanism, culturalism cannot trace an ancient lineage, and it was only with the emergence of the identity politics of the 1960s that it became reasonable to speak of a culturalist movement. In particular, the seventy-two years following the end of the Second World War has featured three fundamental and related events of immediate relevance. The first is the civil rights movement, which raised culturalist consciousness in the pursuit of justice. The second is a post-materialist revolution that lent political voice to elevated consciousness. The third is an ongoing crisis of demographics that has challenged the dominance of the dominant cultural community in liberal republics. Each is of sufficient importance to merit some consideration.

Civil Rights

To the extent that we can assign a cause to any evolutionary social phenomenon, it is reasonable to assert that the ambient conditions for the rise of culturalism came to the fore in the changed environment of post–Second World War America.[1] In particular, it was the civil rights movement that elevated culturalism to the forefront of national consciousness. It is difficult to overestimate the importance of the civil rights movement to the politics of culturalism. Its list of social accomplishments is impressive, even if the baseline from which those accomplishments can be measured is appallingly low. Under the auspices of the civil rights movement we have witnessed the elimination of state-sponsored racial segregation; the moral and legal prohibition against lynching and other (functionally unregulated) racially motivated hate crimes; an equal application of constitutional protection to African-American citizens; a dramatic increase in African-American political participation, and concomitant responsiveness by elected officials; an increased sensitivity to the cultural marginalization of African-Americans; and enormous social pressure to keep such chauvinist sentiments as one possessed either private or confined to the increasingly insular community of like-minded bigots (Vose 1954/1955; Klarman 1994, 11–12).

The crystallizing moment for the civil rights movement was, of course, the US Supreme Court's decision in *Brown v. Board of Education of Topeka* (1954). So definitive was the moment that it is tempting to overstate the importance of the *Brown* decision. In reality, a number of sociological and political conditions emerged in the first half of the twentieth century to make *Brown* and the 1960s civil rights legislation possible (Klarman 1994, 15–23; Spencer 1994; Burstein 1998, ch. 2). The beginning of the modern civil rights movement, which Morris (1984, xi) dates to around 1918, was characterized by sustained and non-violent protests that both challenged existing institutions and (at least in the case of the judicial system) relied upon them (Wasby 1984). The Great Migration of African-Americans from the Deep South, which occurred at the same time, had the effect of raising the consciousness of African-Americans, who found that escape from the rural South hardly constituted liberation from

---

1 This is not to say that the pursuit of justice for subaltern cultural communities began with the civil rights movement or was an entirely mid-to-late-twentieth-century phenomenon. African-American slave revolts were not uncommon before Emancipation, and the protest tradition continued in the immediate decades thereafter. Similarly, the successes of women suffragists and the Women's Christian Temperance Union also speak to this qualification.

discrimination. Indeed, with the countervailing migration of White Americans to the suburbs, the urban experience of de facto residential segregation, inadequately funded schools, and the poverty of the inner city drove home the idea that discrimination was hostage to neither time nor place in America (Hall 2005).

The Second World War provided the opportunity to leverage consciousness with muscle, as the manpower shortage elevated the social utility of African-Americans. Symptomatic was the *Pittsburgh Courier's* 1942 Double V Campaign, which exhorted African-Americans to make support for America's war effort during the Second World War contingent on the war being fought on two fronts – a literal one overseas and a metaphorical one against racism in America (Bailey and Farber 1993). The metaphor was particularly poignant for African-American veterans who witnessed better treatment abroad than they did at home, acquired new job skills, and internalized the irony that the European war was being fought against evil forces claiming racial superiority. They arrived at a sense of justice informed by the idea that if they were good enough to fight and die for their country, they were certainly good enough to reap the benefits that American society had to offer. It is therefore not too surprising that veterans were overrepresented in civil rights leadership, and that membership in the National Association for the Advancement of Colored People (NAACP) increased by a factor of nearly ten during the war (Klarman 1994, 18). Black organizations took advantage of the imperative for national unity during the war effort to extract concessions on limited military desegregation and more equitable employment practices in war-related industries (19–20), a process that continued and intensified into the Cold War (Skrentny 1988).

Politically, one of the keys to the success of the civil rights movement was the litigative strategy employed by the NAACP through the first half of the twentieth century that ultimately paved the way for *Brown* (Tushnet 1987a). The politics of the early civil rights movement turned on the issue of what true equality meant as a result of contending interpretations of the Fourteenth Amendment. In the narrowest sense, equality entailed universally applicable political rights, but no sense of equal dignity. As such, Whites could no longer deny Blacks equality under law. But they did not have to associate with them: eat with them, share athletic endeavours with them, provide goods and services to them, or demonstrate in any way that they recognized that African-Americans had an equal moral claim to dignity (Tushnet 1987b).

The low-water mark of this narrow vision of equality was reflected in *Plessy v. Ferguson* (1896) and the subsequent legitimization of Jim Crow laws. In attacking this legalistic definition of equality, the NAACP rejected the accommodationism of Booker T. Washington's slow integrative strategy reflected in the Atlanta Compromise. Instead, it concentrated on two alternative (and somewhat contradictory) strategies: separatism and litigation aimed toward forced integration. Despite the mainstream hostility to a broader interpretation of equality by the Supreme Court and by various state courts in the first half of the twentieth century, the NAACP's litigative strategy sought to broaden the interpretive impact of the Fourteenth and Fifteenth Amendments in such a way as, employing the language of *Plessy*, to expand the equal and marginalize the separate in American public life. Even before *Brown* the strategy proved fairly successful. Between 1915 and 1948, the organization sponsored twenty-five cases before the US Supreme Court, emerging victorious in twenty-three of them (Vose 1954/1955, 102).

The success of the litigative strategy sent a clear message to culturalist reformers beyond the African-American cultural community. While the gains of the civil rights movement ultimately were consolidated legislatively through the Civil Rights and Voting Rights Acts, those gains were not achieved in the first instance through majoritarian (legislative) institutions. Constitutional rules – the Fourteenth and Fifteenth Amendments and the judicial interpretations thereof – were of far greater efficacy than legislative rules in the struggle for meaningful dignity.

If the effectiveness of constitutional versus legislative rules was the first lesson of the civil rights movement, the second illustrated the inadequacies of the narrow legalistic understanding of equality. Such formal equality proved to be clearly ineffective in the universalization of human dignity. And there was nothing like the televised, aggressive enforcement of narrowly construed conceptions of equality, particularly in the Deep South, to demonstrate to Americans of the dominant culture that equality in law was insufficient to the protection of human dignity.

Just as it is difficult to chart the beginnings of social phenomena, it is treacherous to track their contagion. However, it seems clear that the legacy of the civil rights movement expanded broadly and rapidly in the 1960s. It is surely no coincidence that scholarly interest in the politics of cultural identity rose sharply in the late 1950s.[2] McAdam (1994) suggests that liberation movements should not be considered discrete

2 In tracing the historiography of identity politics, Gleason credits Erik H. Erikson's *Identity and the Life Cycle* published in 1959 as providing the stimulus (albeit not the genesis) for the explosion of academic work on the identity politics manifest in culturalism. Interestingly, the idea of identity politics predates Erikson by over forty years in the work of Horace Kallen, although Kallen's ideas were clearly well ahead of their time (Fishman 2004).

events, but rather manifestations of a common "master protest frame" rooted in the civil rights movement (41–2). They represent, in other words, a broad alliance of forces designed to address a common problem manifested in the hegemony of a dominant culture oppressive in similar ways across different types of groups (see Meyer and Whittier 1994, 281–2).

In part, what linked the women's and civil rights movements was personal contacts and experience. Many of the pioneers of the women's movement beginning in the mid-1960s were veterans of the Mississippi Summer Project (McAdam 1988, 183; see also Evans 1980); although the modern homosexual movement, the catalyst for which was a New York City police raid on the Stonewall Inn on the night of 27 June 1969, enjoyed far fewer personal links to the civil rights movement.[3] However, what they did share was the existence of a symbolic focus of oppression: segregation for African-Americans, and sodomy laws (later same-sex marriage and military service bans) for gays. They also shared a litigative strategy targeting these symbolic icons of oppression (Neal 1995/1996).[4]

The contagion effect of the civil rights movement moved beyond both the personal and the proximate. In Northern Ireland, which witnessed the breakout of "the troubles" in 1969, Catholic protestors borrowed the slogans and symbolism (albeit not the passive resistance) of the civil rights movement (Dooley 1998, ch. 3). Quebec's Quiet Revolution of the 1960s, although tied to the declining influence of the Catholic Church, was also a manifestation of increased activism and raised political consciousness that arose from the civil rights movement in the United States (Baum 1992, 141; see also Vallières 1971).

Post-Materialism

Reinforcing the underlying commitment to culturalism was the post-materialist revolution of the 1960s (Inglehart 1971). Broadly contemporaneous with the civil rights and other social movements, the post-materialist revolution traces its roots to the Keynesianism of the 1930s and 1940s which ultimately stimulated the construction of welfare

3 In fact, there was a degree of resentment on the part of many African-Americans that groups such as gays and lesbians, whose identity was a product of lifestyle, should seek to appropriate moral claims that had been forged through centuries of slavery and other forms of oppression (Russell 1994).

4 While the modern gay rights movement might have been stimulated by Stonewall, the history of homosexual political activism in the United States dates to the early part of the twentieth century. For a good study of that history see McCain (1993).

states in the developed (liberal republican) world. Keynesianism, a product of the sort of activist thinking that characterized the US New Deal, mandates a proactive role for the state in countering the often pathological effects of the demand cycle. Specifically, when demand outpaces supply, judicious application of braking mechanisms (most prominently raising interest rates) serves to dampen inflationary pressures; when demand lags, significant public (usually welfare) spending can serve to stimulate an economy trending toward deepening recession.

One of the effects of the welfare state was to relegate bread and butter *material* political issues to a less prominent role. Where a social safety net exists, material issues like public spending, taxes, wage rates, etc. still matter in people's lives, but they compete with more philosophically substantial *post-material* issues (Inglehart 1971; 1990). To put it in the language of Abraham Maslow's well-known hierarchy of needs, the welfare state services lower-order needs, liberating young people to pursue higher-order objectives.[5] These objectives informed the politics of what came to be known as the new left, dedicated to the sorts of goods money can't buy, such as peace, a sustainable environment, and social justice.

The last is of particular relevance. For society in general, and subaltern cultural communities in particular, post-materialism brought to the forefront of consciousness the manifold forms that social injustice could take. Indeed, the pursuit of social justice might reasonably be considered the first salient post-material value in the developed world. Post-materialism broadened the political base of social movements that historically had been marginalized from mainstream politics. And while it was not just the young who came to embrace the cause of opposition to racial discrimination, the institutionalization and expansion of identity politics was driven by the baby boomers and subsequent post-materialist generations.

Brodie and Nevitte (1993) find that post-materialism has affected patterns of political participation and representation. Specifically, subaltern cultural groups empowered by the post-material left's emphasis on social justice have tended to reject traditional, majoritarian (or legislative), elite-driven forms of political representation as overly reflective of the narrowly-construed secondary values of the dominant culture. As an

5 The distinction between young and old matters here. Values are a product of socialization. And while socialization takes place throughout one's life, the values that one learns as an adolescent and young adult tend to become foundational to one's lifelong value system (Butler and Stokes 1976, esp. ch. 10). As such, the first post-material generation – the first generation to come of age and be politically socialized under the material protection afforded by the welfare state – was the baby boomers.

alternative, Inglehart (1990, 339–40) notes, they have increasingly relied on more issue-specific means of effecting significant political change
manifested by the emergence or empowerment of organizations that
claim an explicit mandate to speak for the values of "their people." In
part, what Inglehart describes reflects increasing efficacy on the part of
subaltern groups to assert their voices in support of policy change
through the legislative process. However, mirroring the litigative strategy
of the NAACP Legal Defense Fund, subaltern groups have sought to
effect change through constitutional jurisprudence and concomitant
expansion of constitutional rules.

The post-material revolution represented a challenge to traditional
liberal republican values. For his part, Bork sees the social disruption of
the 1960s and beyond as a failure on the part of liberal republics to civi-
lize the baby boom generation. In the 1960s, the traditional process of
socialization became overwhelmed, with the baby boomers resisting incorporation into the prevailing values of the generation before them,
and instead creating their own *sui generis* prioritization of primary values
(1997, 21). This accident of demographics, combined with what Bork
sees as the inherent instability of liberal republicanism – the liberal (selfishness) will ultimately outpace the republican (moral obligation) – has
conspired with culturalism (radical egalitarianism, in Bork's parlance)
to put America on the road to Gomorrah. Similarly, Bellah understands
the dislocation of the age as part of a generalized historical pattern in
America away from the Hegelian moral synthesis (albeit one grounded
in Christian principles) of its covenantal founding and toward a society
suffering from an "erosion of common meanings" (1975, x; see also
Anthony and Robbins 1982; Glendon 1991; Popenoe 1993; Etzioni
1996; Roof 1999).[6]

---

6 One of the problems with the apocalyptic diagnoses advanced by Bork and Bellah is
that the appearance of calamity is always magnified by its proximity. History, from Sodom
and Gomorrah onwards, is rife with episodic breakdowns of the perceived moral order,
with concomitant and gloomy predictions about the fate of society. Progressive, genera-
tional moral breakdown was a fairly common theme in Elizabethan England (Lake and
Questier 2002, esp. 467), and Puritan New England (Batinski 1996). It was prevalent in
nineteenth-century America. Indeed, in 1835, for example, American William Ellery
Channing warned amid the disturbing trend of youth violence, general crime, and sexual
luridness that "even in families we see jarring interests and passions, invasions of rights,
resistance of authority, violence [and] force" (Mintz 1995, 3).

The Crisis of Demographics

The Keynesian economics that gave rise to the post-materialist revolution left a legacy that has contributed to a demographic crisis in liberal republics with significant implications for cultural diversity. The point is not to articulate the inherent flaws of a welfare state. Indeed, we have already gone to some lengths to demonstrate that Rawls's prescription for redistribution represents a significant element of the liberal republican understanding of justice.[7]

At the same time, however, the welfare state also represents a set of potential moral hazards, fostering negative behaviour patterns that would not otherwise be as likely to occur if citizens were subject to greater risk exposure. Over time the provision of benefits creates greater demand for such benefits. As with any institution, the welfare state creates a set of predicted income streams (Bates 1990). The effect is manifold. First, for a subset of the population, welfare benefits create a disincentive to engage in more socially productive activity. Second, and related, entrenching these benefits creates a sense of social entitlement. As such, rolling back the welfare state demands a great deal of political capital and runs the risk of significant backsliding as legislators lose their political will in the face of political opposition (Moffitt 1992; Lindbeck 1995; Pierson 1996; Van Keersbergen 2002; Prinz 2005; Robson 2006). Third, as Allison's bureaucratic policy model makes clear, agencies stake proprietary claims to areas of administrative competence that cause them to seek to protect resources (in terms of budgets, personnel, policy responsibilities, etc.) and, where possible, to expand such resources (Allison and Halperin 1972; Allison 1999, ch. 5). Finally, the paternal role of the welfare state in many ways serves as a substitute for the role traditionally played by the family, and therefore contributes to higher illegitimacy rates (Becker 1993). While this can have the effect of offsetting declining population rates, other social costs – increased crime and poverty rates, for example – often accompany higher rates of illegitimacy (Phelps 1996).

---

7 The general acceptance of a welfare state in liberal republics is reflective of the reality that self-reliance alone is insufficient to ensure fairness or material survival in the increasingly complex economies of the post-industrial age. Far more than in Emerson's America, when healthy young men could always migrate West in search of economic opportunities, modern economies offer extremely restricted means of self-reliance in the amelioration of poor people's economic situations. One exception to this in the United States is the role played by the volunteer army, which represents prospects for upward social mobility not through land acquisition, but through job training and veteran benefits.

Despite periodic calls for restraint and reform, it would not appear that welfare spending is going to decrease by a whole lot. While some countries were able to achieve modest retrenchment during the 1990s and early 2000s, liberal republics' long-term trend in social spending is generally upward. In 1980, on the cusp of a dramatic ideological shift away from statism, characterized by the Reagan-Thatcher years, the average percentage of GDP dedicated to social spending in Organisation for Economic Co-Operation and Development (OECD) countries was 15.6 per cent. By 2005, that figure had increased to 19.8 per cent (OECD 2011). Obviously these averages obscure some successful attempts at retrenchment. And some countries have actually reduced social spending from 1980 levels. However, with aging populations and therefore increasing social expenditure demands, spending cuts are difficult to make and even harder to sustain.

If aging populations help to entrench welfare spending, it is important to understand why populations age, particularly in wealthy societies. Indeed, one might intuit that as societies get richer they will get younger. Traditionally, affluence and population growth have been positively correlated. Easterlin (1976) contends that the decision to have children is tied to the relationship between parents' resources and their aspirations, or desired lifestyle. Traditionally, resources were measured by the earning capacity of the husband. Where that capacity was high relative to the couple's aspirations, they were more likely to have children. By contrast, where resources were scarce relative to aspirations, there was more pressure on the wife to work and hence less opportunity for her to have children. Assuming that aspirations stayed constant, increased affluence resulted in increased births (417).

But the post-material age has been one in which aspirations have kept pace with, or even outpaced, resources. Aspirations have become post-material as well, as individuals strive for non-traditional means of fulfillment that focus more on the actualization of the self and less on moral obligations. The focus on the self as a being in search of post-material, and hence non-traditional, means to fulfillment is suggestive of a different sort of individualism than had previously characterized liberal republican societies.

Liberal republics, which have never wholly reconciled the Hegelian dialectic between self and other, have tended to experience a fluctuating equilibrium between focus on the self and focus on the community. Thomson (1997) notes that in the United States of the 1920s, for example, social criticism focused on the excessively individualistic culture that prevailed. By contrast, the next three decades were characterized by what social critics perceived to be an unhealthy conformity, a sentiment embodied at the culmination of the era by Sloan Wilson's classic *Man in the Gray Flannel Suit.* By the 1960s, the counterculture movement represented a widespread reaction against the traditional symbols and manifestations of conformity. It represented, if you will, a post-material manifestation of liberty as that which frees the individual from the oppressive cultural values of the preceding generation who dared not question them. The hip and individualistic (in their own conforming ways) sought personal fulfillment and authenticity through, among other things, drugs, music, and sexual liberation.

The last is particularly relevant. Freedom finds its natural enemy in authority, and the counterculture movement sought to resist what its members perceived to be the illegitimate exercise of authority manifest in marriage. As such, Lesthaeghe (1995, 25) notes, cohabitation emerged as a rite of passage for the protest generation. And while cohabitation is not solely the cause of the declining birth rates, it has been a significant factor. Of course, many couples choose to have children out of wedlock, but many choose not to, a decision facilitated by the ease with which women have been able to get abortions in most liberal republican societies since the early 1970s. At the same time, increased focus on the self has resulted in weaker bonds within dyadic relationships (see also Carmichael and Whittaker 2001).

In addition to creating greater preferences for common-law living arrangements, these weaker bonds manifest themselves in higher separation rates than during previous eras. Strong dyadic relationships demand a deep commitment to incorporating one's spouse's needs into his own utility functions. As individual autonomy and the quest for post-material self-fulfillment has increased, dyadic relationships have become less about merging utility functions and more about finding compatibility between subjectively guarded individual utility functions. Because of this imperative, marriages are delayed in lieu of a prolonged courtship/testing period manifest in cohabitation. Separation, when it occurs, tends to be a product of the difficulty in sustaining the match between two discrete and subjective utility functions. It is for this reason, Lesthaege argues, that marriages in which there has been a trial run of cohabitation are less likely to survive than ones in which the couple go the traditional route directly into marriage (1995, 22–4).

It is not just self-absorption that has contributed to declining birth rates. Gender equality and an increase in women's economic and career opportunities have also played an important part. As women came to acquire a public presence in the postwar period, their educational and hence career opportunities improved (Caldwell 1982). Many decided to have babies later in life, or to forego motherhood in favour of their careers (Lesthaeghe and Willems 1999; Caldwell and Schindlmayr 2003; Offer 2006, 268–9).

There should be no mistaking the empirical message as a normative one. There is no wistful gaze back to a happier time when women were marginalized in the public sphere. Similarly, the reinvigorated individualism of the post-material age does not necessarily alienate liberal republicanism from its individualist roots. Even in the glory days of liberal republicanism, Emerson admonished lovers to "guard their strangeness" (1951c, 359). But the empirical fact remains that the emancipation of women from traditional gender roles, and post-materialist individualism, has contributed to a decline in total fertility rates during a period when increased affluence should have produced the opposite effect.

As noted in the previous chapter, the combination of a declining birth rate and robust, institutionalized welfare spending is an unfortunate one. Even if welfare spending remains steady, falling populations place an increasing burden on those in the active workforce. As longevity increases and technology improves, for example, enormous pressure is placed on health-care systems. Fewer workers, to take another example, are supporting greater demand for Social Security. And while some of the effects can be offset by raising retirement ages and seeking to improve labour productivity, if demographic trends hold it is inevitable that ever greater shares of the working (and aging) population's paycheques will be earmarked to support those benefiting from some form of state assistance (Börsch-Supan 2003; Bongaarts 2004).

The obvious solution is to increase immigration, in the United States a process that was facilitated by the Immigration Act of 1965.[8] But such increases will have to be large if they are to have much impact on prevailing demographic trends. Espenshade, for example, finds that even at the high end of the Census Bureau's expected immigration levels, the overall effect of immigration on the rapidly aging US population would lower the median age by only about a year by 2040 (1994, 762). The oft-proposed alternative of guest-worker programs is also unlikely to offer a realistic alternative. The experiences of Germany and France suggest that the temporary status of guest workers is illusory. As the United States has found with illegal immigration – its own unofficial "guest worker program" – not only do such workers often remain

---

8 The 1965 Immigration Act replaced the emphasis on diffusion of immigrants' heritage toward a greater emphasis on skills and/or kinship ties to American citizens. In the United States, the immigrant population has quadrupled since 1970 and doubled since 1990; to look at it another way, the immigrant population has expanded at twice the rate of the host population (Vigdor 2008, 1).

permanently, they have an incentive to bring relatives into the country as well (764–5).

Not that immigration is a bad thing. Putnam (2007, 138–9) concludes that as ethnic diversity in developed countries increases in the coming decades there will be significant net benefit to host nations. Indeed, the success of immigrant societies such as Canada and the United States over the past century are clear indications of just how beneficial immigration can be. While ethnic conflicts and chauvinism on the part of host societies accompanied such immigration, old prejudices in most cases vanished (which is not to say they have not been replaced by newer ones) as different ethnic groups partook of the integrating effect of liberal republican, market-based pluralism.

Putnam notes that cultural diversity brings with it tangible advantages. One is creativity. First-generation immigrants have accounted for "three to four times as many Nobel Laureates, National Academy of Science Members, Academy Award film directors, and winners of Kennedy Center awards in the performing arts as native-born Americans" (2007, 140). Another is economic growth. While there is no consensus within the economics literature, income growth among native-born Americans appears to increase in regions that feature high immigrant populations (140, 166 fn 4). To the extent that increased wealth fosters democratization (Lipset 1981) and democratization of other countries makes liberal republics more secure (Russett 1993), immigration from poorer regions of the world can be said to contribute to national security. Putnam cites World Bank data that suggests that remittances (economic, creative, and technological) to immigrants' relatives in their former homelands generated through increasing annual immigration from South to North by 3 per cent could have the effect of exceeding development assistance targets and eliminating Third World debt (2007, 141).

On the other hand, a second effect of increased ethnic diversity noted by Putnam is that over the short to medium terms, social capital – or the propensity to fulfill moral obligations –will be threatened. The relationship between social capital and immigration is a controversial one. The "contact hypothesis" of social interaction suggests that social capital is fostered when culturally diverse groups have greater social interaction with one another (e.g., Allport 1979, ch. 16). Conversely, the "conflict hypothesis" makes precisely the opposite claim (e.g., Anderson and Paskeviciute 2006; cf. Stolle, Soroka, and Johnston 2008). The conflict hypothesis suggests that, in large part due to intergroup conflict over scarce resources such as jobs, greater social interaction among cultural groups leads groups to become inwardly focused. Rather than creating so-called bridging social capital – where the radius of trust extends across social groups – the conflict hypothesis predicts an increase only in bonding social capital, where the radius of trust remains focused within discrete social groups (Putnam 1995, 22–4). The result is often chauvinism rather than social integration (2007, 142–3).

Putnam's empirical findings support neither the contact nor the conflict hypotheses. His study examines forty-one geographically diverse communities, from broadly diverse cities such as San Francisco, Houston, and Boston, to extremely homogenous communities like rural South Dakota (where, Putnam suggests, commitment to cultural diversity entails inviting a few Norwegians to the Swedish picnic). Respondents were coded according to one of four ethnic designations – Hispanic, non-Hispanic White, non-Hispanic Black, and Asian – and asked how much they trusted members of all four categories. Superficially, the results supported the conflict hypothesis. There was far greater evidence of bridging social capital in culturally homogenous communities than in culturally diverse ones. People, in other words, trust members of other races far more in theory than in practice. However, when Putnam looks at intra-group trust, he finds the results to be almost precisely the same. Citizens in culturally heterogeneous communities tended not to trust members of their own ethnic group any further than they trusted members of other ethnic groups. Cultural diversity, in other words, fostered neither bonding nor bridging social capital, whereas cultural homogeneity fostered both. The results, then, are a good-news/bad-news proposition. The good news is that the conflict hypothesis does not hold; the bad news is that "[m]any Americans today are uncomfortable with diversity" (Putnam 2007, 158).

As Putnam notes, his findings reflect static attitudes. His surveys, from 2000, represent opinions gathered at a particular point in time. Missing, and highly relevant, is the dynamism that accompanies social change. Social identities change. The overt racism of pre–civil-rights-movement America disappeared incredibly quickly as these things go. Social identities pertaining to women in the workplace and professions, and to gay marriage have undergone, or are undergoing, similar changes. Putnam believes that social identities also will change to become more accommodating of ethno-cultural diversity. And although research into whether that is indeed happening is preliminary, we can look to history to demonstrate areas where it has happened. One good example is the Protestant-Catholic divide that through the early post–Second World War era was a politically salient cleavage in numerous liberal republics, including Canada and the United States. Over the past half-century or so, this cleavage has lost its political relevance. Similarly, waves of early-twentieth-century immigration in North America created culturally insular dominant groups. But, as Putnam points out, where the cultural divide was once caste-like, roughly 80 per cent of White Americans now have spouses with different ethnic backgrounds (2007, 162).

Of course, implicit in Putnam's plausibly optimistic long-run prediction is acculturation – the incorporation of new immigrants into the mainstream of the host political culture. That is, to refresh an earlier discussion, acculturation demands that the (primary and secondary) values of the host society be internalized. Broadly speaking, we can think of acculturation as operating across two dimensions. Economic acculturation can be evaluated by indicators such as workforce participation, education levels, types of employment, and home ownership. Cultural and civic acculturation relies on proxies such as rates of intermarriage, willingness to learn the language dominant in the host society, rates of naturalization, and military service. Collectively, they represent the willingness to acquire a sense of community (or usness) with the host society (Eisenstadt 1951, 224; Gordon 1964, 71; Vigdor 2008, ch. 1).

WHERE WE ARE GOING

Having discussed where we have been, the second mandate of this chapter is to examine where we are going. Increased immigration – and hence increased cultural diversity – is an inevitable consequence of the demographic crisis in liberal republics. This means it is of fundamental importance how a country regulates its intake of immigrants. By regulation I mean both the number of immigrants permitted entry and the means by which these immigrants are socialized. Through the first half of the twentieth century, acculturation in immigrant society conformed to the assimilationist ideal.[9] This ideal went largely unquestioned. Even for indigenous subordinate groups, the struggle was for the right to be accepted into the cultural mainstream (Higham 1993, 200). However, as noted, since the mid-1960s, there is a growing sentiment (a virtual consensus in certain academic circles) that assimilation is merely code for coercion to comply with a set of primary and secondary values established as a means of perpetuating the cultural hierarchy that privileged the dominant group as it then was and typically still is (Glazer 1993; Alba and Nee 2003, ch.1).

9 We have already distinguished assimilation from integration as forms of acculturation. Both demand that immigrants embrace the core values of the host society; they differ, however, as to the desirability of immigrants retaining ties to the heritage culture. To put it in the language employed in this book, assimilation places far greater emphasis on secondary values than tertiary ones.

The disfavour into which the assimilationist ideal has fallen has given rise to two issues that bear examination. The first is a call for open borders. The second is the potential for cultural appropriation, both in the form of cultural contestation and versoculturalism. We examine the former through a brief case study of Mexican immigration to the United States and explore the latter by looking at Muslim immigration in Europe.

Open Borders

Advocates of open borders suggest that regulation of immigration is a natural corollary to assimilation. Both are meant to ensure the dominance of the dominant cultural community. Both suggest a cultural hierarchy in which some are implicitly less desirable than others so that in order to enter a country, one must be cleansed of his cultural impurities. Since the capacity to cleanse is limited, so too must be access to entry.

Carens likens first-world citizenship to a neo-feudal social structure. It provides unequal opportunities for authentic life chances for citizens of rich and poor countries, bestowing unwarranted status and privilege on the former while condemning the latter to second-class status (Carens 1987). It is cultural hierarchy transposed onto the global stage. Carens's analysis is grounded in the reasonable claim that "no defensible moral theory can reject [the assumptions] that our social institutions and public policies must respect all human beings as moral persons and that this respect entails recognition, in some form, of the freedom and equality of every human being" (1987, 265). The question is, can we reconcile border control with defensible moral theory? The answer turns on the fundamental issue of whether or not individuals have a moral claim to organize themselves into governing units of their own choosing, and, within certain reasonable parameters consistent with other primary values, establish the rules governing these units and determining their membership.

What reasons are there to think that this moral claim does not exist? Carens identifies a number of them. One is that restricting national group membership is inconsistent with Rawls's theory of justice. While Rawls assumes a certain moral consensus as to the sorts of primary values that inform the good society, there is no logical prohibition from extending his principles of justice – which are, after all, expressly liberated from all but the most basic elements of social context (Carens 1987, 257). This being the case, it seems reasonable to assert that individuals operating from behind a veil of ignorance would assign greater utility to mobility than they would to restricting that mobility and therefore would select total freedom of mobility as a primary social good.

Carens's interpretation of Rawls is not, however, dispositive. Carens himself qualifies his position on the reconcilability of border control with Rawlsian justice when he concedes that Rawls's theory of justice would allow for immigration control if the public order were threatened due to a country's capacity to accommodate new citizens being overwhelmed by sheer numbers (1987, 259). Rawls's qualification is that "in limiting liberty by reference to the common interest in public order and security, the government acts on a principle that would be chosen in the original position" (Rawls 2003, s. 34, 187). Carens's is a fairly large concession. Immigration control would seem fairly central to public order and security. Certainly (as Native Americans might attest) it has the potential to undermine prevailing values and property rights. This being the case, a strong claim can be made that it reflects the common interest such that it would be chosen in the original position. By extension, we move from an argument about kind (whether or not immigration should be allowed) to one about degree (how much immigration would adversely affect the "common interest in public order"?).

Carens's argument turns on the assumption that national boundaries stand for little more than means to determine who shares in, and who is precluded from sharing in, the material benefits that accrue in a particular national society (cf. Berlin 2001). In this sense, a nation is simply an aggregation of individuals – individuals who may have more cultural affinity for foreigners (think of citizens in Seattle and Vancouver) than they do for people in their own nation (think New York City and Waycross, Georgia). National borders in this case are more social artifice than demarcations of cultural distinction (1987, 266–7).

But this line of reasoning significantly discounts the cultural identification that citizens of Seattle have (but Vancouverites do not have) for the United States; and which the latter, but not the former, have for Canada. Rather than looking at this in terms of cultural affinity, it is more reasonable to consider how important it is for people in Seattle (or New York or Waycross) to identify as Americans; and for that matter, how important it is for citizens of Monterrey to identify as Mexicans, or citizens of Tokyo as Japanese, or citizens of Buenos Aires as Argentinians. If we assume that such identification with secondary values is important, it is by no means clear that individuals behind a veil of ignorance would place greater utility on cross-border migration rights than they would on preserving national identities.

Of course, since one's national identity would not travel with her to the original position, we have to argue from the universal and not the particular. But there are universal principles that inform group identities such that national identity is not a function of one's Americanness or

Chineseness. Rather, it is a function of her humanness. One would not have to know if she were German or Australian or Dutch to know that she values the usness that comes with a shared social identity. Whether she would value it more than freedom of mobility cannot be answered. But the very fact that one counterfactual argument is as reasonable as the other undermines the persuasiveness of Carens's claim that rational individuals would choose freedom of mobility from the original position.

Another argument that Carens presents against border control is that it cannot be reconciled with liberty as a primary value. Just because you might *want* to restrict liberty does not mean that you can do so ethically. There are numerous reasons why individuals within liberal republican communities might want to restrict others' right to migrate. These include the desire to preserve existing ways of life, or the desire not to share group resources with those who would represent a net drain on those resources. Carens notes that Californians were not enthused about the prospect of welcoming Oklahoman dust bowl refugees in the 1930s, just as contemporary Oregonians look askance at Californians who migrate northward. However, the *liberal* part of liberal republicanism makes prohibiting individuals' freedom of movement within a society a moral non-starter.

Similarly, there are reasons why individuals might want to band together to deny other individuals benefits on the basis of ascriptive characteristics such as race or gender. Some people desire racially exclusive neighbourhoods, and some have sought to hire only people of their own kind, or admit only such people into universities, or rent their property in a way that is racially exclusive. While liberal republican societies do allow private organizations to establish criteria to determine their own membership, these criteria typically do not permit exclusion based solely on ascriptive characteristics.

Thus, Carens's logic goes, even if we are willing to admit that the right of a group of people to determine its own membership constitutes a primary value within society, clearly it is a subordinate value – one that must give way in the face of higher priority values such as justice, freedom, and equality. And because justice, freedom, and equality are *cosmopolitan* liberal republican values, they ethically cannot be denied to citizens of other societies. The restricted-country-club model does not work within a liberal republic's borders and it should not work outside of those borders either.

Carens is correct to note that liberal republican cosmopolitanism imposes a moral obligation that all world citizens have to all others. But he is incorrect in the implicit corollary that this moral obligation extends to everyone in equal measure. There is nothing about the liberal republican commitment to moral obligation that precludes differential levels of such obligation. Nor could there reasonably be. It is all but universally believed that a person's moral obligation to his family is greater than to his friends, to his friends than to his neighbours, to his neighbours than to strangers, etc. If we look at liberty, we can argue that we owe all citizens a degree of equal liberty – let us say for argument's sake, the basic liberties that constitute part of Rawls's thin theory of the good. As such, I am no more entitled to enslave a stranger than I am to enslave my children.

But liberal republican freedom is greater than simply freedom from constraint. There is an affirmative dimension to freedom that is not equally provided even within those liberal republics most scrupulous in the preservation of primary values. Equal freedom does not mean, therefore, that it is morally inappropriate to afford my children a greater degree of liberty – say through more expensive education as a means to enjoying a broader and more authentic set of life choices – than I afford to others. I certainly owe strangers something in this respect. I am obliged to pay school taxes that go toward helping others achieve an education. But few would find it reasonable to say that I owe others' children as much as I owe my own.

This idea of concentric levels of obligation is inherent in other ways as well. Even though I live in a liberal republic that offers its citizens free mobility, in my state school tax dollars go disproportionately to funding neighbourhood schools, as opposed to schools in other districts, counties, or states. When citizens in states with state income taxes pay those taxes, the expectation is that tax dollars will provide goods and services in-state and not be exported to other states. And when the federal government provides goods and services in the form of welfare or health care spending, there is no expectation that *equal* concern will be offered to citizens in other countries.

Rather than dismiss border control as an anachronistic cultural hierarchy, it is reasonable to posit that border control represents an essential element in safeguarding the primary values of a liberal republic. We have already established that border control is integral to a sense of usness as reflected in secondary values. Usness is foundational to moral obligation and moral obligation to good governance. But immigration control would seem to be central to primary values as well. A world of fluid population movement is more likely to be a world of tyranny, against which civic obligation is the primary breakwater (Walzer 1981, 8). Political societies form from the inside out. Trust and mutual obligation radiate outward, being strongest at the centre. In this sense large societies are merely an artifice of social construction, and require affirmative measures such as federalism and other mechanisms of localized government to maintain. To try to engineer a global society would undoubtedly create a structure in which load exceeds tolerance, and which could be expected to fracture into smaller and more sustainable units. It is for this reason that Walzer claims, "[t]o tear down the walls of the state is not ... to create a world without walls, but rather to create a thousand petty fortresses" (9).

Cultural Appropriation

Does a moral claim of a people to control its own borders translate into a moral claim to make newcomers conform to the primary and secondary values of the host society? Proponents of what has come to be known as the Copenhagen School argue that societal security – the defence of what makes a people a people – is an important element of national security (Buzan, Waever, and de Wilde 1998, ch. 6; also Buzan 1983; Waever et al. 1993). Insofar as states (as an aggregation of individuals) have a moral claim to defend themselves against threats to their own security, it is not unreasonable to extend that claim to the preservation of primary and secondary values. Indeed, there is not always a great distinction between physical and societal security since the flip side of acculturation is separation, marginalization, and possibly ultimately rebellion (Huntington 2004a, 182; Tubalado 2007).

How do we know when the societal security of a state is threatened? When it comes to physical security, it is pretty clear when such a threat occurs. Hostile forces mobilize, threaten, and even attack the physical space controlled by a nation-state. But threats to cultural security are far more subtle. For one thing, often they are not the result of some planned assault on the primary or secondary values of a state. American immigration into Texas in the first decades of the nineteenth century was not the first stage of an organized campaign against the cultural (and ultimately territorial) integrity of Mexico even though that is how it worked out. Greek irrendentism in the late Ottoman Empire similarly was not the product of careful long-term planning, and instead was a reaction to circumstances that favoured it.[10]

10 Stimulated by a Greek Orthodox Church wary of what it saw as a syncretic drift, the cultural revolution reversed the assimilative process that had seen Greek immigrants culturally and linguistically immersed in host societies throughout Asia Minor. Facilitating this destabilizing cultural revolution was the Ottoman Empire's accommodationist shift toward cultural neutrality and tolerance in the aftermath of the Crimean War. Such tolerance

Cultural threats are also subtle in the sense that they are often ambiguous. Unlike physical security threats, which oblige states to defend themselves against changes to the status quo (pertaining to territorial integrity, · for example), cultural threats cannot be understood in these terms. Secondary values in particular are dynamic in ways that national boundaries are not. Change in secondary values is endemic, with rigid adherence to anachronistic values inherently unhealthy. This suggests that cultural threats can be more apparent than real; or, conversely, they can be more real than apparent. As to the former, the experiences of the United States and Canada suggest that taking in large numbers of immigrants, even those from countries with different linguistic and religious traditions, does not constitute an inherent cultural threat, contemporaneous angst and hand-wringing notwithstanding. At the same time, though, the good intentions of those committed to a multiculturalist conception of justice may well serve as a cloak for significant cultural threats represented by groups appropriating primary or secondary values.

To ensure that the analysis stays on point, the argument here is not that increased levels of immigration will inherently result in threats to secondary or even primary values. In the vast majority of instances it will not, and indeed is far more likely to strengthen a republic than weaken it. But the point here is not the norm, but rather the exception. In that respect, the most common threat of appropriation is to a host country's secondary values.

Cultural appropriation can begin innocently enough, as rejection of the host society's secondary values. While such rejection can occur in a number of ways, the most significant cultural indicator is linguistic (Telles and Ortiz 2008, 186). Where immigrants are resistant to learning the language of the host country and prefer instead to retain the heritage language, the prospects for acculturation decrease. As discussed in the last chapter, cultural appropriation is typically a product of opportunity rather than strategy. Individuals emigrate for any number of reasons, with cultural appropriation being fairly low on most people's lists. On the other hand, people tend to feel more comfortable in the cultural milieu in which they are socialized. And while cultural values are not invulnerable to change, they are resistant. Where there is not strong

---

mandated non-interference in the cultural, intellectual, and educational practices of religious (and hence often ethnic) minorities. Kitromilides notes the irony of the fact that this "attempt to save the empire by elaborating a policy of mutual toleration of its component ethnic groups ... only facilitated the more effective growth of nationalism which eventually destroyed both the empire and the subject nationalities in Asia Minor" (1990, 9; see also Davison 1954; Göçek 2002).

pressure for immigrants to acculturate, and where large numbers of culturally similar immigrants are massed, the potential exists for cultural colonization (Lazear 1999).

Both the United States and Europe face potential cultural challenges from immigration. In the United States, cultural conservatives such as Huntington (2004b) have warned that Hispanic immigration threatens to overwhelm the host culture since the sheer number of immigrants has created a disincentive for their communities to acculturate. In Europe, there are signs that Muslim immigrants have resisted acculturation. Indeed, opinion polls suggest that an unhealthy degree of mutual antipathy exists between host and heritage cultures in Europe. The remainder of this chapter is dedicated to examining the extent to which cultural dynamics in the US and Europe represent legitimate threats to primary or secondary values.

Mexican Immigration: A Threat to Secondary Values in the US?

Huntington's inquiry into what constitutes the cultural identity of Americans sounds a pessimistic note as to the degree to which Hispanic – largely Mexican – immigration threatens secondary values. It is important to note that Huntington's is not a nativist position in the ugly sense that "people like us" have to be people who look and sound like us. Rather, his definition of Americanness is civic, not ascriptive – anyone can become American as long as she accepts the values of what it means to be American. Huntington's problem with Mexican immigration is not cultural in that he does not like what Mexicans stand for. Rather, his is a logistical problem. There are simply too many people from a common cultural heritage for the host society to acculturate (Huntington 2004b, esp. ch. 2; also Gleason 1980; Citrin, Wong, and Duff 2001, esp. 76).

Other analysts are more optimistic, arguing that while Mexican immigrants have a greater propensity than most immigrant groups to retain their cultural heritage even into the third and fourth generations, this does not come at the expense of their cultural integration to the United States (e.g., Telles and Ortiz 2008). As noted in the previous chapter, the logic of acculturation holds that retaining heritage culture does not in and of itself constitute a rejection of host cultural values, and that, indeed, heritage and host cultural affinity vary independently (Phinney et al. 2001).[11] Thus, for Huntington's pessimistic scenario to be a realistic

---

11 To revisit our terms briefly, acculturation is taken to encompass both assimilation (rejection of the heritage culture in favour of the host culture) and integration (retention of the heritage culture in the private sphere and acceptance of the host culture in the public space).

threat, we need to see more than mere retention of the sort of cultural affinity associated with integration. For Mexican immigration to become a significant cultural threat, we would need to see instead widespread rejection of American values, or at least a strong preference for heritage values over the host values of American public life.

The rise of culturalist politics in the 1960s reawakened a sense of cultural threat in America reminiscent of that associated with the wave of immigration from Southern and Eastern Europe at the beginning of the twentieth century. Indeed, it was not until the Immigration Act of 1924 established national origin quotas that the "crusade for Americanization" on the part of both private organizations and public agencies subsided (Higham 2002, ch. 9). In 1965, however, the Immigration Act was amended to abolish national-origin quotas, a move that opened the door to wide-scale Mexican immigration. The coincidence (although it likely was not one) of the emerging culturalist movement and the 1965 Immigration Act gave rise to a growing sentiment on the part of Hispanic activists to assign a moral entitlement to linguistic rights. One of the fruits of this activism was the Bilingual Education Act. This law putatively sought to ease the linguistic acculturation of immigrants through creation of bilingual education as a prelude to educational mainstreaming. In practice, however, it has led to a perpetuation of Spanish-language retention (Citrin et al. 1990, 537; Huntington 2004a, 319–21).

Why pick on Mexico? Certainly there would appear to be nothing ideologically pernicious about Mexican immigration; there is nothing about Mexicanness that makes Mexican immigrants systemically less willing to accept the values of the United States than immigrants from other countries. Still, Huntington (2004a, ch. 9) points to a number of factors that distinguish Mexicans from other immigrant nationalities in the United States. First, Mexico is the only developing nation contiguous with a liberal republic, making it significant, if not surprising, that the income gap between the United States and Mexico is greater than for any other contiguous dyad (222–3). Second, Mexican immigration is numerically impressive. If we look only at those granted permanent resident status, Mexico has consistently outpaced all other countries in supplying immigrants to the United States over the past forty years. In each decade beginning in the 1950s, Mexico has supplied at least 10 per cent of all immigrants granted green cards, with a high-water mark in the 1990s of 28.2 per cent (United States 2011, Table 2).

Obviously these figures do not include illegal immigrants. As of 2008, the Pew Hispanic Center put the number of illegal immigrants in the United States at around 11.9 million. From the late 1990s through 2007, the Center estimates that the number of illegal immigrants to the United States outnumbered legal ones. Of the illegal immigrant population, roughly 60 per cent are estimated to have come from Mexico, although there is some evidence that the rate of illegal immigration to the US has levelled off or even declined in recent years (Passel and Cohn 2008).

Another distinguishing feature of Mexican immigration is geographic concentration. Mexican immigrants are not unique in their propensity to cluster (generally in the southwest and especially in California), but they are more likely to cluster than are members of other immigrant groups (see below). Family and cultural ties tend not to be randomly dispersed and immigrants are naturally drawn toward communities in which these ties exist. This is especially so for illegal immigrants, whose prospects for successful transition are greatly enhanced where there are personal contacts in place to assist them upon arrival (Massey and Capoferro 2008).

High levels of immigration from a particular ethno-national source tend to have three long-term consequences. First, immigration patterns are self-perpetuating, with immigrants facilitating the immigration of others through information on means of migration, resources to assist in migration, and logistical assistance with employment and housing in the host society. Second, critical mass allows for the creation of successful immigrant lobby groups which elevates pressure on the host society for, among other things, increased immigration (or associated issues such as decreased enforcement of border controls). These lobby groups find willing allies among those who for ideological (culturalists), economic (those to whose advantage it is to keep wages lower), or socio-cultural (members of linguistically compatible immigrant communities) reasons create political obstacles to stemming the tide of immigration.[12] Finally, high levels of immigration from a single heritage culture have the effect of retarding acculturation. Not only is the heritage cultural tradition kept alive with successive waves of new immigrants, but the expansion of heritage cultural communities creates less of a logistical impetus for immigrants to acculturate. If one can work and/or exist on a daily basis in her mother tongue, there is no pressing need to learn the language of the host society (Huntington 2004a, 228–9).

It is therefore not terribly surprising that Mexican immigrants have been comparatively slow to acculturate. Vigdor (2008) seeks to measure rates of immigrant acculturation in the United States along indices of

12 Evidence for the political power of Mexican immigration advocates can be seen in the facts that a) US immigration policy has favoured Mexico ahead of any other country with respect to legal immigration in recent years, and b) in far greater proportions than for other countries, Mexican immigrants are admitted on the basis of family (and not employment aptitude) criteria (Lazear 2007, 120).

economic issues, cultural issues,[13] civic issues, and a weighted composite of these three issue clusters.[14] There tends to be a good deal of variance in acculturation among immigrants from different heritage societies. In comparing ten large heritage groups,[15] immigrants from Mexico score the lowest on the composite, civic, and composite indices, below only China and India on the cultural index.[16] Although the process is beset with measurement issues, there is evidence that slow acculturation of Mexican immigrants persists into the second generation,[17] with (non-citizen) second-generation immigrants being considerably less integrated than similar immigrants from other countries. Indeed, the aggregated composite acculturation score for non-Mexican immigrants was 62, compared to 18 for Mexican immigrants (Vigdor 2008, ch. 5).

Symbolically, the most important indicator of acculturation is linguistic. Language, Horowitz suggests, represents a proxy for the relative importance of cultural groups in the public life of a society (1985, 219–24). Because logistics limit the number of public languages a nation can accommodate, the competition for linguistic status can be emotive and conflictual. This is especially so when we consider that knowledge of the prestige language is tied to economic life chances in a way that is mutually reinforcing (Horowitz 1985, 220–1). Even though the United States has no official language, English retains high cultural salience in terms of Americans' sense of Americanism, and as such, Americans feel the need to reaffirm that Americanism in the face of potential cultural threat (Citrin et al. 1990).

The politics of language turns on the extent to which linguistic retention represents a means for preservation of a private heritage culture, or, alternatively, serves as a basis for appropriating American secondary

13 Unfortunately, Vigdor does not disaggregate clear cultural indicators such as learning English and intermarriage rates from the far more ambiguous indicators of marital status and number of children.

14 Vigdor does not distinguish between assimilation and acculturation. Using data from 2006, Vigdor measures assimilation on a 100-point scale with 0 indicating perfect predictive distinction between an immigrant and a native-born American and 100 representing distinction that is no more predictive than tossing a coin.

15 Canada, China, Cuba, Dominican Republic, El Salvador, India, Korea, Mexico, the Philippines, and Vietnam.

16 Ordinal rankings mask some large differences. Mexican immigrants score just over 10 on the composite index, and is one of just four heritage groups to score under 30. On the civic assimilation index, Mexican immigrants score just over 20; with the exception of El Salvadorans, immigrants from all other heritage groups score at least twice as high.

17 This second generation, in order to maintain consistency in the data over time, consists of children who might have been born abroad, but were raised in the United States.

values. Potentially problematic for liberal republicanism is what has come to be known as cultural citizenship – the idea that integration into American society is insufficient for Mexican immigrants to retain authenticity.[18] From this perspective, true authenticity demands that retention of heritage culture not be restricted to the private realm, and instead be manifest in the public life of the host society (most pertinently with respect to linguistic education). Indeed, failure to create a public space for heritage values represents an intolerable violation of immigrants' citizenship rights (Rosaldo 1994; 1999). Cultural citizenship implies not only difference, but distinction. "A key element of cultural citizenship," according to a concept paper put forth by a working group of Latino cultural studies academics, is the ability of a cultural community to define "its interests, its binding solidarities, and its membership (who is and who is not part of the 'community')" (quoted in Silvestrini 2004, 44). The creation of a public space designed for, and quite possibly restricted to, certain immigrant cultures creates the potential for deep cultural fault lines that could threaten the integrity of the republic. Indeed, Americans need look no further than their northern border to see how potentially destabilizing such deep diversity can be.

Have Mexican immigrants acculturated sufficiently to ease fears of a cultural threat? The evidence is mixed. Lazear (2007) looks at data from the 2000 US Census to measure linguistic acculturation. Those data show that roughly 49 per cent of first-generation Mexican immigrants to the United States were fluent in English, compared with around 80 per cent for non-Mexican immigrants (see also similar interpretations of the data in Citrin et al. 2007, 35–7).

In addition to slower rates of language acquisition among first-generation immigrants, Mexican-Americans are more likely to retain heritage-language competence than most immigrant groups. Even by the fourth generation, almost half understand Spanish, a significant difference from European heritage groups, who are typically assimilated as monolinguistic by the third generation (Telles and Ortiz 2008, 187–8). Mexican immigrants' slower language acquisition reflects, but is not wholly explained by, the greater propensity of Mexican immigrants to cluster. On average, Mexican immigrants live in communities where about 15 per cent of the population is Mexican-born. By contrast,

18 The term is meant to connote the inherent incompatibility between formal citizenship on the one hand, and cultural authenticity on the other (Rosaldo 1994).

non-Mexican immigrants live in communities where less than 3 per cent of the population were born in their respective homelands.

In and of itself, of course, heritage-language retention constitutes no cultural challenge. By the second generation, Mexican immigrants generally acquire English-language competence. However, there are straws in the wind to suggest that this trend might be weakening. Huntington notes that bilingual education, particularly in New York State, is a euphemism for Spanish-language education. Children in some schools have exclusively Spanish curricula, come home from school and watch Spanish-language television, and can generally acquire goods and services in their native language. And while some English-language skills are generally acquired along the way, these skills are often insufficient for the requirements of all but the lowest-paying jobs, thereby perpetuating underclass status (2004a, 320–1).

Other variables contribute to the slowness of Mexican immigrants to achieve English-language competence. One is that on average, Mexican immigrants in the 2000 Census had been in the US for a shorter duration than immigrants from other countries. Another is that given the proximity of the two countries, many Mexican immigrants expect to return to Mexico and thus do not bother to invest the resources necessary to acquire linguistic competence. Yet another is that the numbers are skewed by the disproportionately large number of illegal Mexican immigrants who, while counted in the Census, are not in a position to avail themselves of resources that would allow them to learn English fluently (Lazear 2007). Finally, Mexican immigrants tend to be of lower socio-economic status than immigrants from other nations. In a dynamic similar to residential clustering, occupational concentration tends to foster linguistic retention and ethnic identification (Yancey, Ericksen, and Juliani 1976, 392–4).

How problematic is it for Spanish to have a place in the American public space? For many Americans, the answer is that it is deeply problematic. If we look at the distinction between mass and (political) elite preferences with respect to English as the official language of the United States, we can see that the cultural citizenship initiative has a good deal of political influence. Citrin and his colleagues examine "official English" initiatives in various states, finding that in states with large Hispanic populations, elected officials were uniformly unwilling to pass legislation privileging English as the official language of the state. This speaks either to the fact that host-culture citizens in those states were not particularly preferential on the matter, or that they were, but Hispanic activists were sufficiently mobilized to have such legislation defeated or tabled.

The latter appears to be the case (or at least was during the 1980s). Of the six states that are currently at least 20 per cent Hispanic, four permit popular plebiscites.[19] In each of these cases, voters overwhelmingly passed unsuccessful initiatives to make English the state's official language (Citrin et al. 1990, 541–4).

Los Angeles County Social Surveys from 1994 through 2000 show that Hispanics as a whole are far less likely than Asians, Blacks, or Whites to favour making English the official language (for the purposes of conducting government business) of the United States. Indeed, if we combine both immigrants and American Hispanics, we find that only 32 per cent favour making English the official language, as opposed to 69.8 per cent of Asians, 71.2 per cent of Blacks, and 73.7 per cent of Whites. On the other hand, much of the distinction melts away by the third generation, with 67.5 per cent advocating English as the official language of the US. It would therefore seem that English is not under immediate threat in America. Certainly the vast majority of Hispanics in all immigrant generations surveyed in a 2002 Pew Latino Survey believe that success in America is contingent upon learning English, with only 16 per cent of third-generation Hispanics believing otherwise (Citrin et al. 2007, 38–40).

A second dimension of acculturation to American secondary values is national identification. As with linguistic assimilation, descendants of Mexican immigrants are less likely than descendants of other immigrant groups to share a cultural affinity with America's secondary values. Telles and Ortiz (2008) find that in the fourth generation, 29 per cent of Mexican immigrant descendants identified as both Mexican and American, and 37 per cent as just American, meaning that roughly two-thirds of the great-grandchildren of Mexican immigrants can be said to have assimilated or integrated.[20] That leaves one-third who have not.

19 The six are Arizona, California, Colorado, Florida, New Mexico, and Texas. Only the first four permit popular initiatives.

20 The population from which Telles and Ortiz draw their sample is descendants of immigrants who were part of Grebler, Moore, and Guzman's (1970) study of immigrant attitudes in San Antonio and Los Angeles. De la Garza, Falcon, and Garcia's (1996) findings are less ominous. Their sample of 1,546 Mexican-Americans and 456 Anglos were asked two questions: 1) How strong is your love of the United States? 2) And how proud are you to be an American? For both questions respondents were given four options: Extremely strong (proud); very strong (proud); somewhat strong (proud); or not very strong (proud). Respondents were classified according to level of acculturation. Anglos were assumed to be completely acculturated. For the other respondents, classifications were based on native or foreign birth, and dominant language (English, bilingual, or Spanish). The authors found an apparent distinction between Anglos and less-acculturated

The cultural destiny of this one-third informs the threat level associated with large-scale Mexican immigration. And while roughly half of these individuals are socially marginalized insofar as they fail to identify with either culture, the other half (or 17 per cent of the whole fourth-generation sample) born and raised in America continues to reject its secondary values in favour of identifying (largely or exclusively) with the values of a foreign country.[21]

High heritage-language retention rates combined with significant levels of alienation from American secondary values creates a large pool of potential cultural appropriationists. Of course, that is not the same thing as saying that these individuals are anything more than passive cultural separatists, or that their long-term aspirations are cultural appropriation. However, given the success of Hispanic activists in carving out a public space for Spanish in America, it is of some concern that there exists a significant constituency that is at least ideologically predisposed to the creation of a parallel set of secondary values in America.

All in all, while the evidence suggests some worrisome facts about the potential for cultural colonization, it is far too early to say that Mexican immigration represents a cultural threat to America. Within three or four generations, two-thirds to three-quarters of Mexican immigrants appear to acculturate. Indeed, if we look at patriotism as another means of getting at national identification, it is pretty clear from National Election Survey data that Hispanics as a whole are patriotically indistinct from other groups. Questions from 2004 pertaining to love of America and pride in the flag suggest that the percentage of Whites who respond positively is 91 and 85 per cent respectively. For Hispanics the numbers are 91 and 86 (Citrin et al. 2007, 42–3). The aforementioned study by de la Garza, Falcon, and Garcia (1996) supports the finding that Mexican-Americans are no less patriotic than any other segment of the US population.[22]

Mexican-Americans when it came to patriotism and other elements of civic integration. However, after controlling for salient demographic factors such as social class, the authors found no statistically significant differences in patriotism between Anglos and any of the six classifications of Mexican-Americans (1996, Table 2).

21 Rejection of host values can be taken coming or going. It can reflect chauvinism on the part of the immigrant group, or it can reflect nativism on the part of the host society. But the purpose here is less to assign blame than to assess the threat.

22 Another measure of patriotism is voluntary membership in the US Armed Services. While Hispanics have generally been under-represented in the military relative to their share of the population, the past two decades have seen an increase in Hispanic enrollment. Under-representation is not ipso facto proof of a weaker commitment to country. Since Hispanics are significantly under-represented in the officer corps, it is possible that

This is not to say that Hispanics may not have a different vision than non-Hispanics for the America they both love. But such is the history of America, with each successive wave of immigration being accommodated through cultural give and take. Indeed, it would appear that despite the tidal wave of Mexican immigration, acculturation has significantly outpaced cultural colonization. This could change if some indeterminate demographic tipping point is reached, but America's relatively stable TFR (which is helped, incidentally, by Mexican immigration) and comparatively modest rates of welfare spending suggest that America will be able to regulate its (legal) immigration flow without dire socio-demographic consequences.

Islamic Immigration: A Threat to European Primary Values?

While a threat to secondary values is cause for concern, of even greater worry is the threat that immigration poses for liberal republican primary values. This is the cultural challenge that Europe appears poised to confront. With levels of cultural homogeneity historically greater than the United States, Europe has been less successful in acculturating immigrants. The problem has not been uniform within Europe: some countries have been guilty of excessive nativism; others have been deficient in promoting secondary values.

France and Germany are good examples of the former. In those countries, the cultural isolation of Muslim immigrants, justified in the latter case on the fictive grounds that migrants were but temporary guest workers, has resulted in a greater challenge to cultural norms than would have been the case had there been greater emphasis on integration during the first waves of Muslim immigration in the 1960s. Conversely, countries such as Britain and the Netherlands appear inadvertently to have facilitated cultural separatism by being hypersensitive to cultural autonomy. Indeed, it was not until the middle of the 2000s that seminal incidents of terror in Great Britain (the 2005 subway bombing), the Netherlands (the 2004 murder of Theo Van Gogh), and Spain (the 2004 train bombings) compelled these countries toward more acculturalist strategies (Van den Brink 2007; Vaisse 2008; Cherribi 2010, ch. 2).

This is not to say that the shift has been absolute. The government of the UK, for example, still recognizes (through social and inheritance

---

differential treatment has contributed to under representation. This hypothesis is bolstered by the fact that Hispanic high school students show a greater propensity to serve than do non-Hispanic White students (Segal, Thanner, and Segal 2007, esp. 58; Segal et al. 1999).

benefits) polygamy. And the Archbishop of Canterbury created a buzz in 2008 when he proclaimed the inevitability of sharia law creeping into British public life (Bano 2008; Lebl 2010, 50; Bennett 2011). The shift in the Netherlands might be the most extreme. The success of its consociational model in mediating religious differences between Catholics and Protestants presumably led to the same pillarization strategy with Muslims.[23] Cultural autonomy, in other words, was the prevailing ethos – even to the point of state-sanctioned cultural separatism. This pillarization strategy as it pertained to Catholics and Protestants, which collapsed in the aftermath of secularization in Europe, represented so much social scaffolding. With the disintegration of the religious pillars came the integration of Dutch Catholics and Protestants. As such, there was cause for optimism that the same dynamic would occur for Muslims. But by the mid-2000s, the Dutch government conceded that social pillarization had failed as an integrative strategy for Muslims and sought more overtly assimilationist policies (Lenard 2010, 310).

Why pick on Islam? As with Mexican immigration to the United States, Islamic immigration is important in the sense that Muslims represent the largest immigrant group (if we can classify these diverse national populations as a single group) in the EU.[24] Moreover, and again like Mexican immigration to the US, there is a tendency for Muslim immigrants to cluster in urban neighbourhoods. In distinction to Mexican immigrants to America, though, there is far more evidence of Muslim cultural separatism (as well as host-society nativism) than we see with Mexicans in the United States.[25] Even more significantly, what distinguishes Muslim immigration is the source of tension, bordering on incompatibility, between the primary values of liberal republicanism on the one hand and resurgent, fundamentalist Islam on the other.

23 Pillarization represents extreme insularity among social groups. In a pillarized system, the masses within a social pillar will have only limited social interaction with the masses in other pillars.

24 That said, Muslims make up a relatively small percentage of the total Western European population of just over 400 million. According to the Pew Foundation, there were approximately 17 million Muslims in Western Europe in 2010, up from under 10 million in 1990 (Pew Forum on Religion and Public Life 2010). Savage, relying on numbers from the State Department, put the number of Muslims in Europe at 23 million as of 2003. Hard numbers are not easy to come by given that many European countries prohibit questions pertaining to religious affiliation on their official census forms (2004, 26).

25 This is not to suggest that the United States is free of nativism. However, there is a greater historical tradition of cultural diversity within immigrant societies like the US than there is in countries whose nationality has traditionally been informed by cultural homogeneity and reinforced in many cases through ethno-linguistic distinctiveness.

There is nothing theologically determinative in Islam that makes it incompatible with liberal republican values. As with members of other faiths, Muslims run the gamut from secular to devout, and from apolitical to extremist. Those most committed to a public face for Islam are fundamentalists. By fundamentalism I mean commitment to the construction of a society in which the primary values are informed by the founding principles of a faith. Where the Islamic moral law, sharia, is confined to the private sphere, it is reasonable to treat Islam like any other faith in a pluralistic society, which is to say one that must reconcile itself to liberal republican primary values. However, the public face of sharia in resurgent Islam rejects a number of liberal republican values – including the idea of a public place for women; Western conceptions of freedom, particularly as they pertain to issues of sexual behaviour and materialism; tolerance of other faiths within the public square; and even the locus of moral obligation, which resides within the *ummah* (or localized community) rather than the republic itself – in favour of a moral code that conflates the public and private spaces (although see Esposito and Mogahed 2007, ch. 2).[26]

Perhaps most problematic for liberal republicanism is the fundamentalist imperative that the teachings of the faith, in particular the Koran and the traditional ways of the prophet (Sunnah), take precedence over the positive law such that the mullah maintains ultimate authority to condemn by edict violators of the moral law to death. This adherence to traditional ways is particularly problematic as it pertains to the rights of women, many of whom find themselves under the total control of their fathers or husbands. This control is reinforced by the acceptance of domestic violence, including rape and honour killings, as a means of disciplining women who refuse to wear a veil or keep themselves at home (Lebl 2010, 49–50).

The Koran implies a binary vision of the world: the *Dural Iman* (abode of belief) and the *Dural Kufr* (abode of disbelief). Radical fundamentalist theology modifies this distinction to reflect the *Dural Islam* (abode of peace, characterized by Muslim governance) and *Dural Harb* (abode of war, characterized by pre-Muslim governance) (Ali 2010, 184).

It is important to recognize that while fundamentalism is the source of most terrorist violence, not all fundamentalists advocate or even support such actions (Benard 2003, 4). Islamic fundamentalism can be broken down into two sub-categories. Scriptural fundamentalists are those

26 An aphorism of the Muslim Brotherhood in Europe is revealing in this sense: "Allah is our objective; The Prophet is our leader; The Qur'ân is our constitution" (Laurence 2012, 72).

whose political actions are instrumental to the realization of objectives grounded in literal, if sometimes selective, readings of the Koran. Radical fundamentalists are those for whom Islam is instrumental to the realization of political goals. In its radical manifestation, Islamic fundamentalism represents the ultimate anti-system movement in liberal republics, seeking to Islamize the West through any means, including political violence. That said, fundamentalists represent a minority among Muslims. Even in predominantly Islamic countries such as Egypt, Indonesia, Jordan, Pakistan, and Turkey, when asked if they identified more closely with groups who want to modernize their countries or with Islamic fundamentalists, a significant majority in each country (60 to 70 per cent) identified with modernizers. Only in Pakistan did as many as one-third (34 per cent) identify with fundamentalists (Pew Global Attitudes Project 2006).

Despite the fact that Muslims represent a small percentage of the total Western European population, there are significant pockets of Muslim concentration. In numerous European cities such as Amsterdam, Copenhagen, Berlin, Birmingham, Brussels, London, Malmo, Marseilles, Oslo, Paris, Rotterdam, and The Hague, predominantly Muslim neighbourhoods make up significant portions (10 to 25 per cent) of the urban populations. Muhammed is the second most popular boy's name in the United Kingdom. And while demographic trends are notoriously fickle, Muslim populations in Europe have significantly higher TFRs – in some cases up to three times as high – than do members of the cultural mainstream. Indeed, as of 2003, roughly one-third of the Muslim populations in Belgium, France, and Britain were under the age of twenty (and under the age of fifteen in the case of Britain). The comparable figure for the mainstream populations in these countries is closer to one-fifth (Savage 2004, 28–9; Jenkins 2006, 521, 533; Lebl 2010, 48). If present trends continue, despite a fairly modest population base, some analysts conclude that Muslims could represent majority populations in some parts of Europe by the middle of this century (Savage 2004, 29, esp. fn. 14). While in all likelihood this will not be the case, it is reasonable to assume that between European immigration demands and comparatively lower TFRs among mainstream Europeans, Muslims will not remain numerically marginal in Europe for long.

This demographic change is not, of course, evidence of cultural threat. It is reasonable to assume that as the Muslim population expands, Islamic culture will become less marginal and as a result less insular. For the present, however, relatively marginal Muslim populations find it difficult to influence public life through the normal political process. Muslim political leaders have found it more efficacious to rely on community organization and cultural separation from the mainstream. It is through social and religious organizations that putatively operate outside of the political process that Islamic fundamentalists construct their power base.

Strategically, fundamentalist Islamic leaders have sought to politicize the young, principally second-generation Muslims living in Europe (Laurence 2012, 72–104).[27] As with immigrant populations everywhere, second- and third-generation European Muslims tend toward cultural ambivalence. On the one hand, there is the attractive side of liberal republicanism – freedom and attendant economic and educational opportunities. On the other, the repulsive side concerns that self-same freedom as it pertains to the sexualization of women and rampant consumerism, as well as cultural exclusivity and secularism (Shore 2006, 7–8). The danger is that by seeking to win the hearts and minds of young Muslims, Islamic fundamentalists have both a head start and a greater commitment to winning a culture struggle that many European governments enamoured of cultural sensitivity have been slow to acknowledge (see Niblett 2006, 4).

Herein lies the potential for a silent revolution, which Jenkins (2006, 519) calls the greatest threat to many European countries since the 1930s. This strategy relies on the camouflage afforded by multiculturalism to create separate, all but self-sufficient communities within European states (Benard 2003; Weissberg 2005; Jenkins 2007, esp. 187). Cultural appropriation is made easier by the relative isolation of Muslim cultural communities in Europe. As noted, European countries have espoused a curious mix of nativist and culturalist policies toward Muslim immigrants. Such imposition of cultural isolation on the one hand, and tolerance for it on the other, has afforded a convenient cover for social radicalization within the private sphere. As Leslie Lebl puts it, this "tone-deaf approach that ignores the danger of [culturally] accommodating people who don't play by the same rules has helped to create a new form of European Islam" (2010, 49).

This tone-deafness has been reinforced by the possibly mistaken idea that strong European economies will smooth over minor religious and cultural differences in the long run. Economic modernity, this logic goes, has a secularizing effect that will militate against conflict. We have already noted the potential flaw in the logic that modernity will militate

27 The most important politically active fundamentalist networks in Europe are grounded in the tradition of three principal Islamic movements: the *Ikhwan al-Muslimin* (Muslim Brotherhood) which is Arab, principally Egyptian, in origin; the *Jama'at-i Islami* (Islamic Community) of Indo-Pakistani beginnings; and the *Millî Görüş* (National Vision) which emanated out of Turkey (Laurence 2012, ch. 3).

against theological conflict. But whether or not it is so is in some ways beside the point. It is important to recognize that Muslims represent an economic underclass in Europe, something that economic modernization will be slow or even inadequate to address. When the secular/religious divide is superimposed on a reinforcing class cleavage, as the case of Northern Ireland, or Lebanon in the mid-1970s suggests, the effect can be volatile (Jenkins 2006, 536).

High rates of unemployment among Muslim youths – 40 to 50 per cent in Germany and France for example – have cultural implications as well.[28] Generous welfare provisions have kept this from becoming a serious economic issue as it pertains to inter-cultural relations. But welfare provisions have other cultural repercussions. For example, rather than serving as a bridge to integration and social cohesion, some Muslims interpret welfare payments as *jiziya*, or the tax paid by non-Muslims in Muslim societies in deference to their submission to Islam. Furthermore, generous welfare provisions have not prevented violent crime. Indeed, many European cities feature infamous no-go zones, neighbourhoods that police and municipal officials have more or less ceded to Muslims who have proclaimed non-Muslims to be unwelcome (Carr 2006; Lebl 2010, 51). These neighbourhoods effectively represent Islamic microstates governed by sharia law. An attempt to formalize the status of such microstates in Britain, by a group called Muslims Against the Crusades, has resulted in a campaign to declare twelve British cities (including what they call Londonstan) into independent emirates (Kern 2011).

Obviously it is difficult to get a handle on how many European Muslims advocate fundamentalism and imposition of sharia law. A study by the Pew Global Attitudes Project (2006)[29] finds that almost half (47 per cent) of British Muslims felt that a natural conflict exists between being

---

28 While the unemployment rate for non-EU migrants (albeit not all Muslim) is typically double the rate for EU natives, the Netherlands has fared particularly poorly. In 1999, to cite the high-water mark, non-EU migrants were almost 5.5 times more likely to be unemployed than native Europeans in the Netherlands. In 1998, about one-fifth of all non-Western migrants were on welfare; native Dutch were less likely to be on welfare by a factor of 10. Despite disproportionately high state funding, immigrants were 2.5 times more likely to drop out of high school than native Dutch; almost two-fifths of Moroccan immigrants and over one-third of Turkish immigrants were dropouts. In 1997, almost one-third of inmates in Dutch prisons were foreign (Joppke 2007, 6).

29 Based on over 14,000 interviews in thirteen nations. The project featured oversampling of Muslims in Western Europe. The number of Muslim respondents in the four Western European countries discussed in the survey was as follows: France N=400; Germany N=413; Great Britain N=412; Spain N=402. In predominantly Muslim countries, the breakdown was Egypt N=936; Indonesia N=1223; Jordan N=972; Pakistan N=909; Turkey N=1001. In addition, 468 Muslims in Nigeria were included in the sample.

a devout Muslim and living in a modern (liberal republican) society.[30] A significant majority of Muslims in each of the four Western European countries considered by the Pew survey believed that violence against civilian targets in defence of Islam from its enemies was never justified. Of course, that leaves a considerable minority, ranging from about a quarter to about a third in most cases, who believed that civic violence was at least sometimes justified.[31] An ICM poll taken in the aftermath of the 2005 subway bombing revealed that 20 per cent of British Muslims felt some sympathy with the feelings and motives of the bombers. The same poll found that 40 per cent of British Muslims favoured there being areas of Britain that are predominantly Muslim and in which sharia governed at least part of the public space (ICM 2006, 11, 14). As reported in the previous chapter, a survey of young German Muslims' attitudes reported in the mid-1990s by Wilhelm Heitmeyer and colleagues found that nearly one-third believed that Islam should come to power in every country (Shore 2006, 42–3).

Even among the less radicalized, relations between Muslims and non-Muslims in Western Europe are not good. There are deep cultural divisions between Westerners and Muslims living in Europe. At least a quarter of Muslims in each of the four Western European nations surveyed found Westerners to be selfish, arrogant, violent, greedy, immoral, and fanatical.[32] British Muslims held particularly negative views, with a majority agreeing with each of these descriptions, save for the last. To look at this another way, only 10 per cent of British Muslims found that none of these six descriptors applied to Westerners (16 per cent of French Muslims, 20 per cent of German Muslims, and 26 per cent of Spanish Muslims also found that none of these descriptors portrayed Westerners accurately). A sizable percentage of Muslims in four large Western European countries thus would appear to be at least somewhat alienated from their fellow citizens. A majority of both Muslims and non-Muslims in these countries considered relations between Muslims around the world and people living in Western countries to be bad.[33] This does not

30 Of French Muslims, 28 per cent believed this, as did 36 per cent of German Muslims and 25 per cent of Spanish Muslims.

31 In France the percentage was 35; Spain followed, with 25 per cent believing this; 24 per cent of British Muslims believed that violence against civilians was sometimes justified. German Muslims were considerably less likely to support violence, with only 13 per cent believing that violence was sometimes justified.

32 Minor exceptions are that only 24 per cent of Spanish Muslims found Westerners to be violent, and only 21 per cent found them fanatical.

33 An exception is Spanish Muslims, only 23 per cent of whom considered such relations to be bad.

translate directly into a failure to accept the values of Western societies, although it is suggestive of a significant cultural divide.[34]

European governments have started to fight back. The first step has been to recognize the pernicious effects of cultural separatism, which, born of either nativism or excessive cultural tolerance, has contributed to the alienation of Muslims in Europe. One goal has been to integrate Muslims, long economically marginalized in many European countries, more fully into the economy. France, for example, while not targeting Muslims specifically, has sought to offer incentives to businesses that introduce young, not previously employed individuals into the workforce.

Another objective has been to make cultural integration a requirement of citizenship. As such, in 2004, Britain began making a degree of English proficiency, as well as knowledge of British history and culture, a precondition to receive citizenship. The (post–Van Gogh) Netherlands implemented an imperative for all immigrants to take almost 400 hours of Dutch language classes. An additional requirement, implemented in 2006, mandated immigrants to watch the film *To the Netherlands*, which features topless women and homosexual intimacy (Niblett 2006, 7–8; Associated Press 2006), although how efficacious this is in combating Islamic fundamentalism is open to question. Denmark and Sweden raised the age at which spousal immigration is permitted to a minimum of twenty-four so as to limit the practice of arranged marriages with young brides.

European governments have also adopted a stronger commitment to law and order as a means of limiting their countries' exposure to terrorism. As such, in 2002, the Single Warrant Act gave police in one European country the ability to arrest suspects on crimes committed in another. Britain, France, Germany, Italy, and Spain have begun immigration restrictions and fingerprinting requirements as a condition of obtaining visas. Denying admittance to, and expelling, radical imams is another means by which European governments have sought to protect themselves, as is criminalizing such activity as incitement to terrorism and violence (Niblett 2006, 7–9).

As with the case of Mexican immigration to the United States, it is too early to reach for the panic button in Europe. But the prospect of Islamic appropriation of primary values in Europe is not to be dismissed lightly.

---

34 This point must be qualified by the fact that European populations in general either have not been, or currently are not, the most accommodating of hosts. In addition to the *hijab* and burka controversies in France, Swiss voters, for example, decided in 2009 to ban minarets from mosques. Anti-Muslim xenophobia extends to the mainstream media (see Carens 2006), further exacerbating the cultural division in Europe.

Clearly there is a hard core of Islamic fundamentalism that, while not all that numerically impressive as compared to the population of Europe as a whole, has been far more dedicated to the cause of value appropriation than European governments have been in defending themselves against such appropriation. But this is not, as Schulman (2009) suggests, a case of continental Stockholm Syndrome. European publics have begun to articulate their concerns forcefully and unambiguously. And governments have started to take notice. New Left European governments' wholehearted acceptance of cultural separatism has begun to give way to a greater emphasis on acquiring host society values. There is no reason to believe that this trend will reverse itself. Nor are there good grounds to catastrophize the gap in TFRs between host and immigrant populations in Europe. While this demographic disparity will no doubt have an effect, demographic trends are already showing a moderation in TFRs throughout the developing world.

Europe does have a problem, born both of nativism and culturalism. Its TFRs are too low, its reliance upon immigration is too high, and its commitment to social welfare is too deep simply to dismiss the problem out of hand. But there would appear to be time to address the problem by recognizing and reversing the threat before it becomes too large to contain.

CONCLUSION

If we look at where we have been and where we are going, the challenges faced by liberal republics in the coming years become clearer. The postwar rise of culturalism – manifest most obviously in the civil rights movement, the post-materialist revolution, and the demographic crisis that has seen declining fertility rates, static welfare spending, and increased immigration – has forced liberal republics to examine how they deal with increased diversity. That examination suggests that countries have made a number of false steps. Indeed, the timidity with which liberal republics have asserted the imperative for immigrant acculturation has helped to stimulate the challenge of cultural appropriation in liberal republics.

Weak acculturation policies make it more difficult for countries to defend their primary and secondary values in the face of large-scale immigration. The obvious threat is that raised by cultural contestation and versoculturalism. However, the more clear nature of these threats should not blind us to less momentous challenges. More benign forms of culturalism may enhance justice in liberal republics, but even the most benign – multiculturalism – brings with it externalities that need to be recognized. That is, cultural appropriation might represent the death of the organism, but more benign forms of culturalism have the potential to put it in its weakened condition. One of the lessons of the European case is that well-intentioned culturalism can bring with it negative externalities. It can, as we have noted, affect the imperative to acculturate new citizens of different political backgrounds. More critically, multiculturalism provides effective camouflage for more sinister forms of culturalism.

Even the most benign forms of culturalism – forms that enhance liberal republican understandings of justice – can place stress on a society's sense of usness.· Factionalism – the breakdown of a sense of usness – is therefore a source of concern to those with an interest in the stability of liberal republics. This is no great insight; traditional republicans dedicated tremendous effort to counteract the evils of faction. The Madisonian solution articulated in *Federalist 10* (Publius 1961) militated against the threat of faction, such that the term has lost many of its negative connotations. However, the Madisonian defence against the negative effects of faction is operative only in the context of an active and involved citizenry. The Madisonian solution, in other words, is institutionally conditioned. It is not universally applicable. Where institutions are constructed in such a way as to undermine the effects of civic participation, factions become less benign.

The mandate of the next chapter is to examine the institutional structure of liberal republics with an eye toward the effects institutions have on a society's sense of usness. We will therefore look at the challenge to liberal republicanism in the context of what we have called primary (constitutional and jurisprudential) and secondary (legislative) rules.

8

Challenging the Participatory Ideal

IN THE LAST CHAPTER WE EXPLORED culturalist challenges to liberal republicanism, suggesting that while cultural appropriation represents an obvious and overt threat, milder forms of culturalism pose their own challenges. Specifically, we suggested that cultural separatism can help to pave the way for cultural appropriation, or indeed can metamorphose into it. The corollary to changes in values is changes in rules. Here, cultural appropriation is not particularly interesting insofar as a revolutionary change in rules represents a coup, not a cultural challenge. In this chapter I wish to explore the challenge to liberal republican rules posed by status-seekers, whom we have defined as those pursuing institutionalized political privilege for discrete essentialist groups.

Status-seeking is not dedicated to cultural appropriation or challenging the dominance of the dominant group. That is, the privilege sought by status-seeking groups is not the same sort of privilege enjoyed by the dominant group. I use the term *privilege* in two ways. First, privilege constitutes an enhanced recognition of the relevance – or status – of an essentialist culture compared to the recognition afforded the cultures of other essentialist communities. Second, privilege reflects procedural modifications designed to skew outcomes in favour of the privileged essentialist community. It represents, in other words, status afforded through specially constructed rules.

Privilege can attach to legislative or constitutional rules. For legislative rules, the most common form of privilege is special representation, or modifying electoral rules to skew the distribution of legislative seats, for example, legislative seat quotas for representatives of essentialist communities. Quotas have been a particularly popular means of ensuring gender equality in representative bodies. Indeed, more than one hundred countries currently employ, for example, some form of legislative gender quota (Caul 2001; Krook, Lovenduski, and Squires 2009,

781). Additionally, Belgium, France, Italy, New Zealand, Portugal and Spain all maintain quotas for members of other subaltern communities in their lower legislative chambers (Krook and O'Brien 2010, 257–8).

Special representation also takes the form of essentialist group vetoes over applicable legislation. Belgium and Hungary are examples of countries that have afforded privileged groups cultural vetoes (Krizsán 2000; Swenden 2002). Canada's failed Charlottetown Accord of 1992 would have gone even further, and provided Aboriginal peoples with a sovereign level of government, coordinating with the federal government and the provinces.

Less formally, creative re-districting is an effective and less overt means of privileging discrete groups. Over thirty countries use some form of unofficial seat reservation (Reynolds 2005). The United States, for example, has long relied on such affirmative gerrymandering to ensure minimally adequate levels of African-American congressional representation. Similarly, Dutch consociationalism through the 1960s was an uncodified arrangement among elites to privilege relevant essentialist communities in the name of political stability (Lijphart 1977). Consociational principles have been applied prescriptively in some form or another to a number of other countries, perhaps most successfully in Northern Ireland.

Obviously, privilege in the form of special representation does not just happen. It is the product of political activism – status-seeking – on the part of subaltern essentialist communities. In the strictest sense, of course, special representation is antithetical to liberal republicanism. As we have already discussed, liberal republicanism conceives diversity of tertiary values in *spatial,* not essentialist, terms. In practice, however, particularly when they are informal, liberal republics often accept qualifications to the spatial imperative.

For culturalist status-seekers, legislative privileges are meaningful. However, they are rarely sufficient for overcoming what can be thought of as the majoritarian bias of legislatures. Where the cultural values of even privileged essentialist communities clash with the salient values of the dominant community, legislatures are considered more likely to gratify the demands of the more powerful group. For this reason, privileges institutionalized through constitutional rules constitute a far more highly prized objective. As we have discussed, such pre-commitment to essentialist tertiary values immunizes these values from change through the normal political process. Even more important, it can serve as a launching pad for extending political privileges (Cairns 1990; Manfredi and Lusztig 1998).

FACTION AND PRE-COMMITMENT

As it pertains to liberal republicanism, constitutional status-seeking is problematic in a number of ways. First, it has the potential to intrude into areas of public policy that previously had been contested through the normal political process. It represents, in other words, an erosion of the capacity of individuals to govern themselves in that it restricts the range of issues subject to political contestation. Second, it represents a qualification to formal equality. Constitutional status effectively affords individuals differential protection under law. The same can be said of federalism, of course. However, the difference is that successful status-seeking results in differential protection based upon who a person happens to be and not on where she chooses to live. Third, status-seeking is potentially erosive of a sense of national identity or usness insofar as it takes policy contestation out of the iterative legislative arena in which civic dialogue and compromise hold sway.

There are implications here that need unpacking. We have already noted that a significant advantage of civic participation is popular input into contestation over legislative rules, as well as popular legitimization of that process. Eventual losers in the political process go in with the recognition that they will not necessarily have their objectives gratified, but at least they will have their voices heard. Indeed, even if the outcome is not to their liking, they may well effect a degree of compromise in the final legislative product.

Losers in the constitutional process, by contrast, are assured of no such mitigation. With respect to formal constitutional rules, they are relatively far removed from the process, although they may have some input into the ratification process. As discussed below, this was among the problems that Canada experienced when it patriated its Constitution in 1982, and with the 1987 Meech Lake Accord, designed to correct some of the hard feelings born of patriation. Losers are often even more removed when it comes to evolutionary constitutional rules. Indeed, unless their representatives are granted *amicus* status, their voices are excluded from the process altogether. In such cases, popular governance is replaced by elite governance. The implication is that erstwhile self-governing citizens do not exercise sufficiently good judgment prudential to arrive at appropriate policy outcomes.

Given the potential for the procedural exclusion of losers, constitutional status-seeking has the propensity to factionalize. While factionalism is inherent in meaningful political participation, it also has the potential to be corrupted where rival sources of political authority

– legislatures and courts, for example – compete for the loyalty and support of discrete constituents (Dobel 1978).

The Madisonian, free-market solution is to permit political contestation within clearly delineated bounds. The process, in other words, mandates consensus as to the rules of the game. Functionally this means that factionalism is benign only where there is reasonableness and tolerance – where there is a greater commitment to procedural order than to substantive victory along any one policy dimension. Generally speaking, what this means is that factionalism is healthier when it pertains to contestation over legislative rules than when it pertains to contestation over constitutional rules.

To make sense of the complex relationship between constitutional and legislative rules, we need to be more nuanced in our understanding of the former. Constitutional rules are necessary, both as a means to, and a necessary restriction on, civic self-governance. When we speak of *means* we recognize that some constitutional rules are process-enabling (Ely 1980, 74–5; Monahan 1987, 136–8). They are rules for making rules, laying out the formal distribution of authority for the various departments and levels of government. When we speak of *restriction* we recognize that some constitutional rules represent protection against a collective failure of rationality.

Societies are as vulnerable to akratic distortion of rational choices as individuals are. They are capable of passing laws, in other words, that magnify the importance of short-term objectives that come at the expense of more cherished long-term values. It is to protect against social akrasia that societies put themselves under some form of voluntary constraint through the use of constitutional rules (Publius 1961, No. 49; Elster 1979; Holmes 1988; Waldron 1999a, 266–70). Voluntary constraint preserves society's capacity to govern itself by immunizing rules that are fundamental to self-government from transitory social preferences. Pre-commitment to voluntary constraint protects primary values from change through the normal political process.

Pre-commitment to What?

The constitutional rules of restrictions on civic self-governance are of two types: rules that pre-commit to primary values, and rules that pre-commit to the *prioritization* of primary values. The former represents a catalogue of primary values; the latter discriminates among these values so that we privilege some values ahead of others. Value-prioritization occurs under two types of circumstance. The first is where there is social consensus. Under these conditions, it is reasonable to institutionalize value-prioritization through formal constitutional rules. An example is the Fourth Amendment right against unreasonable search and seizure which Americans generally consider to be more important than the right to security of the person that a preventive invasion of privacy might help to ensure.

The second circumstance is where no social consensus exists. Here value-prioritization is settled reasonably by deferring to legislative rules at either the federal or state level. It is not conducive to political stability, in other words, to pre-commit to value-prioritization on which we cannot generally agree. This is why liberal republics generally do not seek to establish official religions; or if they do, it does not intrude into religious tolerance. Where no social consensus can be said to exist, reasonableness demands tolerance instead of pre-commitment.

Liberal republics occasionally do, but generally do not, violate standards of reasonableness through formal constitutional rules. Indeed, it is to ensure against this that amending formulae are constructed so as to ensure broad and deep value consensus. But liberal republics often do violate the standards of reasonableness through evolutionary constitutional rules. To give a more descriptive name to the juridical resolution of value-prioritization I will call this creeping pre-commitment.

Rules, Values, and Pre-commitment

So far the argument has been rather neat and tidy. Constitutional rules for value-prioritization should exist only when a reasonable standard of social consensus has been realized. But in reality, things are not often so clear. Sometimes there is no consensus as to whether or not there *is* social consensus. Sometimes a strong majority of individuals might have a preference to prioritize a certain set of values, but an intensely preferential minority might not. How large and how diverse does a social consensus have to be before it is considered reasonable to pre-commit to formal constitutional rules?

Moreover, even where a consensus about a consensus exists, it is not always clear how far that consensus extends. For example, we can assume the existence of a social consensus that the right to life takes priority over all other rights. This being the case, the prescriptive solution for reproduction rights would be to impose formal constitutional rules outlawing abortion. However, there is *not* a social consensus as to whether or not the fetus constitutes a rights-bearing entity. This being the case, constitutional rules outlawing abortion would not be appropriate.

Such ambiguity does not stop the argument in its tracks. Just the opposite, in fact. Ambiguity as to reasonable social consensus speaks to the argument that in a self-governing liberal republic, constitutional rules must be imposed with a light hand. If there is no social consensus as to whether or not there *is* social consensus, constitutional rules are not appropriate to regulate the issue at hand. Dedicated as it is to liberty, equality, and a common social purpose, the liberal republican default position on value-prioritization lies in deference to *legislative* rules.

Because liberal republicanism holds that all individuals are equal in their capacity for moral agency, there is no justification for removing contentious issues from the hands of a self-governing people. Where such removal occurs – where issues best regulated through legislative rules are instead regulated by constitutional ones – the effect is to undermine equality and self-government. This is one of the dangers of creeping pre-commitment. Recasting legislative rules as constitutional ones devolves ethical responsibility away from a morally endogenous populous as a whole and instead places moral authority in the hands of a neo-Socratic, juridical elite the implicit mandate of which is to protect society from its collective lack of moral wisdom.

In depoliticizing contentious issues, creeping pre-commitment imposes a static solution to a dynamic problem. Indeed, without reasonable consensus on value-prioritization, the relevant issue remains dynamic and unconsolidated. Over time, consensus might emerge or it might not. (It did on slavery; it is showing few signs of doing so on abortion.) Where an issue is dynamic and unconsolidated, the only justification for regulating the issue through constitutional rules is if one side of the dissensus is consistent with liberal republican values and one side is not.

In the absence of general consensus, liberal republican justice mandates universal civic participation in the construction of legislative rules, but does not exclude civic participation in the construction of constitutional ones. The logic of liberal republicanism suggests there are manifold social advantages to universal civic participation. For one thing and as noted in Chapter 4, civic participation helps to foster common purpose, a sense of usness, that informs the secondary values of liberal republican societies. This usness does not mandate that citizens come to consensus on all issues; they will not. Rather, common purpose is to be understood in the sense expressed by Thomas Gilby that "[c]ivilization is formed by men locked together in argument" (in Murray 2005, 24; see also Hirschman 1994; Waldron 1999b, chs. 4–5). The values that bind us are constructed and perpetuated through refinement born of debate and dialogue. Our understanding of value-prioritization is examined, and sometimes re-evaluated, through the process of debate.

While well-constructed constitutions restrict liberty through formal constitutional rules as a bulwark against social akrasia, there is no substitute for an engaged citizenry. One need not look beyond the former Soviet bloc to find well-constructed constitutions in nations that suffer despotic government. A people who wish to be free must act to support that freedom. Participation broadens the locus of political power. The more citizens who participate in public life, who mobilize in support of a particular form of value-prioritization, the broader the distribution of authority, and hence the protection afforded to liberty. If concentration of power is the very definition of despotism, its distribution is the best protection against despotism (see Dahl 1961).

It is in recognition of the importance of civic participation that some constitutional rules *prohibit* state regulation of a particular issue. Here I am speaking of so-called gag rules which ensure state neutrality when it comes to the prioritization of primary values, such as the freedom to worship as one pleases (Holmes 1995, ch. 7). Gag rules are designed to ensure that the state not pre-commit to what Hirschman (1994, 214) calls *live-and-let-live* issues – those most appropriately banished from public regulation. Live-and-let-live issues can be defined as those for which the absence of state regulation is content-neutral; that is, the lack of regulation privileges no one set of citizens and has no negative impact on any set of citizens. The best example is the freedom to worship as one pleases. Another example, albeit one that comes with certain exceptions, is freedom of speech. We will examine this second example below.

PRE-COMMITMENT AND THE PURSUIT OF STATUS

As noted, pre-commitment can take two distinct forms. The first is formal constitutional amendment. The second, what we have called creeping pre-commitment, is the judicial expansion of the rules to which society pre-commits. Both represent potential vehicles for status-seeking groups to acquire political privilege by constitutionally entrenching value-prioritization.

Formal Constitutional Amendments

Given its recent constitutional upheavals, Canada represents an excellent illustration of status-seeking by formal constitutional amendment. Between 1982 and 1995, Canada underwent three major constitutional reform initiatives, only the first of which was ultimately successful. In 1982, Canada patriated its constitution by constructing an indigenous amendment process that replaced the archaic practice of constitutional amendment through the Parliament of Great Britain.[1] The genesis of the patriation initiative was a promise made by then prime minister Pierre Trudeau that if citizens in Quebec voted *non* in the upcoming referendum on (quasi) independence for Quebec, he would engage in constitutional renewal. The implication, obviously, was that such renewal would satisfy Quebec's long-standing concerns about its place in the Canadian federation. And so it was with no small degree of controversy that the only province *not* to give its ultimate blessing to the patriation package was Quebec itself.

To ameliorate this unsuitable state of affairs, another constitutional reform package was negotiated and unanimously reached by heads of the provincial and federal governments. The centrepiece was a constitutional filter that obliged courts to recognize Quebec as a distinct society within the Canadian federation. As such, Quebec's distinctiveness would have to be read as prior to the application of other constitutional rules. This attempted reform, part of the Meech Lake Accord of 1987, failed to be ratified in all provincial (and federal) legislatures within the three-year time frame mandated by the Constitution.

Meech Lake failed for two principal reasons. First, many in English Canada saw the asymmetrical nature of the distinct society clause as an unreasonable prioritization of Quebec's distinctiveness ahead of the symmetrical federalism most consistent with formal equality. Second, other subaltern cultural communities failed to appreciate the reasons as to why Quebec's distinct status should be recognized while their own cultural distinctiveness was not similarly affirmed. Aboriginal and women's groups in particular felt alienated and unrepresented by the process (Breton 1992).

As a result, leaders of these essentialist groups ultimately became the first non-governmental actors formally to negotiate constitutional amendments in Canada when yet a third initiative was launched in the early 1990s. This initiative, the Charlottetown Accord – weighing in at a hefty sixty amendments and seeking to satisfy the constitutional demands

1 The British North America Act (1867) was an act of the British Parliament that in terms of substance still constitutes a large portion of Canada's constitution. Because it was an act of Parliament that governed the operation of a country that was still not fully sovereign (and would not become so for more than half a century), there was no thought of including an indigenous constitutional amending formula. Like all legislation, acts of the British Parliament can be amended by subsequent legislation by the same body. The patriation package consisted in the main of the articulation of an indigenous amending formula and the Charter of Rights and Freedoms (for a discussion of how the Charter affected the roles of both courts and interest groups, see Banting and Simeon 1983; Romanow, Whyte, and Leeson 1984).

of as many different groups as could logistically be achieved – was put to a referendum in all ten provinces in 1992. It too was defeated, leading to a second referendum on independence in Quebec that failed by a spread of barely more than 1 per cent.[2]

The Canadian case illustrates the logistical perils of status-seeking through formal constitutional amendment. It is a tough sell to pre-commit to values that prioritize the cultural status of discrete identity-creating communities ahead of others. Even if a social consensus could be reached that essentialist tertiary values should be protected through constitutional rules, there is no logistical way of cataloguing all of the discrete identity-creating communities whose values might be prioritized. (And all this assumes that it is even reasonable to speak of such generalized status as *prioritization.*) No distinct boundaries separate one identity-forming community from others, only stipulated lines. Thus, asked the Native Women's Association of Canada quite reasonably, if Aboriginal groups were to be invited to the negotiating table for the Charlottetown Accord, why were Native women's groups being excluded? There was no good answer to that question. The exclusion was arbitrary, but such arbitrariness was necessary to avoid *reductio ad absurdum.* If Native women's groups were to be included it would then be arbitrary to exclude lesbian Native groups; and if the process was pluralized to include lesbian Native groups, there would be no legitimate basis to exclude transgendered lesbian Native groups, and so forth.

Creeping Pre-commitment

If the Canadian example is anything to go by, status-seeking through using formal constitutional amendment is unlikely to get essentialist

---

2 The referendum was defeated by a vote of 50.58 per cent to 49.42 per cent. It should be noted, however, that the language of the referendum question was designed to obscure the starkness of the prospect of outright independence: "Do you agree that Québec should become sovereign after having made a formal offer to Canada for a new economic and political partnership within the scope of the bill respecting the future of Québec and of the agreement signed on June 12, 1995?" The 12 June "agreement" was not between Canada and Quebec on a new economic and political partnership as might be implied from the referendum question. Rather, it was an agreement among leaders of secessionist parties and movements on the proposal to be made to the government of Canada as to what a new economic and political partnership would look like. The bill referred to, *An Act Respecting the Future of Quebec*, represented the legislative manifestation of the June 12 Agreement, and was a creature of the Quebec National Assembly and not, as also might be accidentally perceived, the Parliament of Canada. Finally, although the language somewhat obscures the intent, the referendum was not to give Quebec a mandate to negotiate with the government of Canada under threat of secession, but a mandate to secede and then negotiate.

community representatives further than the negotiating table. Far more efficacious has been the use of creeping pre-commitment to acquire constitutional status.

Courts in liberal republics find themselves forced to maintain a precarious balance. Despite the challenge posed by creeping pre-commitment, judicial review is not inconsistent with liberal republicanism. As with its formal constitutional amendment, judicial involvement in the protection of constitutional rules often proves central to enhancing equality, liberty, obligation, and purpose. Indeed, to the extent that judicial review keeps the branches (and levels) of government in check, it protects the rules fundamental to the preservation of primary values. Courts serve an important role as trustees of the nation's most cherished values, ensuring that values and the prioritization of those values to which society has pre-committed are not subsequently eroded through the legislative or executive process (Knopff 2003, 201–2). The *Brown* decision represents an obvious case in point.

But judicial review becomes problematic if it extends the scope of pre-commitment. As such, creeping pre-commitment is problematic when it alters the prioritization of primary values in ways that do not reflect the social consensus inherent in the reasonableness standard. Similarly problematic, creeping pre-commitment can intrude on civic participation in a fashion erosive of liberty and moral obligation, the former through limitations on civic self-government, the latter through entrenching deep lines of factionalization (see Ajzenstat 2007, ch.3, esp. 70–2). Finally, it can undermine formal constitutional rules to which society has already pre-committed, thereby undoing their effects.

To Gag or Not to Gag? Pre-commitment to Either-Or Issues

The line between creeping pre-commitment on the one hand, and judicial protection against social akrasia on the other is often a very fine one. However, there is one set of rules – gag rules – where the distinction is relatively stark. As noted, many countries' constitutions impose gag rules for what we have called these live-and-let-live issues (Hirschman 1994, 214). From the liberal republican perspective, one problem with creeping pre-commitment is that it has the potential to distort the intended impact of gag rules. It can do so in two ways. First, creeping pre-commitment can impose gag rules on other than live-and-let-live issues, violating the criterion of content-neutrality. Second, creeping pre-commitment can erode the gag rule on live-and-let-live issues which results in public regulation intruding in areas reserved for the private space. Let's take these in order.

When the criterion of content-neutrality is violated, the effect is to extend gag rules beyond live-and-let-live issues and onto what Hirschman calls *either-or issues*, those in which resolution must favour one position or another (1994, 213).

In their respective landmark decisions on abortion, the Supreme Courts of both Canada and the United States effectively imposed gag rules on the issue of reproductive freedom.[3] In so doing, they sought to protect a tertiary value of fundamental importance to feminists who have taken a proprietary view of reproductive freedom as a distinctly gender-specific issue (McDaniel 1985; Fine 2006). The logic behind the respective courts' decisions was clear. Abortion not only liberates women from the unwanted burden of carrying a fetus to term, but also frees them from the difficult choice of raising the child, often at great personal sacrifice, or putting the child up for adoption. Symbolically, freedom to choose whether or not to carry a fetus to term represents liberation from an expansive patriarchy that extends to even the most personal choices that women might make – those about control over their bodies (Cannold 2000, esp. ch. 5; Smyth 2002).

At issue here is not whether abortion rights are justified. Rather, the discussion turns on the locus of regulation, and in particular whether or not pre-commitment to a gag rule is appropriate in this case. The argument from the liberal republican perspective is that it is not, since abortion is not a live-and-let-live issue. It is not content-neutral. Given the lack of social consensus as to whether or not abortion is morally justifiable, abortion is a classic either-or issue. The very debate turns on the issue of whether or not abortion should be subject to public regulation.[4] Again, to be very clear: the argument is not that abortion must be regulated by the state, or that the pro-choice position is untenable. Rather, the point is that from the perspective of liberal republicanism, without a prevailing social consensus to prioritize one set of primary values (the right to liberty) ahead of another (the right to life), the appropriate regulatory tool is legislative rules and not constitutional ones.

There are good reasons for not pre-committing to the prioritization of primary values in circumstances where social consensus is lacking.

---

3 In Canada, the corollary to *Roe v. Wade* (1973) is *R. v. Morgentaler* (1988).

4 Whether or not this is a legitimate debate is also open to question. For proponents of reproductive freedom rights, the issue is a private one between a woman and her (1973) doctors. To the extent it becomes relevant for public policy discussion, some culturalists demand what amounts to a cultural veto such that abortion is an issue that involves women and as such should not be regulated by men (e.g., MacKinnon 1989, ch. 10). Against this is the fact that the fathers of unborn children would seem to have a stake in the regulation of abortion. Moreover, there is a generalized tradition in liberal republics – perhaps itself born of dominant-group dominance – that criminal law is not subject to differential regulation and oversight depending on the constituencies most affected.

Institutionalizing what are in effect unsettled social issues does not solve the problem. The point can be made through an analogy between social and individual pre-commitment. In exploring the latter, Waldron (1999a) asks us to imagine Bridget, a young woman who after much soul-searching definitively decides upon a particular theological course for her life. Reinforcing her commitment to this path, she pre-commits to this decision. She locks up her private library of theological books, which previously had stimulated her self-doubt, and gives the keys to a friend with instructions that the friend is not to return the keys, even if Bridget makes such a demand in the future.

But new issues and old doubts start to creep into Bridget's mind after a while ... and a few months later she asks for the keys. Should the friend return them? Clearly this is quite a different case from (say) withholding car keys from the drinker at midnight. Both involve forms of pre-commitment. But in Bridget's case, for the friend to sustain the pre-commitment would be for the friend to take sides, as it were, in a dispute between two or more conflicting selves or two or more conflicting aspects of the same self within Bridget, each with a claim to rational authority. It would be to take sides in a way that is simply not determined by any recognizable criteria of pathology or other mental aberration. To uphold the pre-commitment would be to sustain the temporary ascendancy of one aspect of the self at the time the library keys were given away, and to neglect the fact that the self that demands them back has an equal claim to respect for its way of dealing with the vicissitudes of theological uncertainty. (268–9)

Waldron's point is not that that either-or issues are easily resolved. They are not, and regulation of them through legislative, as opposed to constitutional, rules hardly guarantees a salutary outcome. But among the advantages of trying to settle such issues through legislative rules is that doing so, to reprise Gilby, "locks men together in argument." It lends itself to bargaining, persuasion, and the prospect, however difficult, of arriving at a reasonable solution that, should it prove unsatisfactory over the course of time, can be amended through the normal legislative process. It is the impermanence of the solution, in other words, that allows outcomes to be acceptable, if less than optimal for the parties involved.

The rough and tumble of public discourse – of intergroup competition for political influence – renders legislation but a system of semi-stable equilibria, which can be altered by shifting social understandings of what constitutes appropriate social purpose (Riker 1980). Unlike pre-commitment, contestation over conflicting value-prioritization encourages popular discourse rather than shutting down, or at least rendering much less efficacious, subsequent discussion and the prospect of finding a more palatable equilibrium.

Perhaps the most pernicious element of creeping pre-commitment as it pertains to either-or issues is that it narrows the boundaries of political contestation by taking political issues out of play. This has the effect of limiting civic participation and the catalogue of advantages that come with it. Surprisingly, this fact has not generated a good deal of resistance to judicial activism. There is a general sense that judicial review represents the triumph of justice over politics (Waldron 1999b, 2, 128). Judicial social policy making is imbued, in other words, with a myth of the sacred (James, Abelson, and Lusztig 2002) – a sense that judicial interpretation of the constitution is the next best thing to divine interpretation. Even within academic circles, removing issues from political contestation has been understood as somehow conducive to civic participation. Dworkin (1996, 345) argues, for example, that

[w]hen a constitutional issue has been decided by the Supreme Court, and is important enough so that it can be expected to be elaborated, expanded, contracted and even reversed by future decisions, a sustained national debate begins, in newspapers and other media, in law schools and in classrooms, in public meetings and around dinner tables. The debate better matches [the] conception of republican government, in its emphasis on matters of principle, than almost anything the legislative process on its own is likely to produce.

Dworkin cites *Roe v. Wade* as an example. *Roe* certainly brought the issue of abortion to the forefront of public consciousness by reviewing the constitutionality of laws criminalizing abortion. But to say that the court can perform the task of bringing issues to the forefront of public consciousness is not to say that it is the only or best vehicle for such consciousness-raising (Waldron 1999a). Indeed, public consciousness also is likely to be heightened when debate takes place within a representative legislature as opposed to a court room. The difference is that Supreme Court decisions are for all intents and purposes dispositive. Dworkin is correct that courts do indeed reverse precedent. But the intervening period typically stretches to decades – far longer than the electoral cycle that facilitates policy changes in the legislative arena. The precedent set in *Plessy v. Ferguson* was reversed, but the intervening years witnessed more than a half-century of Jim Crow laws.

Dworkin also is correct to note that constitutionalizing an issue does not wholly remove it from political contestation. But it certainly changes the terms of such contestation. Indeed, it changes contestation from an active political enterprise to little more than an intellectual one – one that can be debated ad infinitum, but to no practical effect. Judicial disposition of a case effectively closes the door to civic participation in the resolution of the issue in question. But it is participation, and not merely awareness, that informs the mandate of the liberal republican citizen. Such participation is born of proprietorship of the public square. It represents the active obligation of the steward and not the passive attendance of the spectator, however piqued her interest might be.

More important perhaps, the judicial process promotes factionalism insofar as it does not lend itself to bargaining. The system is adversarial. There is no imperative to construct and maintain alliances. There is not, in other words, a long-term integrative effect born of recognizing that one's adversaries on one issue might well be one's allies on the next. For most who appear before the courts, the process is not iterative. There is no incentive to be sensitive to the compromise demanded by future political alliance; indeed, the process itself precludes such mechanisms as issue linkage as the route to compromise.

The adversarial nature of the judicial process is underscored by the prizes at stake. When a status-seeking group's objectives are gratified through constitutional rules, the benefit is both substantive and symbolic. Substantively, and as noted, unlike legislation that represents a temporary equilibrium that can be upset by something as anodyne as the electoral cycle, constitutional victories are all but invulnerable to change in the short to medium terms. Symbolically, constitutional victories elevate a group's status. They suggest that the cultural values of an essentialist community are sufficiently important to warrant special constitutional status. The essentialist community is thus raised from being one voice among many to one worthy of enhanced cultural recognition.

Status represents a group's position as a veto player on issues pertaining to its vital interests. Indeed, its claim to *frame* the relevant policy issue is recognized. The way in which an issue is framed has implications for the framing of cognate issues (Stetson 2001, 4). To use Dworkin's example of *Roe v. Wade*, the decision not only secured reproductive freedom rights for women, but it also served notice of the claims of women's groups to assert their privileged status in defining the parameters of the abortion debate. It is to protect this status (as opposed to inherent animus toward the partially born) that feminist groups have fought vigorously against legislation banning partial-birth abortions (Sharrin 1989/1990; Brenner 1996; Meyer and Staggenborg 2008).

When civic participation is eroded, so too is moral obligation. The legislative process is intersubjective. Through the construction of legislative rules, the desires and preferences of others must be factored into the demands one makes on society. The mere fact of compromise, in other words, serves as a constant reminder of our obligation to others, and of our own interest in remaining sensitive to that obligation. But when a society pre-commits to either-or issues, citizens lose the incentive to compromise. Subjectivity once again holds sway. If the benefit of contestation over legislative rules is to be found in the (obligation-enhancing) *process*, the cost of litigative contestation over constitutional rules is to be found in the (obligation-depleting) winner-take-all *outcome*. Bonds of community are enhanced by forming and preserving shared values, of the sense of common purpose that gives meaning to our understanding of civil society. Where pre-commitment to value-prioritization is deeply contested, the mitigating imperative to compromise is trumped by the unadulterated incentive to win. The result is that community-enhancing values such as trust and efficacy, and ultimately, moral obligation are depleted. Without common purpose, we are left with the malignant form of factionalization so feared by traditional republicans.

As noted, the Madisonian solution to the pernicious effects of factions was to temper them through the countervailing forces of rival factions. The wider the boundaries of political contestation – the greater the number of intersecting cleavages – the greater the likelihood that the evils of faction could be neutralized through the legislative process. But integral to the Madisonian solution is an underlying commitment to formal equality. Group mobilization is a product of free and equal individuals choosing to come together to support some form of value-prioritization.

However, where the imperative for formal equality of interest is subordinated to the situational equality of cultural identity, the Madisonian logic breaks down. Rather than shifting alliances born of intersecting cleavages across a broad range of salient issues, the culturalist worldview sees group membership as the product of essentialist – substructural – characteristics that do not lend themselves to shifting alliances across different policy issues. Instead, factions take on greater rigidity. Because identity is prior to interest, group members will tend to view all issues through the same cultural lens, which is to say a different lens than other cultural groups used. While this does not preclude the formation of social coalitions in pursuit of common objectives, the most important issues in recognizing group status do not lend themselves easily to such coalitions. As such, the pursuit of status is an entirely minoritarian proposition, which is therefore far more likely to find remedy in a minoritarian institution (courts) than a majoritarian one (legislatures).

The effect is judicial appropriation of the legislative process. In the process, the deliberative filter that traditionally accompanies the prioritization of values in liberal republics is lost. Removing the value-prioritization of either-or issues from the scrutiny afforded by public discourse has the effect of raising the stakes on contentious issues. Rather than temper the socially disintegrative effects of faction, it heightens them, building antagonism, resentment, and distrust and undermining the sense of common purpose of a working liberal republic. Marrying factionalism to the winner-take-all process embodied by judicial policy making, in other words, does nothing to militate against the theocratic temptation and hence does nothing to enhance tolerance or reasonableness.

Creeping Erosion of Gag Rules

Just as creeping pre-commitment can impose gag rules on either-or issues, it also has the effect of eroding the effectiveness of the gag on live-and-let-live issues. A good example is the gag rule prohibiting a state religion from being established. Here the obvious intent of the gag rule is content-neutrality so that each is free to worship how she chooses. However, this gag rule has occasionally been interpreted not as a prohibition against establishing a religion, but rather a prohibition against non-secularism. For example, when the European Court of Human Rights upheld French law banning students from wearing conspicuous symbols of their religions in school, it cannot reasonably be said to have protected students' freedom to worship as they chose.[5] Indeed, instead of regulating a content-neutral live-and-let-live issue, the court effectively ruled on an entirely different, either-or issue – whether or not to permit organized religion in the public space. The same criticism can be levelled at the US Ninth Circuit Court of Appeals, which ruled in *Newdow v. Congress* (2002) that the words "under God" in the Pledge of Allegiance violated the First Amendment.

When gag rules on live-and-let-live issues are eroded, the effect is sometimes to undermine process-enabling rules that preserve citizens'

---

5 Article 9 of the European Convention on Human Rights holds that "Everyone has the right to freedom of thought, conscience and religion; this right includes freedom to change his religion or belief and freedom, either alone or in community with others and in public or private, to manifest his religion or belief, in worship, teaching, practice and observance." Additionally, "Freedom to manifest one's religion or beliefs shall be subject only to such limitations as are prescribed by law and are necessary in a democratic society in the interests of public safety, for the protection of public order, health or morals, or for the protection of the rights and freedoms of others."

ability to participate in public life. A good example is the right to freedom of political speech and expression. For it to be meaningful (with
the exception of speech that incites violence or sedition), political
speech and expression must be protected. Freedom of political expression represents the freedom to join the public discourse that shapes legislative rules and all forms of values. Of course, in order to arrive at
appropriate rules and values, logic dictates that *inappropriate* ones need to
be voiced, debated, and rejected. People are not locked in argument
when all agree, or are forced to agree, or are insulated from the offensive
nature of particularly inappropriate values. Take the case of flag-burn-
ing. While revolting to most, especially given that citizens have given
their lives to defend the values for which their national flag stands, as the
Supreme Court found in *Texas v. Johnson* (1989), prohibiting such expression represents an intolerable intrusion into citizens' ability to participate in the political process.

Equally repulsive as expressions desecrating iconic symbols of nationhood is speech intended to incite or perpetuate hatred against discrete
subaltern cultures. Speech and other symbolism is one of the principal
battlegrounds on which culturalists have sought to realize the situational
equality of subaltern groups. To advance this end, culturalists have
sought to reform both legislative and constitutional rules as a means of
pre-empting the cultural harm inflicted by offensive speech. The issue is
a controversial one. So offensive is hate speech that many jurisdictions
have prohibited it.

Prohibition of hate speech, backed by sanctions, proliferated on college campuses in the wake of the political correctness movement of the
late 1980s and early 1990s. Hate speech is that which expresses a moral
or political viewpoint that goes beyond mere annoyance and disruption
of an individual's life. It is sufficiently offensive to one or more discrete
cultural communities to transcend the merely offensive. Rather, such
speech inflicts the sort of psychological harm manifest in the Clarks' doll
test and inherent in stereotype threats (Matsuda 1989; Altman 1993).

The argument here is not that hate speech does not exist. Of course it
does. And its capacity to inflict harm is clear. The problem is that it is
extremely hard to regulate and indeed in many cases regulating it may
be more problematic than the fact of it. A manifestation of this is that
one person's hate speech can be another person's moral conviction. In
2008, for example, the Reverend Stephen Boisson and the Concerned
Christian Coalition were convicted before the Alberta Human Rights
Panel. Boisson's offence was a 2002 letter that he wrote to the *Red Deer
Advocate* in which he remonstrated with citizens to defend traditional
social values against the inroads made by homosexual activists since the

1960s. The tone of the letter, while hardly equivocal, was not mean-spirited. It did not advocate violence toward, or even hatred of, homosexuals. In its decision, the Alberta Human Rights Panel ordered Boisson and the Concerned Christian Coalition to pay $7,000 in compensation; Boisson was prohibited from any public disparagement of homosexuals and was ordered to write a letter of apology to the complainant. On top of that, the *Red Deer Advocate* was ordered to publish the Panel's ruling (Alberta Human Rights Panel 2008), the point of which, presumably, was to serve as a warning to other would-be apostate contributors to the debate on gay rights.

The ambiguity that attaches to cases in which offence comes up against conviction suggests that hate speech is akin to Justice Potter Stewart's characterization of pornography. You know it when you see it, but it is difficult to define precisely, or at least sufficiently precisely that excising it will permit the meaningful protection of free speech (Altman 1993, 306). Without a reasonable, and reasonably precise, definition of hate speech, attempts to regulate it risk being seen as arbitrary and *un*reasonable.

For this reason, hate speech prohibition has engendered a good deal of debate on the triadic relationship among political discourse, social purpose, and harm. Gale (1991) has sought to mediate this relationship by prohibiting only a limited range of expression – that which fails to "advance knowledge, seek truth, expose government abuses, initiate dialogue, encourage participation, further tolerance of divergent views, or enhance individuals' dignity or self-respect" (179–80). But even such a narrow prohibition quickly becomes arbitrary. Gale cites an example of someone who snuck into the dorm room of two African-American college students and wrote on the mirror, "African monkeys, why don't you go back to the jungle?" (176) as expression that should be prohibited under these criteria.

Certainly Gale is correct that such expression fails to realize most of the criteria for legitimate speech that she articulates. But it does not violate *all* of them. We already have prima facie evidence of the initiation of dialogue insofar as Gale references the incident in the first place. No doubt it would have caused a great deal of dialogue at the time as well. It is also unclear that such a message, whatever its intent, fails to further tolerance of divergent views: the message is literally repulsive insofar as it provides an excellent illustration of the ugliest side of racial intolerance. It is not unreasonable to assume that the racially ambivalent are as likely to react against such overt racism as to embrace it. In fact, it is sometimes better to air the ugly side of a group's cultural preferences than to drive it underground where it festers, unlikely to wither and die of its own accord, perhaps to emerge in some more virulent form. And in any case, it rarely serves to punish and hence promote the "political sacrifice" made by idiots, a strategy which tends to concentrate attention on the martyrdom rather than the idiocy.

Some jurisdictions go beyond prohibiting hate speech and actually criminalize it. Sweden's Act on Persecution of Minority Groups, for example, makes hate speech criminally justiciable (Houser 2009, 613). The European Council's *Framework Decision on Certain Forms of Xenophobia and Racism by Means of Criminal Law* mandates that member states criminalize genocide-denial when it is likely to engender hatred or violence or when it is threatening, abusive, or insulting (Pech 2009, 1).

While criminalization of hate speech has not met with traction in the United States, it has fared better in Canada, a system with a similar judicial structure and a similar jurisprudential tradition (Manfredi 1990). Hate speech has been criminalized in Canada since the introduction of s. 319 to the Criminal Code of Canada in 1970. Under s. 319(2) it is unlawful publicly or willfully to incite hatred against any group identifiable by colour, race, religion, ethnicity, or (since 2004) sexual orientation. Violations are punishable by up to two years in prison.

In *R. v. Keegstra* (1990), Canada's first Charter of Rights and Freedoms challenge to the hate speech provision of Criminal Code, the Supreme Court ruled 4–3 that the hate speech prohibition trumps the constitutional right to freedom of expression contained in the Charter of Rights and Freedoms. The Charter limits the absolute nature of rights and freedoms in that they are guaranteed "subject only to such reasonable limits prescribed by law as can be demonstrably justified in a free and democratic society" (s. 1). Keegstra, a social studies teacher, subjected his students to the benefits of his vitriolic and manifestly inaccurate diatribes against the evils visited upon the Christian world by Jews, Catholics, and Blacks. Referring to Jews as "sadistic" and "child-killing," he painted the Holocaust as a hoax perpetuated by an international Jewish conspiracy. These were not just off-the-cuff remarks. Students were obliged to replicate these views in their assignments on pain of losing grades. One would have to search long and hard in the hope of finding any redeeming qualities of James Keegstra as a teacher or as a citizen. But offensive as they were, it is difficult to justify the prohibition of such sentiments, far less their criminalization. The worst of the problem could have been solved by the entirely justifiable firing of Keegstra on the grounds of incompetence.

At issue in the Keegstra trial was whether or not the hate speech provision (s. 319(2)) constituted a reasonable limitation on speech rights protected in the Charter of Rights and Freedoms under section 2(b).

After making its way through the appeals process, the case was heard in the Supreme Court. The majority on that court held that

The effects of s. 319(2) are not of such a deleterious nature as to outweigh any advantage gleaned from the limitation of s. 2(b). The expressive activity at which s. 319(2) is aimed constitutes a special category, a category only tenuously connected with the values underlying the guarantee of freedom of expression. Hate propaganda contributes little to the aspirations of Canadians or Canada in either the quest for truth, the promotion of individual self-development or the protection and fostering of a vibrant democracy where the participation of all individuals is accepted and encouraged. Moreover, the narrowly drawn terms of s. 319(2) and its defences prevent the prohibition of expression lying outside of this narrow category. Consequently, the suppression of hate propaganda represents an impairment of the individual's freedom of expression which is not of a most serious nature.

This is a remarkable statement. It is curious to suggest that there are any underlying values, other than freedom, connected tenuously or otherwise with freedom of expression. It is possible to articulate *competing* values, such as public safety, or demonstrable group-based harm, that come from permitting unfettered free speech. But to claim, as the next sentence in the decision does, that underlying the constitutional right to freedom of expression is the imperative to seek the truth smacks of the very distinction between good (i.e., state-sanctioned) speech and bad political speech that pre-commitment to free speech seeks to guard against in the first place. Indeed, rather than constituting a limitation that can be demonstrably justified in a free and democratic society, the wording suggests a limitation inconsistent with a free society. And the idea that limiting citizens' rights to express ideas, even foolish and offensive ones, somehow contributes to the "fostering of a vibrant democracy where the participation of all individuals is accepted and encouraged," is particularly unconvincing.

The point is not that the contribution of Keegstra and his ilk is substantively valuable; although as noted, the case can be made that social opprobrium illustrates the inappropriateness of such sentiments in a far more effective manner than does state prohibition.[6] The greater vice is

---

6 A good case in point occurred during the 2012 elections in the Canadian province of Alberta. In the latter stages of the campaign, a blog post from a Wildrose Party candidate derailed what was shaping up to be a victory for the upstart party. Reacting against Lady Gaga's "Born This Way," Allan Hunsperger posted that if gays and lesbians lived *that way* they could expect to die *that way* as well. "You see," he wrote, "you can live the way you were born, and if you die the way you were born then you will suffer the rest of eternity in a lake

the effect this ruling can have on the actions of others. Even the threat of prosecution under s. 319(2) has a deleterious effect on freedom of expression and civic participation. After the inclusion of sexual orientation as the basis for protection against criminal hate speech in 2004, for example, religious groups in Canada have had to consider the prospect of criminal prosecution for promoting religious beliefs that are inconsistent with homosexuality. In the words of one evangelical Christian, "the wording of the (hate speech) legislation is so vague, there is no way of knowing how it will be interpreted" (quoted in Clausen 2005, 458). Similar fears have been expressed by other religious leaders, academics, and journalists. Given the nebulous definition of what it means to incite hatred, it is hardly inconceivable that a person's stated opposition to public policies such as homosexual marriage could subject a citizen seeking to participate in the vibrancy of democracy to prison time, or at the very least the cost of mounting a defence against criminal prosecution (Clausen 2005, 457–9). The criminalization of hate speech in Sweden, for example, landed Pastor Ake Green a month in prison for publishing a sermon in which he likened homosexuality to a cancerous social tumour (Brammer 2006).

Constitutional endorsement of hate speech criminalization creates what are effectively no-go zones for speech. Not only do such no-go zones institutionalize a form of value-prioritization in which freedom from offence trumps most erstwhile primary values, but they foreclose effective dialogue and debate on such value-prioritization. This raises the stakes of factionalization by giving groups that have won special status through some form of pre-commitment a weapon to protect their gains. To raise a hypothetical question, having established that women have a constitutional right to reproductive choice, a choice that is essential to their identity as women, would it be hateful to accuse women who have abortions as parties to genocide? Whatever one's view on the abortion issue is, and however extreme such a statement might be, it is a sentiment that is heard fairly often, particularly in religious circles. It is also one that is deeply offensive to many women. Since there is, and can be, no non-stipulative line between political speech and hate speech, is

---

of fire, hell, a place of eternal suffering." Whether or not Hunsperger's speech rose to the level of hate speech was never adjudicated, at least not before a court or tribunal. Instead, Alberta's voters passed their own form of judgment, not only against Hunsperger, but against the Wildrose Party as a whole, which wound up winning only 17 of the 87 seats contested.

it possible that such a sentiment might rise to the level of hate speech (Lillian 2007)?

CONCLUSION

It is difficult to criticize the motivation of culturalist status-seekers. Dominant communities, which have enjoyed elevated status and privilege, rarely engage in the constitutionalist strategies employed by culturalist status-seekers. (The case can be made that since legislative rules already serve to preserve their cultural status there is no need to seek change of constitutional rules.) But as this chapter has demonstrated, constitutional status-seeking, however unintentional, has the potential to erode social commitment to primary values.

The constitutional pre-commitment inherent to status-seeking is not axiomatically problematic to liberal republican values. All regimes undertake some form of pre-commitment. Liberal republicanism demands pre-commitment to three sorts of rules: process-enabling rules, rules for which there is social consensus consistent with primary values, and gag rules, which preclude publicly regulating intractable, content-neutral, live-and-let-live issues. Failure to pre-commit to such rules, or pre-committing to rules other than these, constitutes a challenge to the values that sustain liberal republics.

From the perspective of liberal republicanism, "good" pre-commitment (if we may call it that) precludes status-seeking by groups seeking to acquire differential recognition by constructing and interpreting constitutional rules. There may be manifest costs when subaltern cultural communities are able to institutionalize special status. The resulting potential for factionalization, injury to social solidarity, and marginalization of civic participation create the potential for competing sources of legitimate political authority that characterize traditional republican conceptions of corrupted states. Indeed, deeply factionalized societies are vulnerable to conflict that can lead to violence, secession, and other forms of political instability (Dobel 1978).

The "bad" form is often manifest as creeping pre-commitment. This is not to say that constitutional jurisprudence is an inherently pernicious thing. In fact, as the free speech case suggests, a failure by the courts to take a firm stance on gag rules is as bad as substituting constitutional rules for legislative rules on either-or issues. The fact that creeping pre-commitment is an intrusion into civic sovereignty is also not necessarily a bad thing. A social consensus on value-prioritization – Jim Crow laws, to take one example – is not to be prized on that count alone. When social consensus undermines the primary values that inform liberal republicanism in the first place, reimposing such values by non-majoritarian institutions may restore primary values.

On the other hand, there is a paradox insofar as while formal pre-commitment through constitutional amendment is a rigorous process generally subjected to painstaking oversight, what limited oversight is assigned to creeping pre-commitment is wholly at the mercy of an appeals process in which writs of certiorari, depending on the country and courts in question, may or may not be granted. And while this last point is unlikely to be an issue for cases that represent significant change to constitutional rules, the fact remains that popular oversight is divorced from the process.

Establishing decision rules for how courts should exercise their power of creeping pre-commitment is beyond the point of this exercise. I addressed a couple of such rules in this chapter only as they relate to the potential for culturalist erosion of liberal republican values. To this narrow end, the first case, abortion, represents a case of the court regulating an either-or value issue in favour of feminist groups on the issue of reproductive freedom and cognate issues. It imposed, in other words, a gag rule that was in and of itself not content-neutral given the issue at hand. Even if we wish to stipulate that the fetus has no rights, there is still a substantive impact on the father of the fetus. In the absence of a social consensus as to value-prioritization, the court's adjudication of this issue imposed the cost of foreclosing civic participation. There are costs to such action. Among the less obvious, as I have argued, is to shift interest-group politics out of the inclusive and integrative legislative arena and into the more exclusive and factionalizing judicial one.

The second case, pertaining to political speech, represents a manifestation of status-seeking that intrudes upon a gag rule designed to permit equal civic participation in the political process. Here it was up to the Canadian Supreme Court to stand up for a constitutionally articulated gag rule. The point is not that gag rules represent absolutes, for clearly they cannot. Freedom to worship as one pleases cannot, for example, extend to human sacrifice. And so too is it with speech. Speech that has a direct and substantive effect on others cannot claim protection under gag rules. Culturalists argue that hate speech does have a direct and substantive effect insofar as it can serve to marginalize members of subaltern communities (Massey 1992).

There is no question that offensive speech can affect esteem and esteem can affect efficacy and efficacy can affect performance. Hate speech is harmful in that sense. But try as we might, we cannot regulate speech through a refinement process that separates harmful offensiveness from more benign offensiveness because there is no objective understanding of what constitutes hate speech. All reasonable people can agree that "African monkeys, why don't you go back to the jungle?" is extremely offensive. All reasonable people can agree that the authors of such sentiments richly deserve all of the social opprobrium they invite. But what we cannot do is craft a rule with sufficient precision to regulate more ambiguous statements that may or may not represent nuanced ways of saying precisely the same thing. This interpretative ambiguity represents less of a problem for regulators than for citizens whose freedom of speech is filtered through the threat of possibly being cited for offensiveness.

The problem with hate speech regulation is that in theory (and in Canada), all it takes is one person to take offence at a statement for a person to be subjected to official sanction. In Canada, offended individuals acting as proxies for the subaltern communities they putatively represent, use offence as the means to elevate themselves to the status of veto players in determining politically acceptable speech and behaviour. This is one of the fruits of the empowerment of human rights tribunals in the wake of *Keegstra*. Probably most notorious is the decision by the British Columbia Human Rights Commission to proceed against journalist Mark Steyn and *Maclean's Magazine*. In "The Future Belongs to Islam," published by *Maclean's* in October 2006, Steyn highlights the potential demographic threat posed by the likelihood of increased Islamic immigration.

Among those offended by "The Future Belongs to Islam" were three members of the Canadian Islamic Congress, who filed a claim against Steyn. The tribunal ultimately found Steyn not guilty. That result, however, hardly undoes the damage. Despite being a prominent journalist and in the face of strong media opposition, Steyn's case was prosecuted and he was subjected to intense public scrutiny, to say nothing of the prohibitive cost of mounting a defence. For citizens whose visibility is not as high or whose resources are not as great, the prudent move is to refrain from public comment on political issues that might result in someone's feelings getting hurt.

In some cases, offended parties are able to move beyond prohibiting certain forms of political behaviour and actively mandate alternative forms. In *M.J. v. Nichols* (2008), the Saskatchewan Human Rights Tribunal fined Baptist minister Orville Nichols $2,500 for refusing to officiate over a gay marriage ceremony in spite of the tribunal's finding that "the Respondent was acting out of his genuine and sincere religious belief in refusing to perform the marriage ceremony" (Saskatchewan Human Rights Tribunal 2008). The tribunal's implication was not only that it was illegitimate to take a particular position on the issue of gay rights, but that citizens have an affirmative obligation to accept the position deemed most appropriate by those who would be otherwise offended. Once again, the damage in such cases is not limited to the person accused of the offence. It extends to the community of citizens whose political views are silenced out of fear of giving offence to those whose political recourse extends beyond debate and dialogue to cooptation of the coercive organ of the state. Indeed, the Saskatchewan Human Rights Tribunal was able to perform the remarkable feat of simultaneously intruding into two gag rules.

The point of this chapter is not that equalizing cultural status is inherently incompatible with liberal republicanism. As long as status attaches to political privilege for some cultural communities, but not others, the imperative to universalize dignity through formal equality is not violated. Where status-seeking becomes problematic is when groups seek special recognition through formal constitutional rules, through jurisprudential prioritization of primary values in the absence of general social consensus, or through gag rules designed to limit the intrusion of the state into areas where societies have already pre-committed to the illegitimacy of state encroachment.

9

Conclusion

IN THE INTRODUCTION OF THIS BOOK I suggested that liberalism and republicanism offer different visions of the future: the end of history or the end of the world. Neither seems imminent. Perhaps this is because in their classical or traditional manifestations, neither liberalism nor republicanism paints an accurate portrait of modern democratic states. Instead, modern democracies represent an amalgam of liberal and republican theory. Liberal republicanism promotes a theory of the just society predicated on reconciling liberal and republican theories of equality, liberty, obligation, and purpose. Since the end of the Enlightenment, the harmonization of liberal and republican principles has led to remarkable stability and prosperity in modern democratic states.

The mandate of this book has been to assess the prospects for continued stability. Specifically, it has been to systematize the challenges – even the threats – to the stability of liberal republican regimes posed by culturalism. The political causes of regime mortality can be of only two kinds: failure from without or failure from within. External failure is caused by states in an anarchical international environment being vanquished by stronger powers. Internal failure occurs when governments weaken through corruption and ultimately revolution. Of course, quite often there is an interactive effect where, as traditional republicans feared it, internal corruption leaves republics vulnerable to external destruction. Traditionally, the prescription was the inculcation of virtuous citizens, virtuous leaders, and strong armies. *Liberal* republicanism has improved upon the formula. Virtuous leaders are nice but, as experience has shown, hardly necessary for good government where there are well-constructed institutions. Virtuous citizens are important, but given fair rules and a morally endogenous citizenry, we can assume a general degree of intersubjective obligation within liberal republican societies. Strong armies (and a culture that contributes to them) still matter, but international commerce has replaced conquest as a means of acquiring wealth and power.

Yet the traditional republican laments cannot be wholly forgotten. While the mechanisms have changed, liberal republics still face threats. The most significant of these is the cultural appropriation of national identities or even of core values. The threat to national identities, or secondary values, comes from what we have called cultural contestants, which can result in secondary values being appropriated either completely or incompletely. Where it is incomplete, contestation results in the creation of parallel or competing sets of secondary values. The "two solitudes" of English and French Canada are a good example of this. Where it is complete, cultural contestation serves as the basis either for colonizing and displacing extant secondary values, or, more dramatically, seceding outright from an existing nation-state. The threat to core or primary values comes from what we have called versoculturalism – an infinitely more dangerous form of culturalism than cultural contestation. Versoculturalism represents a cultural revolution, in which one set of regime-defining values is replaced with another. As the escalating terrorist violence in Western Europe indicates, versoculturalist revolutions are rarely achieved without tectonic disturbance to the social order.

Cultural appropriation represents a clear and obvious threat. However, what makes it particularly insidious is that its effects can be masked – and state responses limited – by more benign forms of culturalism: status-seeking, cultural separatism, and multiculturalism. In this sense, to the extent that they pave the way for their far less palatable counterparts, these more benign forms constitute indirect challenges for liberal republican stability.

Of the three, status-seeking poses the greatest challenge. Status-seeking represents the attempt to reform constitutional rules – either through formal amendment or through the mechanism of what we have called creeping pre-commitment. The objective of status-seekers is to provide constitutional niches for differential treatment, which in turn represent footholds to further expand privileged status. The problem with status-seeking is not that it pits competing interests against one another. Liberal republican pluralism easily accommodates factionalism. It is that status-seeking contributes to a more malign factionalization than is inherent in the multidimensional issue-space that informs pluralist competition over legislative rules. Particularly when achieved through legal challenges, status-seeking is more likely to promote social discord than social integration.

Most status-seekers presumably have no intention of doing damage to the core values of liberal republicanism. At worst, status-seeking represents the desire to shift the prioritization of certain primary values. Feminists, for example, aren't looking to bring about the revolution that will finally rid society of liberal republican primary values. They simply want the existing primary rules to accommodate their quest for situational gender equality. There are no base motives here. But there are potentially problematic *effects*. As the Canadian example has made clear, factionalization, by reforming constitutional rules, has the potential to weaken the moral obligation requisite to usness. Where the core is weak, in other words, there are few common secondary values uniting disparate interests. There is no common civil religion as it were, no national identity, no common sense of usness that binds a country together, whatever its other differences might be.

While cultural appropriation and status-seeking have received a good deal of attention in this book, the challenges posed by cultural separatism and multiculturalism were addressed less fully. In part this is because both are compatible with liberal republicanism. Indeed, both address weaknesses in liberal republican theories of justice. Unless guarded against, liberal republicanism has the potential for chauvinism. More specifically, there is a propensity to define usness (what it means to be "people like us") in terms of sameness. This usness is expressed through a set of shared secondary values. Oftentimes the common (or at least majority) commitment to these secondary values has the effect of marginalizing the cultural values of subaltern cultural communities. We have called these tertiary values. Culturally diverse liberal republics are sensitive to the imperative to protect tertiary values. However, such values are generally understood in geographic, or spatial, terms and not in terms of the ascriptive, or essentialist, characteristics that define cultural communities born of common race, ethnicity, language, gender, or sexual orientation.

THE CHALLENGE OF CULTURAL SEPARATISM

This book has defined cultural separatism as voluntary withdrawal from the cultural mainstream. It is entirely unilateral in the sense that separatist cultural communities ask little of the dominant culture except to be left alone. Certainly cultural separatism is not ideal. It represents an abdication of the participatory mandate of liberal republican citizenry. In this sense it also constitutes a challenge to social solidarity. Of course, so does the chauvinism of a dominant culture that provokes a separatist response.

Cultural separatism is usually quite benign. With time, the cultural antipathy that divided subaltern and dominant communities dissipates and cultural reintegration is the result. Dutch consociationalism represents a good example of this. While deeply cleaved along religious lines as late as the 1960s, the cultural separatism inherent in Dutch consociation ultimately served as so much social scaffolding. As secularization nullified theologically informed cultural antipathy, social integration rendered the rules of consociation obsolete. Greater sensitivity to issues of race, gender, and sexual orientation in the aftermath of the civil rights movement has similarly, if not yet as effectively, relieved pressure for cultural separatism in the United States as well.

It is important to bear in mind that cultural separatism is not the same thing as secession, although as we have noted, the principal challenge posed by cultural separatism is its potential to evolve into political separatism. The latter is an extreme desire for cultural dissociation that we have associated with cultural contestation and the complete appropriation of secondary values. By contrast, cultural separatism proceeds from the logic that one can feel alienated from the dominant culture without feeling so alienated as to exercise the exit option. Even in deeply ethnically divided societies, secession tends to be favoured only by minorities or transitory (akratic?) majorities of the disaffected group in question. Most cultural separatists, in other words, are more motivated by a desire to reform the dominant culture than by the desire for secession. They might be enticed toward the secessionist position by extremists or self-interested elites. But it is not their natural position.

Spain represents a case in point. Relying on 2003 data we see that only 17 per cent of Catalonians favoured outright independence from Spain. Support for independence was only slightly higher among Basques (23 per cent) (Guibernau 2006, 63). In Canada, despite a referendum on secession that failed by only the narrowest of margins in 1995, the issue of sovereign independence for Quebec appears to be passé in Quebec. A 2011 CROP poll in Quebec found that 71 per cent of Quebeckers felt that the idea of Quebec sovereignty was outmoded, and only 25 per cent wished to create a country separate from Canada (Simpson 2011). In Britain, support among the Welsh and Scots for independence within the European Union was also low in 2003: 6.5 and 18.6 per cent respectively (Guibernau 2006, 65), although the strength of the nationalist vote in the 2014 Scottish referendum does speak to the volatility of these numbers.

Moreover, Guibernau finds that even in ethnic cultural communities where support for outright separation is strongest, most members maintain some identification with the secondary values of the host nation-state. Thus in Spain, only one-quarter of Basques and 16 per cent of Catalonians fail to identify at all with their Spanishness; in Britain, 36 per cent of Scots and 23 per cent of Welsh feel no identification with Great Britain; and in Quebec, only 21 per cent felt no attachment to Canada (Guibernau 2006, 66–8). As such, while clearly these ethnic cultural communities are significantly alienated from the secondary values of the host nation, they also feel a great deal of dual identification.

On the other hand, this dual identification can be exploited by more radical cultural contestants. Cultural contestants might be thought of as extremists within cultural separatist movements who seek to appeal to a comparatively moderate constituency. This colours their strategy to the extent that they have an incentive to mask their extremism. It is for this reason that to these more radical culturalists, cultural separatism is a highly efficacious strategy for appropriating secondary values – either through seceding and creating a new set of secondary values in the brand new state, or by forcing significant accommodations to the secondary values of the old one.

Cultural separatism represents – choose your cliché – the velvet glove or the good cop or the cat's paw. It is the moderate option that, should the dominant group fail to accommodate its narrow (in the sense of being group-specific) cultural demands, can help to persuade the mainstream of the subaltern group to accept more extreme measures. Cultural separatism represents the benign stimulus for popular mobilization that would be much more difficult to achieve if the stark initial choices were the status quo or outright secession. In a cultural separatist milieu, the mandate of more extreme culturalists is simply to nudge moderates further, perhaps by taking advantage of an inflammatory issue (in Canada, the failure of Charlottetown Accord) or perhaps through gradual, intergenerational socialization that turns latent grievance into passionate cause.

Still, in most countries, cultural separatism is not terribly pernicious. For it to have any destabilizing potential at all, relevant subaltern communities have to control territory. Leaving without land is called emigration. Secession is therefore not an option for a number of essentialist communities. Similarly, cultural separatism is no gateway to secession for essentialist communities that cannot sustain their own populations – women and homosexuals, for example. Finally, where essentialist communities are broadly distributed, such as Native Americans and African-Americans, without radical migration shifts, cultural separatism cannot be taken as a threat.

THE CHALLENGE OF MULTICULTURALISM

In this book multiculturalism has been presented as the most benign form of culturalism. Indeed, to the extent that it addresses the weakness of liberal republics' commitment to cultural diversity, multiculturalism can be seen as *conducive* to the stability of liberal republics. There are, of course, points of conflict between multiculturalist and liberal republican theories of justice. To put these in the context of the values we used to reconcile liberalism and republicanism, multiculturalism privileges situational equality ahead of formal equality. It emphasizes identity ahead of liberty. It understands moral obligation in terms of obligation to relevant essentialist communities, sometimes giving such obligation pride of place ahead of obligation to the national community. And by the same token, it understands social teleology as prioritizing values in ways that can work against common national purpose.

But none of these points of conflict are *antithetical* to liberal republicanism. With respect to equality, for example, liberal republicanism does not reject the situational equality mandated by multiculturalist justice. It *assumes* it. The logic is that fair rules produce fair outcomes. Over the long run, formal equality will result in situational equality as the distortions born of past systemic biases slowly fade away. On the other hand, as John Maynard Keynes has put it, in the long run we are all dead. Rather than serving as a threat to liberal republican values, their commitment to hasten the arrival of situational equality makes multiculturalists (to paraphrase Mackenzie King) little more than liberal republicans in a hurry.

The multiculturalist imperative to privilege identity ahead of liberty facially represents a source of incompatibility with liberal republicanism, to which liberty is central. For liberal republicans, liberty is a right to which individuals have a moral claim. That moral claim is grounded in the premise that, as with other rights, liberty is foundational human dignity. By contrast, protecting cultural identity is not generally understood to be a *right*. Instead, for many liberal republicans (e.g., Kukathas 1992) preservation of identity is an objective that can be advanced through exercising individual liberty. Yet whether or not it is a right is somewhat beside the point. To the extent that cultural identity is requisite to human dignity it serves the same purpose as a right, and hence can be seen as a *moral equivalent* to a right. If this is so, then privileging identity ahead of liberty is but a different means to the common end of universalizing human dignity.

Liberal republican and multiculturalist values can be similarly accommodated with respect to both their obligation and purpose. Liberal republicans recognize the importance of both secondary (national) and tertiary (subnational) values. Such recognition is inherent in federalism, for example. Both levels of government inculcate civic virtue in their own ways, and both work to social purposes, albeit slightly different ones. Multiculturalists' commitment to tertiary values simply shifts the nature

– and perhaps degree – of emphasis on tertiary values as it pertains to both obligation and purpose.

Still, to say that multiculturalism is not antithetical to liberal republicanism and indeed might be conducive to liberal republican stability is not the same thing as saying that it poses no challenge. Multiculturalism represents potentially unstable ground between liberal republican values on the one hand, and more radical culturalist values on the other. The ground is unstable because in reality multiculturalism often delivers either more than it advertises or less.

Multiculturalism represents the celebration of difference. Celebrating difference is not difficult if all it demands is appreciating the beauty of Native American cultural traditions, or sympathy for the injustices visited upon members of subaltern cultural communities, or support for the empowerment of groups to realize the situational equality that liberal republicanism promises but seemingly cannot deliver. Celebration is an active cause. One of the fundamental tenets of a multiculturalist universalization of dignity is the idea that subaltern cultures must not merely be tolerated or endured as deviations from the Normal, but actually must be recognized and celebrated as constituent elements of a pluralized normal.

The pluralized normal, manifest in the city-life ideal, brings with it certain logistical concerns, however. Realization of the pluralized normal is less akin to a lavish cultural buffet at which patrons select only the items that most appeal to their tastes than it is to a full-course meal in which some of the food is frankly not too appetizing. Meaningful celebration of subaltern cultural values demands that we celebrate *all* of these values. Truly to recognize and celebrate a culture demands accepting the values and practices that matter most to a culture's most committed members (Fish 1997, 380). This is problematic if what matters most to a culture's most committed members is antithetical to the primary values of a liberal republic. (We can think of any number of cultural practices – female genital mutilation to take just one example – that are difficult to square with liberal republicanism.) But multiculturalism (the full-course kind and not the buffet kind) would preclude such things as subordinating the values inherent in sharia law to the primary values of liberal republicanism. It would not just endure or tolerate certain cultural traditions – the inequality of women for example. It would embrace them whole-heartedly as being the cultural moral equivalent of liberal republicanism's insistence on gender equality. Indeed, in this sense, multiculturalism threatens to deliver more radical forms of culturalism than it promises.

At the same time, however, it also delivers less culturalism than it promises. For Fish, the problem with what he calls (buffet-style) "boutique" multiculturalism is that it is merely liberal republicanism in disguise. Underlying multiculturalism is a latent individualistic core in which celebrating and preserving minority cultures is bounded by a fundamental commitment to the idea that no individual's right to life or self-determination may be sacrificed to anyone else's cultural values (1997, 379). Few multiculturalists, for example, nodded approvingly at the *fatwa* issued against Salman Rushdie, as though such a proclamation was merely part of the rough and tumble of multicultural life. Celebrating cultural traditions that are different from (but not too different from) your own makes you open-minded. It does not make you a celebrator of minority cultures in any meaningful sense. A true multiculturalist cannot use his own cultural experience as a filter through which the traditions of other cultures are measured. To do that, it would seem, defeats the whole point of being a multiculturalist in the first place.

The bad news is that true (full-course) multiculturalism leaves liberal republican primary values vulnerable. To embrace the true multiculturalist logic limits a state's options in addressing versocultural threats. Indeed, to do so would be illegitimate insofar as it represents the breathtakingly condescending act of asserting the primacy of one set of cultural values over another. But as many European governments have found out the hard way, meeting cultural intolerance with full-course cultural tolerance sounds better on paper than it does in fact. The good news, as the belated response of many European governments attests, is that in reality there are not all that many true multiculturalists.

Ultimately, "boutique multiculturalism" provides few prescriptive cues. While it articulates an ideal that all moral agents in a liberal republic should embrace – that greater cultural sensitivity serves to strengthen rather than weaken liberal republican justice – the means to that end are not terribly cogent. The problem is that the solution is less an institutional issue than an attitudinal one. While institutional innovations have made a difference, *Brown* represents the paradigmatic case. Its importance stemmed from the attitudinal changes it provoked on the part of the American cultural mainstream. The issue reflects a much earlier one, pertaining to the locus of moral knowledge. To realize greater cultural sensitivity through rules and sanctions is reminiscent of the traditional republican, elitist principle that moral agency is exogenous to most of humanity. It implies that a neo-Socratic philosopher-king (a philosopher-court?) is necessary to impose justice on an unjust citizenry.

To be sure, the liberal republican assumption of moral endogeneity has hardly proven to be an infallible defence against cultural injustice. An intense historical inquiry is not needed to uncover awful examples of chauvinism and bigotry inflicted by erstwhile moral agents. But moral endogeneity does not promise infallibility; it suggests capacity. The attitudes of moral agents can be changed, and changed for the better. This being the case, multiculturalism can be effective in the same way as American evangelical Protestantism was effective in the early years of the republic. It can work the moral conscience. It performs that role best when it does so without the power of enforcement or sanction. As public policy, multiculturalism delivers either more than it promises or less. As social gadfly, to use the term that Socrates chose for himself, multiculturalism represents an effective tool for perfecting a liberal republican conception of justice that too often conflates usness with sameness.

CULTURALISM: THE ONLY CHALLENGE?

This book has concentrated on two main points: that liberalism and republicanism are inherently reconcilable, and that culturalism poses a challenge to liberal republican values. But there is potentially more to the story. Just because liberalism and republicanism are reconcilable does not mean the alliance is not volatile. If we are addressing the issue of regime stability, we would do well to remember that compounds are often less stable than the units that comprise them.

The persistent tension between republicanism and liberalism has manifested itself many times since the Enlightenment. Perhaps the readiest example is the US Civil War. There is obviously peril in reducing that event to a clash of ideologies tied to slave-holding and emancipation. Clearly there were reinforcing economic and political issues that map less neatly with the two ideological paradigms at issue. But to the extent that ideology was a factor, it turned on the tension between Southern preservation of a system of differential recognition of dignity (in this case based on race) and a Northern commitment to universalization of human dignity.

Since the Civil War, the tension between liberal and traditionally republican understandings of equality has been far less dramatic. But tension between liberal individualism and republican collectivism has not entirely disappeared. We have already noted that the twentieth century witnessed cultural fluctuation between times of greater collectivism and times of greater individualism. The demographic crisis that emerged in the 1960s can be seen as a product of individualist ascendance, resulting in a breakdown of moral obligation in favour of personal gratification that colours even our most intimate relationships.

The struggle between liberal individualism and republican collectivism has not gone unremarked in the literature. Bork, for example, sees America's slouch toward Gomorrah as equal parts hedonism and

multiculturalism (1997). Bellah (1975) understands the American social dislocation of the 1960s and 1970s as a product of the country's
alienation from its socio-religious origins and the icons of the civil religion that gave meaning to nationhood. He begins with the premise that
viable societies demand a generalized system of (typically religious) beliefs pertaining to that which is, or is not, morally appropriate. This moral code provides both cultural legitimation of that for which the society
stands, as well as a standard of judgment for determining when the society has strayed too far from it. For the United States of the eighteenth
century, the moral code was derived from a Christian conception of virtue emphasizing freedom, justice, and charity, and the republican one
which held that a good society relied on a virtuous citizenry (1975, ix–x).
But by the last quarter of the twentieth century, it was clear how far
America had apparently strayed. The fracturing of the generalized system of moral beliefs was manifest across numerous dimensions. The generation gap of the 1960s was but one illustration of what Bellah calls "the
erosion of common meanings." Another, in implicit agreement with
Bork, was an increased atomism and concomitant delegitimization of
traditional institutions of moral authority such as occupation, family,
church, and even nation. Still another was an increase in crimes against
people and property (1975, ix–xi).

From the beginning, Bellah notes, American moral consciousness had
a dualistic nature consistent with our conception of liberal republicanism. Indeed, such duality is endemic in many free societies, representing
the dialectic between private and public, liberty and duty, cupidity and
generosity (1975, 16–21). Thus, in America, on the one hand, there was
the covenantal vision of the United States as an Elect Nation, steeped
in the symbolism of nationhood that reinforced the moral values for
which the republic stood, and without which it could not survive (25). At
the same time, there was a utilitarian vision that underscored the efficacy
of reason and not faith as the foundational basis of the republic. Through
much of the nineteenth century, this duality held firm. Born of the original founding, this duality was institutionalized through the Second Great
Awakening, which emphasized the symbiotic relationship between liberty and moral rectitude. The duality of nineteenth-century America was
born in large part of Protestant Christianity, which reinforced both liberal individualism and republican virtue. It was this powerful nexus that
represented the moral foundation of America, culminating in a process
whereby it became nearly universally accepted that liberty and virtue
were mutually reinforcing values (Noll 2002, 209).

But in the end, for Bellah and others, it appears that the individualist,
rather than the communal, stream of the Evangelical Enlightenment has

taken hold of American culture. In the emerging social order he witnessed from the viewpoint of the mid-1970s, Bellah sees a dangerous
transformation of the meaning of liberty, from the Protestant/republi-
can understanding of it as freedom to live the virtuous (and hence most
rewarding) life to the late-twentieth-century conception as freedom to
live the unconstrained life (1975, 20–5). The former is predicated on
the existence of an objective moral code; the latter represents a utilitarian calculus. The utilitarian theory of freedom is part of what for Bellah
is a larger and more complex set of social phenomena that includes the
triumph of science over faith and the transformation of virtue from its
traditional republican meaning to the Mandevillian one, in which one
serves the greater good by serving oneself. This new "morality of self-
interest," Bellah suggests, is too thin a reed upon which to build a pros-
perous society. The "religion" born of liberal commitment to self-interest,
science, and capitalism cannot account for social context, and is limited
in its capacity for matters of ethics, aesthetics, and religion (xiii–xiv).

Fukuyama (1999) offers a less apocalyptic explanation. He attributes
the social dislocation described by Bork and Bellah to normal, cyclical
fluctuations that periodically punctuate the prevailing equilibrium
(Krasner 1984) of established social values. Fukuyama understands this
social dislocation in terms of the loss of moral obligation manifest as
trust that others within the community share the same norms and values
and that they will honour their commitments to society (1999, 15). The
decline of moral obligation manifests itself in terms of social pathologies, such as anomie and suicide (Durkheim 1979), crime against people
and property, and the breakdown of the family as manifested through a
decline in total fertility rates and an elevation of divorce and illegitimacy
rates (1999, ch. 2). Because trust is a byproduct of obligation, its decline
appears to represent a dangerous atomization of the ties that bind civil
society (51), and the rise of the sort of hedonism inherent in Bork's and
Bellah's diagnoses.

On the other hand, even if what we are witnessing is a depletion of
moral obligation in liberal republics, it is important to note that this has
happened before, most notably in the context of the shift from the agri-
cultural to the industrial mode of production. Using evidence from past
social disruptions in addition to examining the trends of the 1990s,
Fukuyama argues that social tolerance for personal self-indulgence cannot be sustained indefinitely.[1] Ultimately, natural human impulses for

---

1 Using indicators such as increasing rates of violent crime, theft, divorce, and
illegitimacy, as well as decreasing total fertility rates, Fukuyama finds that (with slightly different starting points and differing levels of intensity) these social indicators began to

social order begin to reassert themselves (ch. 16). If this is true, then destabilization of the homeostatic alliance of liberal and republican values is but a temporary phenomenon, magnified in importance in the eyes of those who experience it, but historically insignificant, a temporary blip in the symbiotic relationship that exists between individualism and civil obligation.

The Fukuyama thesis finds support in the social psychological literature. McHugh (1966), for example, looks at radical value transformation in the context of personal rehabilitation from the destructive influence of personal self-indulgence. He finds that in the rehabilitation process, socially disintegrative behaviour – desocialization – is a prerequisite for resocialization into the norms and values of the social mainstream. While his argument is not as deterministic as Fukuyama's, it does warn against assigning too much weight to the symptoms of social dislocation without correctly diagnosing the underlying disorder.

Thus, despite stresses and strains that tear at the resiliency of liberal republicanism, it seems reasonable to assert that there are limits to the pernicious effects of atomism. At some point, it would seem, Hegel's *geist* or Smith's moral sentiment or Kant's pure reason or America's God or Fukuyama's human imperative for moral order or some other homeostatic force reasserts itself to bring the system back into equilibrium before licentious anarchy and corrective tyranny derail the eschatological progression of history.

THE END OF HISTORY OR THE END OF THE WORLD?

It seems pretty clear that we have reached neither the end of history nor the end of the world as we know it. This is a good thing, for neither is an appealing prospect. The end of history represents the end of the culturalist challenge to liberal republicanism. But it also represents the end of usness as a meaningful concept insofar as the end of history represents a cosmopolitan nullification of themness. The end of the world, if we may take licence to call it that, will occur when liberal republics can no

---

trend in the wrong direction for most countries at some point during the 1960s or early 1970s. By the early 1990s, however, we find that these negative indicators have levelled off, and even begun to reverse themselves. If we extend the trend lines for TFR to 2010, we find modest support for the Fukuyama thesis. Australia, Austria, Belgium, Canada, Denmark, Finland, France, Germany, Ireland, Italy, the Netherlands, New Zealand, Norway, Spain, Sweden, the United Kingdom, and the United States have all witnessed increases in TFR from the period 1995–2000 to 2005–2010. On the other hand, most of these increases have been fairly small (an average of .14 children per country) and only Ireland and New Zealand have reached the replacement threshold of 2.09 (United Nations 2011).

longer accommodate the us–them distinction, and the thems and the usses either go our separate ways – the breakup of Canada or Spain, or the cultural dualism of the Huntingtonian United States in the wake of Hispanic immigration – or the thems vanquish the usses, such that one set of primary values replaces another as Islamic fundamentalism threatens to do in contemporary Europe. The trick for liberal republics, then, is to stay the middle course between the elimination of the us–them distinction on the one hand, and the imperialism of the us–them distinction on the other.

Usness, and by extension themness, is critical to liberal republican societies. Without the us–them distinction, as Fukuyama points out at the conclusion of the *End of History*, societies will lose all intrinsic value. Because values acquire value only in the context of countervailing values, the end of history will be a society without values. It is for this reason that Fukuyama fears that the eschatological end of his universal history will in reality mark the beginning of a new recursive cycle. Too much us–them distinction, by contrast, swamps the capacity of liberal republics to retain the sense of obligation – of virtue – necessary for perpetuating a society predicated on a conception of the moral good inherent in liberal republican values. Such obligation represents a tripartite commitment to the self, to the society, and to the moral good. This is accomplished, in a modern manifestation of the Aristotelian ideal of ruling and being ruled in turn, through civic participation in constructing the sorts of secondary rules that guide individuals into more meaningful lives. Civic participation is both source and product of moral obligation to others, of trust and efficacy, of social capital, of the glue that holds societies together, call it what you will. That moral obligation is threatened through the breakdown of reasonableness, or purpose, or social moral consensus, call it what you will. More benign forms of culturalism do not constitute a threat in the same sense that cultural appropriation does. But benign prescriptions can potentially be embraced by more radical culturalists as a necessary first step in their ultimate quest to replace one set of primary values with another.

There are two contradictory implications here for more radical culturalists. The first is that cultural appropriation is a stealthy strategy. Most radical culturalists tend not to advertise themselves as such, finding it far more politic to disguise themselves in the cloak of more benign forms of culturalism. The second, and no doubt more applicable in most cases, is that radicalism is an opportunistic strategy that enters into people's consciousness only when conditions favourable to value appropriation occur. In this sense, radical culturalists are *graduates* of more benign forms of culturalism, if we can put it this way, who somewhere along the line begin to see radicalism as a more pleasing alternative to moderation, as in multiculturalism.

Will we, as liberal republics, survive the potential cultural challenges suggested by this book? It seems likely. We have weathered more overt threats in the past. But it is foolish just to count on past successes to see us through future challenges, to adopt the ostrich theory of good governance. This was the mistake of the Roman republicans of the first century BC. Regimes, even great regimes like the Roman Republic, do fail. We have learned from those mistakes. Universalization of human dignity is a more stable base than differential recognition of great men. Good systems born of good institutions are more stable than good people born of high station. Self-interested political contestation is not the very definition of regime-destroying corruption, but such contestation must take place in the context of a consensual understanding of primary values. Threats will not just melt away as we approach the threshold of some mythical eschatological end. We are very much mired in history as the battle for recognition continues to evolve, allowing us to reach the cusp of historical progression even as the end eludes our grasp.

References

Ackermann, Alice. 2000. *Making Peace Prevail: Preventing Violent Conflict in Macedonia.* Syracuse: Syracuse University Press.

Ajzenstat, Janet. 2007. *The Canadian Founding: John Locke and Parliament.* Montreal: McGill-Queen's University Press.

– 1985. "Modern Mixed Government: A Liberal Defence of Inequality." *Canadian Journal of Political Science* 18:119–34.

Ajzenstat, Janet, and Peter J. Smith. 1995. "Liberal-Republicanism: The Revisionist Picture of Canada's Founding." In *Canada's Origins: Liberal, Tory, or Republican?*, edited by Janet Ajzenstat and Peter J. Smith, 1–18. Ottawa: Carleton University Press.

Alba, Richard, and Victor Nee. 2003. *Remaking the American Mainstream: Assimilation and Contemporary Immigration.* Cambridge: Harvard University Press.

Alberta Human Rights Panel. 2008. "Decision on Remedy: Darren Lund v. Stephen Boisson and the Concerned Christian Coalition Inc." S2002/08/0137.

Ali, Ameer. 2010. "Assimilation, Integration or Convivencia: The Dilemma of Diaspora Muslims from 'Eurabia' to 'Londonistan,' from 'Lakembanon' to Sri Lanka." *Journal of Muslim Minority Affairs* 30:183–98.

Allison, Graham T. 1999. *Essence of Decision: Explaining the Cuban Missile Crisis.* Boston: Little Brown.

Allison, Graham T., and Morton H. Halperin. 1972. "Bureaucratic Politics: A Paradigm and Some Policy Implications." *World Politics* 24:40–79.

Allport, Gordon W. 1979. *The Nature of Prejudice.* New York: Basic Books.

Almond, Gabriel A. 1955. "Comparative Political Systems." *Journal of Politics* 18:391–409.

Almond, Gabriel A., and Sidney Verba. 1965. *The Civic Culture: Political Attitudes and Democracy in Five Nations.* Boston: Little Brown.

Altman, Andrew. 1993. "Liberalism and Campus Hate-Speech: A Philosophical Examination." *Ethics* 103:302–17.

Anderson, Benedict. 2006. *Imagined Communities: Reflections on the Origins and Spread of Nationalism*. London: Verso.

Anderson, Christopher J., and Aida Paskeviciute. 2006. "How Ethnic and Linguistic Heterogeneity Influence the Prospects for Civil Society: A Comparative Study of Citizen Behavior." *Journal of Politics* 68:783–802.

Anthony, Dick, and Thomas Robbins. 1982. "Spiritual Innovation and the Crisis of American Civil Religion." *Daedalus* 111:215–34.

Aquinas, Thomas. 1947. *Summa Theologica*. Translated by Brothers of the English Dominican Province. Cincinnati: Benziger Brothers.

Archibald, Katherine. 1949. "The Concept of Social Hierarchy in the Writings of St. Thomas Aquinas." *The Historian* 12:28–54.

Aristotle. 1999. *Nicomachean Ethics*. 2nd ed. Translated by Terence Irwin. Indianapolis: Hackett.

– 1962. *The Politics of Aristotle*. Translated and edited by Ernest Baker. New York: Oxford University Press.

Arnhart, Larry. 1983. "Statesmanship as Magnanimity: Classical, Christian & Modern." *Polity* 16:263–83.

Arrow, Kenneth. 1972. "Gifts and Exchanges." *Philosophy & Public Affairs* 1:343–62.

Ashcraft, Karen Lee, and Michael E. Pacanowsky. 1996. "A Woman's Worst Enemy: Reflections on a Narrative of Organizational Life and Female Identity." *Journal of Applied Communication Research* 24:217–39.

Associated Press. 2006. "Film Exposes Immigrants to Dutch Liberalism: If You Can't Tolerate Gay Lifestyle, Public Nudity, You Can't Come." 16 March. http://www.msnbc.msn.com/id/11842116/ns/world_news-europe/t/film-exposes-immigrants-dutch-liberalism/. Accessed 16 February 2012.

Saint Augustine. 1943. *The Confessions of St. Augustine*. Translated by J.G. Pilkington. New York: Liveright.

– 1887. *City of God*. In *Nicene and Post-Nicene Fathers of the Christian Church*. Vol. II, translated by J.F. Shaw and edited by Philip Schaff. Buffalo: Christian Literature Company.

Bailey, Beth, and David Farber. 1993. "The 'Double-V' Campaign in World War II Hawaii: African Americans, Racial Ideology, and Federal Power." *Journal of Social History* 26:817–43.

Bailyn, Bernard. 1962. "Political Experience and Enlightenment Ideas in Eighteenth Century America." *American Historical Review* 67:339–51.

Baker, David P., and Deborah P. Jones. 1993. "Creating Gender Equality: Cross-National Gender Stratification and Mathematical Performance." *Sociology of Education* 66:91–103.

Bano, Samia. 2008. "In Pursuit of Religious and Legal Diversity: A Response to the Archbishop of Canterbury and the 'Sharia Debate' in Britain." *Ecclesiastical Law Journal* 10:283–309.

Banting, Keith, and Richard Simeon, eds. 1983. *And No One Cheered: Federalism, Democracy and the Constitution Act.* Toronto: Methuen.

Barron, Robert. 2007. "Augustine's Questions: Why the Augustinian Theology of God Matters Today." *Logos* 10:35–54.

Barton, Carlin A. 2001. *Roman Honor: The Fire in the Bones.* Berkeley: University of California Press.

Baskerville, S.K. 1998. "Puritans, Revisionists, and the English Revolution." *Huntington Library Quarterly* 61:151–71.

Bates, Robert H. 1990. "Institutions as Investments." Duke University Program in Political Economy, Working Paper Number 133.

Batinski, Michael C. 1996. *Jonathan Belcher: Colonial Governor.* Lexington: University Press of Kentucky.

Baum, Gregory. 1992. "The Catholic Left in Quebec." In *Culture and Social Change: Social Movements in Quebec and Ontario,* edited by Colin Leys and Marguerite Mendell, 140–54. Montreal: Black Rose.

Bayertz, Kurt. 1996. "Human Dignity: Philosophic Origin and Scientific Erosion of an Idea." In *Sanctity of Life and Human Dignity,* edited by Kurt Bayertz, 73–90. Dordrecht: Kluwer.

Becker, Gary S. 1993. *A Treatise on the Family.* Enlarged ed. Cambridge: Harvard University Press.

Bellah, Robert N. 1975. *The Broken Covenant: American Civil Religion in Time of Trial.* New York: Seabury Press.

Bellamy, Richard, and Martin Hollis. 1995. "Liberal Justice: Political and Metaphysical." *The Philosophical Quarterly* 45:1–19.

Benard, Cheryl. 2003. *Civil Democratic Islam: Partners, Resources, and Strategies.* Santa Monica: Rand.

Bennett, Rosemary. 2011. "British Muslims Reviving Polygamy." *The Australian.* 27 September.

Benson, Paul. 2004. "Blame, Oppression, and Diminished Moral Competence." In *Moral Psychology: Feminist Ethics and Social Theory,* edited by Peggy DesAutels and Margaret Urban Walker, 183–200. Lanham: Rowman and Littlefield.

Berger, Peter. 1970. "On the Obsolescence of the Concept of Honor." *European Journal of Sociology* 11:339–47.

Berki, R.N. 1971. "Machiavellianism: A Philosophical Defense." *Ethics* 81:107–27.

Berlin, Isaiah. 2001. Nationalism: Past Neglect and Present Power." In *Against the Current: Essays in the History of Ideas,* edited by Henry Hardy, 333–56. Princeton: Princeton University Press.

– 1991. "Two Concepts of Liberty." In *Liberty*, edited by David Miller, 33–57. Oxford: Oxford University Press.

Bernard, G.W. 1990. "The Church of England c.1529–c.1642." *History* 75:183–206.

Berry, J.W., U. Kim, S. Power, M. Young, and M. Bujaki. 1989. "Acculturation Attitudes in Plural Societies." *Applied Psychology* 38:185–206.

Berryman, Sue. E. 1983. *Who Will Do Science?* New York: Rockefeller Foundation.

Beuf, Ann H. 1977. *Red Children in White America.* University Park: Pennsylvania State University Press.

Beza, Theodore. 1969. "Right of Magistrates." In *Constitutionalism and Resistance in the Sixteenth Century: Three Treatises by Hotman, Beza, & Mornay*, edited by Julian H. Franklin, 101–35. New York: Pegasus.

Black, Anthony. 1997. "Christianity and Republicanism: From St. Cyprian to Rousseau." *American Political Science Review* 91:647–56.

Blau, Joseph L. 1977. "Emerson's Transcendent Individualism as a Social Philosophy." *Review of Metaphysics* 31:80–92.

Bonadeo, Alfredo. 1969. "The Role of the 'Grandi' in the Political World of Machiavelli." *Studies in the Renaissance* 16:9–30.

Bongaarts, John. 2004. "Public Aging and the Rising Cost of Public Pensions." *Population and Development Review* 30:1–23.

Bork, Robert H. 1997. *Slouching towards Gomorrah: Modern Liberalism and America's Decline.* New York: Reganbooks.

Börsch-Supan, Axel. 2003. "Labor Market Effects of Population Aging." *Labour* 17:5–44.

Brammer, J. Brady. 2006. "Religious Groups and the Gay Rights Movement: Recognizing Common Ground." *Brigham Young University Law Review* 4:995–1031.

Brenner, Johanna. 1996. "The Best of Times, the Worst of Times: Feminism in the United States." In *Mapping the Women's Movement: Feminist Politics and Social Transformation in the North*, edited by Monica Threlfall, 17–72. London: Verso.

Breton, Raymond. 1992. *Why Meech Failed: Lessons for Canadian Constitutionmaking.* Toronto: C.D. Howe Institute.

Brewer, John D. 1991. "Hercules, Hippolyte and the Amazons – or Policewomen in the RUC." *British Journal of Sociology* 42:231–47.

Brittan, Samuel. 1975. "The Economic Contradictions of Democracy." *British Journal of Political Science* 5:129–59.

Brodie, Ian. 2002. *Friends of the Court: The Privileging of Interest Group Litigants in Canada.* Albany: SUNY Press.

– 1996. "The Market for Political Status." *Comparative Politics* 28:253–71.

Brodie, Ian, and Neil Nevitte. 1993. "Evaluating the Citizens' Constitution Theory." *Canadian Journal of Political Science* 26:235–69.

Brown, Jason W. 2005. *Process and the Authentic Life: Toward a Psychology of Value.* Piscataway: Transaction Books.

Brown, Peter. 2015. *The Ransom of the Soul: Afterlife and Wealth in Early Western Christianity.* Cambridge: Harvard University Press.

Brown, Robert A., and Todd C. Shaw. 2002. "Separate Nations: Two Attitudinal Dimensions of Black Nationalism." *Journal of Politics* 64:22–44.

Buchanan, Allen. 1991. *Secession: The Morality of Political Divorce from Fort Sumter to Lithuania and Quebec.* Boulder: Westview.

Buchanan, James M., and Gordon Tullock. 1962. *The Calculus of Consent: Logical Foundations of Constitutional Democracy.* Ann Arbor: University of Michigan Press.

Buchwalter, Andrew. 1992. "Hegel's Concept of Virtue." *Political Theory* 20:548–83.

Budziszewski, J. 1999. "Why We Kill the Weak." In *The Revenge of Conscience: Politics and the Fall of Man*, edited by J. Budziszewski, 125–35. Dallas: Spence.

– 1997. *Written on the Heart: The Case for Natural Law.* Downers Grove, IL: InterVarsity Press.

– 1988. *The Nearest Coast of Darkness: A Vindication of the Politics of Virtue.* Ithaca: Cornell University Press.

Buell, Lawrence J. 1972. "Reading Emerson for Structure: The Coherence of the Essays." *Quarterly Journal of Speech* 58:58–69.

Burckhardt, Jacob. 1990. *The Civilization of the Renaissance in Italy.* Translated by S.G.C. Middlemore. London: Penguin.

Burstein, Paul. 1998. *Discrimination, Jobs, and Politics: The Struggle for Equal Employment Opportunity in the United States.* Chicago: University of Chicago Press.

Burtt, Shelley. 1993. "The Politics of Virtue Today: A Critique and a Proposal." *American Political Science Review* 87:360–68.

Butler, David, and Donald Stokes. 1976. *Political Change in Britain.* 2nd college ed. New York: St Martin's.

Buzan, Barry. 1983. *People, States and Fear: An Agenda for International Security Studies in the Post-Cold War Era.* Brighton: Wheatsheaf.

Buzan, Barry, Ole Waever, and Jaap de Wilde. 1998. *Security: A New Framework for Analysis.* Boulder: Lynne Rienner.

Cairns, Alan C. 1990. "Constitutional Minoritarianism in Canada." In *Canada: State of the Federation 1990*, edited by Ronald L. Watts and Douglas M. Brown, 71–96. Kingston: Queen's University Institute of Intergovernmental Relations.

Calder, Todd C. 2007. "Is the Deprivation Theory of Evil Dead?" *American Philosophical Quarterly* 44:371–81.

Caldwell, John C. 1982. "An Explanation of the Continued Fertility Decline in the West: Stages, Succession and Crisis." In *Theories of Fertility Decline*

(Population and Social Structure), edited by John C. Caldwell, 233–66. London: Academic Press.

Caldwell, John C., and Thomas Schindlmayr. 2003. "Explanations of the Fertility Crisis in Modern Societies: A Search for Commonalities." *Population Studies* 57:241–63.

Calvert, Clay. 1997. "Hate Speech and Its Harms: A Communication Theory Perspective." *Journal of Communication* 47:4–19.

Calvin, John. 1845. *Institutes of the Christian Religion*. Edited and translated by Henry Beveridge. Edinburgh: Calvin Translation Society.

Cannold, Leslie. 2000. *The Abortion Myth: Feminism, Morality, and the Hard Choices Women Make*. Middletown: Wesleyan University Press.

Carens, Joseph H. 2006. "Free Speech and Democratic Norms in the Danish Cartoon Controversy." *International Migration* 44:33–42.

– 1987. "Aliens and Citizens: The Case for Open Borders." *Review of Politics* 49:251–73.

Carmichael, Gordon A., and Andrea Whittaker. 2001. "Asking the Actors: A Radical(?) Approach to Understanding Ongoing Fertility Decline in Australia." Paper presented to the International Union for the Scientific Study of Population, Salvador, August.

Carr, Matt. 2006. "You Are Now Entering Eurabia." *Race & Class* 48:1–22.

Cassirer, Ernst. 2000. *The Individual and the Cosmos in Renaissance Philosophy*. Translated and edited by Mario Domandi. New York: Dover.

Catsambis, Sophia. 1994. "The Path to Math: Gender and Racial-Ethnic Differences in Mathematics Participation from Middle School to High School." *Sociology of Education* 67:199–215.

Caul, Miki. 2001. "Political Parties and the Adoption of Candidate Gender Quotas: A Cross-National Analysis." *Journal of Politics* 63:1214–29.

Chavous, Tabbye M., Debra Hilkene Bernat, Karen Schmeelk-Cone, Cleopatra H. Caldwell, Laura Kohn-Wood, and Marc A. Zimmerman. 2003. "Racial Identity and Academic Attainment among African American Adolescents." *Child Development* 74:1076–90.

Cherribi, Sam. 2010. *In the House of War*. Oxford: Oxford University Press.

Chung, Kim-Sau. 2000. "Role Models and Arguments for Affirmative Action." *American Economic Review* 90:640–8.

Cicero. 2008a. *The Republic*. In *The Republic and the Laws*. Translated and edited by Niall Rudd. Oxford: Oxford University Press.

– 2008b. *The Laws*. In *The Republic and the Laws*. Translated and edited by Niall Rudd. Oxford: Oxford University Press.

– 1974. *De Officiis/On Duties*. Translated and edited by Harry G. Edinger. Indianapolis: Bobbs-Merrill.

– 1971. *Cicero on the Good Life*. Translated and edited by Michael Grant. London: Penguin.

– 1891. *The Orations of Marcus Tullius Cicero.* Translated by Charles Duke Yonge. London: George Bell and Sons.

Citrin, Jack, Amy Lerman, Michael Murakami, and Kathryn Pearson. 2007. "Testing Huntington: Is Hispanic Immigration a Threat to American Identity?" *Perspectives on Politics* 5:31–48.

Citrin, Jack, Beth Reingold, Evelyn Walters, and Donald P. Green. 1990. "The 'Official English' Movement and the Symbolic Politics of Language in the United States." *Western Political Quarterly* 43:535–59.

Citrin, Jack, Cara Wong, and Brian Duff. 2001. "The Meaning of American National Identity: Patterns of Ethnic Conflict and Consensus." In *Social Identity, Intergroup Conflict, and Conflict Reduction,* edited by Richard D. Ashmore, Lee Jussim and David Wilder, 71–100. New York: Oxford University Press.

Clark, J.C.D. 1994. *The Language of Liberty, 1660–1832: Political Discourse and Social Dynamics in the Anglo-American World.* Cambridge: Cambridge University Press.

Clark, Kenneth B., and Mamie P. Clark. 1947. "Racial Identification and Preference in Negro Schoolchildren." In *Readings in Social Psychology,* edited by Eleanor E. Newcomb and Theodore M. Hartley, 169–78. New York: Holt.

Clarke, Jean Illsley, and Connie Dawson. 1998. *Growing Up Again: Parenting Ourselves, Parenting Our Children.* Center City, MN: Hazelden.

Clausen, Hans C. 2005. "The 'Privilege of Speech' in a 'Pleasantly Authoritarian Country': How Canada's Judiciary Allowed Laws Proscribing Discourse Critical of Homosexuality to Trump Free Speech and Religious Liberty." *Vanderbilt Journal of Transnational Law* 38:443–504.

Coffey, John. 1998. "Puritanism and Liberty Revisited: The Case for Toleration in the English Revolution." *Historical Journal* 41:961–85.

Colish, Marcia L. 1999. "Republicanism, Religion and Machiavelli's Savanarolan Moment." *Journal of the History of Ideas* 60:597–617.

– 1985. *The Stoic Tradition from Antiquity to the Early Middle Ages.* 2 vols. Leiden: E.J. Brill.

– 1971. "The Idea of Liberty in Machiavelli." *Journal of the History of Ideas* 32:323–50.

Connor, Walker. 1973. "The Politics of Ethnonationalism." *Journal of International Affairs* 27:1–21.

Coomarswamy, Radhika. 2002. "Identity Within: Cultural Relativism, Minority Rights and the Empowerment of Women." *George Washington International Law Review* 34:483–518.

Cornish, Paul J. 2010. "Augustine's Contribution to the Republican Tradition." *European Journal of Political Theory* 9:133–48.

Correll, Shelley J. 2001. "Gender and the Career Choice Process: The Role of Biased Self-Assessments." *American Journal of Sociology* 106:1691–730.

Dahl, Robert A. 1961. *Who Governs? Democracy and Power in an American City.* New Haven: Yale University Press.

Damico, Alfonso J. 1984. "Is the Problem with Liberalism How It Thinks?" *Polity* 16:547–66.

Daniels, Norman. 1990. "Equality of What: Welfare, Resources, or Capabilities?" *Philosophy and Phenomenological Research* 50:273–96.

Darwall, Stephen. 2004. "Equal Dignity in Adam Smith." *Adam Smith Review* 1:129–34.

Davies, Godfrey. 1934. "Arminian Versus Puritan in England, ca. 1620–1640." *Huntington Library Bulletin* 5:157–79.

Davison, Roderic H. 1954. "Turkish Attitudes concerning Christian-Muslim Equality in the Nineteenth Century." *American Historical Review* 59:844–64.

De La Garza, Rodolfo O., Angelo Falcon, and F. Chris Garcia. 1996. "Will the Real Americans Please Stand Up: Anglo and Mexican-American Support of Core American Political Values." *American Journal of Political Science* 40:335–51.

De Tocqueville, Alexis. 1969. *Democracy in America.* Translated by George Lawrence. Edited by J.P. Mayer. Garden City: Anchor.

Degutis, Algirdas. 2006. "Reflections on Western Self-Deconstruction: Extinction via Liberal Openness." *Athena* 3:31–51.

Delpit, Lisa. 1998. "What Should Teachers Do? Ebonics and Culturally Responsive Instruction." In *The Real Ebonics Debate: Power, Language, and the Education of African-American Children*, edited by Theresa Perry and Lisa Delpit, 17–28. Boston: Beacon Press.

DeLue, Steven M. 1989. *Political Obligation in a Liberal State.* Albany: State University of New York Press.

Dershowitz, Alan. 2005. *Rights from Wrongs: A Secular Theory of the Origin of Rights.* New York: Basic Books.

Deutsch, Karl W. 1961. "Social Mobilization and Political Development." *American Political Science Review* 55:493–514.

Dobel, J. Patrick. 1978. "The Corruption of a State." *American Political Science Review* 72:958–73.

Donnelly, Jack. 1982. "Human Rights and Human Dignity: An Analytic Critique of Non-Western Conceptions of Human Rights." *American Political Science Review* 76:303–16.

Dooley, Brian. 1998. *Black and Green: The Fight for Civil Rights in Northern Ireland and Black America.* London: Pluto.

Downing, Lyle A., and Robert B. Thigpen. 1993. "Virtue and the Common Good in Liberal Theory." *Journal of Politics* 55:1046–59.

Doyle, Michael. 1986. "Liberalism and World Politics." *American Political Science Review* 80:1151–69.

Durkheim, Emile. 1979. *Suicide: A Study in Sociology.* New York: Free Press.

Dworkin, Ronald. 1996. *Freedom's Laws: The Moral Reading of the American Constitution.* Cambridge: Harvard University Press.

– 1978. "Liberalism." In *Public and Private Morality.* Edited by Stuart Hampshire, 113–143. Cambridge: Cambridge University Press.

Easterlin, Richard A. 1976. "The Conflict between Aspirations and Resources." *Population and Development Review* 2:417–25.

Ehrlich, Susan, and Ruth King. 1992. "Gender-Based Language Reform and the Social Construction of Meaning." *Discourse and Society* 3:151–66.

Eisenstadt, S.N. 1951. "The Place of Elites and Primary Groups in the Absorption of New Immigrants in Israel." *American Journal of Sociology* 57:222–31.

Elster, Jon. 1983. S*our Grapes: Studies in the Subversion of Rationality.* Cambridge: Cambridge University Press.

– 1979. *Ulysses and the Sirens: Studies in Rationality and Irrationality.* Cambridge: Cambridge University Press.

Ely, John Hart. 1980. *Democracy and Distrust: A Theory of Judicial Review.* Cambridge: Harvard University Press.

Emerson, Ralph Waldo. 2008. "Uses of Great Men." In *Representative Men,* 7–21. Rockville: Arc Manor.

– 2007. "Power." In *The Conduct of Life,* 29–46. New York: Cosimo.

– 1951a. "Self-Reliance." In *Emerson's Essays,* 31–66. New York: Harper and Row.

– 1951b. "History." In *Emerson's Essays,* 1–30. New York: Harper and Row.

– 1951c. "Manners." In *Emerson's Essays,* 345–73. New York: Harper and Row.

– 1951d. "Experience." In *Emerson's Essays,* 292–323. New York: Harper and Row.

– 1891. *The Complete Prose Works of Ralph Waldo Emerson.* London: Ward, Lock and Co.

Englard, Izhak. 1999/00. "Human Dignity: From Antiquity to Modern Israel's Constitutional Framework." *Cardozo Law Review* 21:1903–27.

Espenshade, Thomas. 1994. "Can Immigration Slow U.S. Population Aging?" *Journal of Policy Analysis and Management* 13759–768.

Espenshade, Thomas J., Juan Carlos Guzman, and Charles F. Westoff. 2003. "The Surprising Global Variation in Replacement Fertility." *Population Research and Policy Review* 22:575–83.

Esposito, John L. 2003. "Introduction: Modernizing Islam and Re-Islamization in Global Perspective." In *Modernizing Islam: Religion in the Public Sphere in Europe and the Middle East,* edited by John L. Esposito and François Burgat, 1–16. New Brunswick, NJ: Rutgers University Press.

Esposito, John L., and Dalia Mogahed. 2007. *Who Speaks for Islam? What a Billion Muslims Really Think.* New York: Gallup Press.

Etzioni, Amitai. 1996. *The New Golden Rule: Community and Morality in a Democratic Society.* New York: Basic Books.

Euben, Roxanne L. 1999. *Enemy in the Mirror: Islamic Fundamentalism and the Limits of Modern Rationalism, A Work of Comparative Political Theory.* Princeton: University Press.

Eulau, Heinz, and John C. Wahlke. 1978. *The Politics of Representation: Continuities in Theory and Research.* Beverly Hills: Sage.

Evans, Sara. 1980. *Personal Politics: The Roots of Women's Liberation in the Civil Rights Movement and the New Left.* New York: Vintage.

Ewin, R.E. 1970. "On Justice and Injustice." *Mind* New Series 79:200–16.

Eyerman, Ron. 1981. "False Consciousness and Ideology in Marxist Theory." *Acta Sociologica* 24:43–56.

Feagin, Joe R., and José A. Cobas. 2008. "Latinos/as and White Racial Frame: The Procrustean Bed of Assimilation." *Sociological Inquiry* 78:39–53.

Fearon, James. 1999. "Why Ethnic Politics and 'Pork' Tend to Go Together." Paper Presented at MacArthur Foundation Conference on Ethnic Politics and Democratic Stability, University of Chicago, May 21–3.

Feinberg, Joel. 1980. "The Nature and Value of Rights." In *Rights, Justice, and the Bounds of Liberty: Essays in Social Philosophy*, 143–58. Princeton: Princeton University Press.

Ferejohn, John, Jack N. Rakove, and Jonathan Riley. 2001. "Editors' Introduction." In *Constitutional Culture and Democratic Rule*, edited by John Ferejohn, Jack N. Rakove, and Jonathan Riley, 1–40. Cambridge: Cambridge University Press.

Fichte, J.G. 1869. *The Science of Rights.* Translated by A.E. Kroeger. Philadelphia: J.B. Lippincott.

Fine, Terri. 2006. "Generations, Feminist Beliefs and Abortion Rights Support." *Journal of International Women's Studies* 7:126–40.

Fink, Zera S. 1945. *The Classical Republicans.* Evanston: Northwestern University Press.

Fish, Stanley. 1997. "Boutique Multiculturalism, or Why Liberals are Incapable of Thinking about Hate Speech." *Critical Inquiry* 23:378–95.

Fishkin. James. 1983. *Justice, Equal Opportunity, and the Family.* New Haven: Yale University Press.

Fishman, Donald A. 2004. "Mainstreaming Ethnicity: Horace Kallen, the Strategy of Transcendence, and Cultural Pluralism." *Southern Communication Journal* 69:157–72.

Flew, Antony. 2001. *Equality in Liberty and Justice.* New Brunswick, NJ: Transaction.

Folger, Robert, and Russell Cropanzano. 2001. "Fairness Theory: Justice as Accountability." In *Advances in Organizational Justice*, edited by Jerald Greenberg and Russell Cropanzano, 1–55. Stanford: Stanford University Press.

Foster, Herbert D. 1927. "International Calvinism Through Locke and the Revolution of 1688." *American Historical Review* 32:475–99.

Freedman, Estelle. 1979. "Separatism as Strategy: Female Institution Building and American Feminism, 1879–1930." *Feminist Studies* 5:512–29.

– 1974. "The New Woman: Changing Views of Women in the 1920s." *Journal of American History* 61:372–93.

Freeman, Samuel. 2007. *Justice and the Social Contract: Essays on Rawlsian Political Philosophy.* Oxford: Oxford University Press.

Frey, William H. 1996. "Immigration, Domestic Migration and Demographic Balkinization in America: New Evidence for the 1990s." *Population and Development Review* 22:741–63.

Frost, S.B. 1952. "Eschatology and Myth." *Vetus Testamentum* 2:70–80.

Frye. Marilyn. 1993. "Some Reflections on Separatism and Power." In *The Gay and Lesbian Studies Reader*, edited by Henry Abelove, Michèle Aina Barale, and David M. Halperin, 91–8. New York: Routledge.

Fukuyama, Francis. 2002. *The End of History and the Last Man.* New York: Perennial.

– 1999. *The Great Disruption: Human Nature and the Reconstitution of Moral Order.* New York: Free Press.

– 1989. "The End of History?" *National Interest* 16:3–18.

Fuller, Graham E. 2003. "The Youth Factor: The New Demographics of the Middle East and the Implications for U.S. Policy." http://www.brookings.edu/fp/projects/islam/fuller2003.pdf. Accessed 15 November 2011.

– 1991. *Islamic Fundamentalism in the Northern Tier Countries.* Santa Monica: Rand.

Gale, Mary Ellen. 1991. "Reimagining the First Amendment: Racist Speech and Equal Liberty." *St. John's Law Review* 65:119–185.

Galston, William A. 1995. "Two Concepts of Liberalism." *Ethics* 105:516–34.

– 1991. *Liberal Purposes: Goods, Virtues, and Diversity in the Liberal State.* Cambridge: Cambridge University Press.

– 1982. "Defending Liberalism." *American Political Science Review* 76:621–9.

Gauvreau, Michael. 2005. *The Catholic Origin of Quebec's Quiet Revolution.* Montreal: McGill-Queen's University Press.

Geertz, Clifford. 1963. "The Integrative Revolution: Primordial Sentiments and Civil Politics in the New States." In *Old Societies and New States: The Quest for Modernity in Asia and Africa*, edited by Clifford Geertz, 105–19. New York: Free Press.

Geise, Jack P. 1989. "The Rhetoric and Politics of Liberty." *Social Science Quarterly* 70:836–50.

George, Katherine, and Charles H. George. 1955. "Roman Catholic Sainthood and Social Status: A Statistical and Analytical Study." *Journal of Religion* 35:85–98.

Germino, Dante. 1969. "Hegel as a Political Theorist." *Journal of Politics* 31:885–912.

Gewirth, Alan. 2007. "Duties to Fulfill the Human Rights of the Poor." In *Freedom from Poverty as a Human Right: Who Owes What to the Very Poor?*, edited by Thomas Pogge, 219–36. Oxford: Oxford University Press.

Gilpin, Robert. 1983. *War and Change in World Politics.* Cambridge: Cambridge University Press.

Glazer, Nathan. 1993. "Is Assimilation Dead?" *Annals of the American Academy of Political and Social Science* 530:122–36.

Gleason, Philip. 1980. "American Identity and Americanization." In *Harvard Encyclopedia of American Ethnic Groups*, edited by Stephan Thernstrom, Ann Orlov, and Oscar Handlin, 31–58. Cambridge: Harvard University Press.

Glendon, Mary Ann. 1991. *Rights Talk: The Impoverishment of American Political Discourse.* New York: Free Press.

Göçek, Fatma Müge. 2002. "The Decline of the Ottoman Empire and the Emergence of Greek, Armenian, Turkish, and Arab Nationalisms." In *Social Constructions of Nationalism in the Middle East*, edited by Fatma Müge Göçek, 15–83. Albany: State University of New York Press.

Göle, Nilüfer. 2000. "Snapshots of Islamic Modernities." *Daedalus* 129:91–117.

Gordon, Milton M. 1964. *Assimilation in American Life.* New York: Oxford University Press.

Gordon, Philip H. 2002. "Iraq: The Transatlantic Debate." Institute for Security Studies. Occasional Paper No. 39.

Graglia, Lino A. 1992. "Of Rights and Choices." *National Review* February 17.

Greaves, Richard L. 1982. "Concepts of Political Obedience in Late Tudor England: Conflicting Perspectives." *Journal of British Studies* 22:23–34.

Grebler, Leo, Joan W. Moore, and Ralph C. Guzman. 1970. *The Mexican-American People: The Nation's Second Largest Minority.* New York: Free Press.

Guibernau, Montserrat. 2006. "National Identity, Devolution and Secession in Canada, Britain and Spain." *Nations and Nationalism* 12:51–76.

Guicciardini, Francesco. 1994. *Dialogue on the City of Florence.* Edited and translated by Alison Brown. Cambridge: Cambridge University Press.

Gurin, Patricia, Shirley Hatchett, and James S. Jackson. 1989. *Hope and Independence: Blacks' Response to Electoral and Party Politics.* New York: Russell Sage Foundation.

Gutmann, Amy. 1985. "Review: Communitarian Critiques of Liberalism." *Philosophy and Public Affairs* 14:308–22.

Hababi, Don A. 1995. "The Positive / Negative Liberty Distinction and J.S. Mill's Theory of Liberty." *Archives for Philosophy of Law and Social Philosophy* 81:347–68.

Hadas, Moses. 1943. "From Nationalism to Cosmopolitanism in the Greco-Roman World." *Journal of the History of Ideas* 4:105–11.

Hall, Jacquelyn Dowd. 2005. "The Long Civil Rights Movement and the Political Uses of the Past." *Journal of American History* 91:1233–63.

Harper, Brian E., and Bruce W. Tuckman. 2006. "Racial Identity Beliefs and Academic Achievement: Does Being Black Hold Students Back?" *Social Psychology of Education* 9:381–403.

Harrell, Shelly P. 2000. "A Multidimensional Conceptualization of Racism-Related Stress: Implications for the Well-Being of People of Color." *American Journal of Orthopsychiatry* 70:42–57.

Harrington, James. 1770. *The Commonwealth of Oceana*. In *The Oceana and Other Works of James Harrington, with an Account of His Life*, edited by John Toland. London: T. Becket and T. Cadell.

Harter, Susan. 1999. *The Construction of the Self: A Developmental Perspective*. New York: Guildford.

Hartz, Louis. 1955. *The Liberal Tradition in America: An Interpretation of American Political Thought since the Revolution*. New York: Harcourt Brace.

Hatch, Nathan O. 1989. *The Democratization of American Christianity*. New Haven: Yale University Press.

Hegel, Georg Wilhelm Friedrich. 2001. *Philosophy of Right*. Translated by S.W. Dyde. Kitchener: Batoche Books.

– 1977. *Hegel's Phenomenology of Spirit*. Translated by A.V. Miller. New York: Oxford.

Heimert, Alan. 1966. *Religion and the American Mind: From the Great Awakening to the Revolution*. Cambridge: Harvard University Press.

Hendrickson, Kimberly A. 2002. "The Survival of Moral Federalism." *The Public Interest* 148:96–111.

Herdt, Jennifer A. 2016. "Aquinas and the Democratic Virtues: An Introduction." *Journal of Religious Ethics* 44:232–45.

– 2015. "Eudaimonism and Dispossession: Augustine on Almsgiving." In *Augustine and Social Justice*, edited by Teresa Delgado, John Doody, and Kim Paffenroth, 97–112. Lanham: Lexington Books.

Higham, John. 2002. *Strangers in the Land: Patterns of American Nativism, 1860–1925*. New Brunswick: Rutgers University Press.

– 1993. "Multiculturalism and Universalism: A History and Critique." *American Quarterly* 45:195–219.

Hill, Christopher. 1997. *Society and Puritanism in Pre-Revolutionary England*. New York: St. Martin's.

Hirschman, Albert O. 1997. *The Passions and the Interests: Political Arguments for Capitalism Before its Triumph*. Princeton: Princeton University Press.

– 1994. "Social Conflicts as Pillars of Democratic Market Society." *Political Theory* 22:203–18.

– 1982. "Rival Interpretations of Market Society: Civilizing, Destructive, or Feeble?" *Journal of Economic Literature* 20:1463–84.

Hoagland, Sarah Lucia. 1988. *Lesbian Ethics: Towards New Value*. Palo Alto: Institute of Lesbian Studies.

Hobbes, Thomas. 1976. *Leviathan*. London: Dent.

Holmes, Stephen. 1995. *Passions and Constraint On the Theory of Liberal Democracy*. Chicago: University of Chicago Press.

– 1993. *The Anatomy of Antiliberalism*. Cambridge: Harvard University Press.

– 1988. "Precommitment and the Paradox of Democracy." In *Constitutionalism and Democracy*, edited by Jon Elster and Rune Slagstad, 195–240. Cambridge: Cambridge University Press.

Honneth, Axel. 1996. *The Struggle for Recognition: The Moral Grammar of Social Conflicts*. Translated by Joel Anderson. Cambridge: MIT Press.

Hoover, Kenneth R., and Vernon D. Johnson. 2003/2004. "Identity-Driven Violence: Reclaiming Civil Society." *Journal of Hate Studies* 3:83–94.

Höpfl, Harro. 1982. *The Christian Polity of John Calvin*. Cambridge: Cambridge University Press.

Horowitz, Donald L. 1985. *Ethnic Groups in Conflict*. Berkeley: University of California Press.

Houser, Justin Kirk. 2009. "Is Hate Speech Becoming the New Blasphemy? Lessons from an American Constitutional Dialectic." *Penn State Law Review* 114:571–619.

Howard, Rhoda E., and Jack Donnelly. 1986. "Human Dignity, Human Rights, and Political Regimes." *American Political Science Review* 80:801–17.

Howe, Irving, 1986. *The American Newness: Culture and Politics in the Age of Emerson*. Cambridge: Harvard University Press.

Hughey, Michael. 1984. "The Political Covenant: Protestant Foundations of the American Political State." *State, Culture and Society* 1:113–56.

Hume, David. 1994. "Of the Original Contract." In *David Hume, Political Essays*, edited by Knud Haakonssen, 186–201. New York: Cambridge University Press.

– 1896. *A Treatise of Human Nature*. Edited by L.A. Selby-Bigge. Oxford: Clarendon.

– 1751. *An Enquiry Concerning the Principles of Morals*. London: A. Millar.

Huntington, Samuel. 2004a. *Who Are We? The Challenges to America's National Identity*. New York: Simon and Schuster.

– 2004b. "The Hispanic Challenge." *Foreign Policy* 141:30–45.

– 1996. *The Clash of Civilizations and the Remaking of the World Order*. New York: Simon and Schuster.

Hurley, Susan L., and Matthew Nudds, eds. 2006. *Rational Animals?* Oxford: Oxford University Press.

ICM. 2006. "Muslims Poll – February 2006." http://www.icmresearch.com/pdfs/2006_february_sunday_telegraph_muslims_poll.pdf. Accessed 17 February 2012.

Inglehart, Ronald F. 1990. *Culture Shift in Advanced Industrial Society*. Princeton: Princeton University Press.

- 1971."The Silent Revolution in Europe: Intergenerational Change in Post-Industrial Societies." *American Political Science Review* 65:991–1017.

Iyer, Aarti, Colin Wayne Leach, and Faye J. Crosby. 2003. "White Guilt and Racial Compensation: The Benefits and Limits of Self-Focus." *Personality and Social Psychology Bulletin* 29:117–29.

Jackson, Pamela Irving. 1991. "Crime, Youth Gangs and Urban Transition: The Social Dislocation of Postindustrial Economic Development." *Justice Quarterly* 8:379–97.

Jackson, Timothy P. 2011. "General Introduction." In *The Best Love of the Child: Being Loved and Being Taught to Love as the First Human Right*, edited by Timothy P. Jackson, 1–38. Grand Rapids: William B. Eerdmans.

Jacobs, Jerry A. 1995. "Gender and Academic Specialties: Trends among Recipients of College Degrees in the 1980s." *Sociology of Education* 68:81–98.

James, Patrick, Donald E. Abelson, and Michael Lusztig, eds. 2002. *The Myth of the Sacred: The Charter and Judicial Politics in Canada*. Montreal: McGill-Queen's University Press.

Jenkins, Philip. 2007. *God's Continent: Christianity, Islam, and Europe's Religious Crisis*. Oxford: Oxford University Press.

- 2006. "Demographics, Religion, and the Future of Europe." *Orbis* 50:519–39.

Joppke, Christian. 2007. "Beyond National Models: Civic Integration Policies for Immigrants in Western Europe." *West European Politics* 30:1–22.

Kant, Immanuel. 2006. *Anthropology From a Pragmatic Point of View*, edited and translated by Robert B. Louden. Cambridge: Cambridge University Press.

- 2005. *Groundwork for the Metaphysics of Morals*. Edited by Lara Denis. Translated by Thomas Abbott. Revised translation by Lara Denis. Peterborough: Broadview.

- 1996. *The Metaphysics of Morals*. Edited and translated by Mary Gregor. Cambridge: Cambridge University Press.

- 1987. *Critique of Judgment*. Edited and translated by Werner S. Pluhar. Indianapolis: Hackett.

- 1795. *Perpetual Peace: A Philosophical Essay*. Edited and translated by M. Campbell Smith. London: George Allen & Unwin.

Kashlinsky, Mark. 1977. "The Emergence of Adversary Politics in the Long Parliament." *Journal of Modern History* 49:617–40.

Kateb, George. 2011. *Human Dignity*. Cambridge: Harvard University Press.

- 2002. *Emerson and Self-Reliance*. Lanham: Rowman and Littlefield.

Kennedy, Paul. 1988. *The Rise and Fall of the Great Powers: Economic Change and Military Conflict from 1500 to 2000*. London: Fontana.

Keohane, Robert O., and Joseph S. Nye. 1977. *Power and Interdependence*. Boston: Little, Brown.

Kern, Soeren. 2011. "European 'No-Go' Zones for Non-Muslims Proliferating: 'Occupation without Tanks or Soldiers.'" *Stonegate Institute,* 22 August.

Kitromilides, Paschalis M. 1990. "Greek Irredentism in Asia Minor and Cyprus." *Middle Eastern Studies* 26:3–17.

Klarman, Michael J. 1994. "*Brown*, Racial Change, and the Civil Rights Movement." *Virginia Law Review* 80:7–150.

Knopff, Rainer. 2003. "How Democratic Is the Charter? And Does It Matter?" In *The Canadian Charter of Rights and Freedoms: Reflections on the Charter after Twenty Years*, edited by Joseph Eliot Magnet, Gérald-A. Beaudoin, Gerald Gall, and Christopher P. Manfredi, 199–218. Markham, ON: Butterworths.

– 1998. "Populism and the Politics of Rights: The Dual Attack on Representative Democracy." *Canadian Journal of Political Science* 31:683–705.

Knopff, Rainer, and F.L. Morton. 1992. *Charter Politics*. Scarborough: Nelson.

Krasner, Stephen. D. 1984. "Approaches to the State: Alternative Conceptions and Historical Dynamics." *Comparative Politics* 16:223–46.

Kraynak, Robert P. 2003. "'Made in the Image of God': The Christian View of Human Dignity and Political Order." In *In Defense of Human Dignity: Essays for Our Times*, edited by Robert P. Kraynak and Glenn Tinder, 81–118. Notre Dame: University of Notre Dame Press.

Kristeller, Paul Oskar. 1979. *Renaissance Thought and its Sources*. New York: Columbia University Press.

– 1939. "Florentine Platonism and its Relations with Humanism and Scholasticism." *Church History* 8:201–11.

Krizsán, Andrea. 2000. "The Hungarian Minority Protection System: A Flexible Approach to the Adjudication of Ethnic Claims." *Journal of Ethnic and Migration Studies* 26:247–62.

Krook, Mona Lena, Joni Lovenduski, and Judith Squires. 2009. "Gender Quotas and Models of Political Citizenship." *British Journal of Political Science* 39:781–803.

Krook, Mona Lena, and Diana Z. O'Brien. 2010. "The Politics of Group Representation: Quotas for Women and Minorities Worldwide." *Comparative Politics* 42:253–72.

Kukathas, Chandran. 1992. "Are There Any Cultural Rights?" *Political Theory* 20:105–39.

Kymlicka, Will. 1995a. *Multicultural Citizenship*. Oxford: Oxford University Press.

– ed. 1995b. *The Rights of Minority Cultures*. Oxford: Oxford University Press.

Lake, Peter, and Michael Questier. 2002. *The Anti-Christ's Lewd Hat: Protestants, Papists and Players in Post-Reformation England*. New Haven: Yale University Press.

Latham, Earl. 1952. *The Group Basis of Politics*. Ithaca: Cornell University Press.

Laurence, Jonathan. 2012. *The Emancipation of Europe's Muslims: The State's Role in Minority Integration*. Princeton: Princeton University Press.

Lawrence, Charles. 1987. "The Id, the Ego and Equal Protection: Reckoning with Unconscious Racism." *Stanford Law Review* 39:317–88.

Lazear, Edward P. 2007. "Mexican Assimilation in the United States." In *Mexican Immigration to the United States,* edited by George J. Borjas, 107–22. Chicago: University of Chicago Press.

– 1999. "Culture and Language." *Journal of Political Economy* 107:95–126.

Lebl, Leslie S. 2010. "Radical Islam in Europe." *Orbis* 54:46–60.

Leets, Laura, Howard Giles, and Kimberly Noels. 1999. "Attributing Harm to Racist Speech." *Journal of Multilingual and Multicultural Development* 20:209–15.

Lenard, Patti Tamara. 2010. "What Can Multicultural Theory Tell Us about Integrating Muslims in Europe?" *Political Studies Review* 8:308–21.

Lesthaeghe, Ron. 1995. "The Second Demographic Transition in Western Countries: An Interpretation." In *Gender and Family Change in Industrialized Countries,* edited by Karen Oppenheim Mason and An-Magritt Jensen, 17–62. Oxford: Oxford University Press.

Lesthaeghe, Ron, and Paul Willems. 1999. "Is Low Fertility a Temporary Phenomenon in the European Union?" *Population and Development Review* 25:211–28.

Levy, David M., and Sandra J. Peart. 2004. "Sympathy and Approbation in Hume and Smith: A Solution to the Other Rational Species Problem." *Economics and Philosophy* 20:331–49.

Lijphart, Arend. 1977. *Democracy in Plural Societies: A Comparative Exploration.* New Haven: Yale University Press.

Lillian, Donna. 2007. "A Thorn by Any Other Name: Sexist Discourse as Hate Speech." *Discourse and Society* 18:719–40.

Lindbeck, Assar. 1995. "Hazardous Welfare State Dynamics." *The American Economic Review* 85:9–15.

Lindberg, Carter. 1993. *Beyond Charity: Reformation Initiatives for the Poor.* Minneapolis: Augsburg Fortress.

Lipset, Seymour Martin. 1981. *Political Man: The Social Bases of Politics.* Baltimore: Johns Hopkins University Press.

– 1959. "Some Social Requisites of Democracy: Economic Development and Political Legitimacy." *American Political Science Review* 53:69–105.

Locke, John. 1974. "The Second Treatise of Civil Government." In *Two Treatises of Government,* edited by Thomas I. Cook. New York: Hafner.

Lopez, Michael. 1996. *Emerson and Power: Creative Antagonism in the Nineteenth Century.* DeKalb: Northern Illinois University Press.

Lukes, Steven. 2006. *Individualism.* Colchester: European Consortium for Political Research.

Lusztig, Michael. 2002. "Deeper and Deeper: Deep Diversity, Federalism, and Redistributive Politics in Canada." In *The Myth of the Sacred: The Charter, the Courts, and the Politics of the Constitution in Canada,* edited by Patrick James, Donald E. Abelson, and Michael Lusztig, 207–18. Montreal: McGill-Queen's University Press.

MacCallum, Gerald C. 1991. "Negative and Positive Freedom." In *Liberty*, edited by David Miller, 100–22. Oxford: Oxford University Press.

Machiavelli, Niccolo. 1975. *The Discourses of Niccolo Machiavelli*. Edited and translated by Leslie J. Walker. Boston: Routledge and Paul.

MacIntyre, Alasdair. 1981. *After Virtue: A Study in Moral Philosophy*. Notre Dame: University of Notre Dame Press.

MacKinnon, Catharine. 1989. *Towards a Feminist Theory of the State*. Cambridge: Harvard University Press.

Macklin, Ruth. 2003. "Dignity Is a Useless Concept." *British Medical Journal* 20:1419–20.

Maddox, Graham. 2002. "The Secular Reformation and the Influence of Machiavelli." *Journal of Religion* 82:539–62.

Mandeville, Bernard. 1924. *The Fable of the Bees: Or Private Vices, Publick Benefits*. Oxford: Clarendon.

Manfredi, Christopher P. 1990. "The Use of United States Decisions by the Supreme Court of Canada under the Charter of Rights and Freedoms." *Canadian Journal of Political Science* 23:499–518.

Manfredi, Christopher P., and Michael Lusztig. 1998. "Why Do Formal Amendments Fail? An Institutional Design Analysis." *World Politics* 50:377–400.

Margalit, Avishai. 1996. *The Decent Society*. Translated by Naomi Goldblum. Cambridge: Harvard University Press.

Markus, R.A. 1965. "Two Conceptions of Political Authority: Augustine, *De Civitas Dei*, XIX. 14–15, and Some Thirteenth Century Interpretations." *Journal of Theological Studies* New Series 16:68–100.

Massey, Calvin R. 1992. "Hate Speech, Cultural Diversity and the Foundational Paradigms of Free Expression." UCLA *Law Review* 40:103–97.

Massey, Douglas S., and Chiara Capoferro. 2008. "The Geographic Diversification of American Immigration." In *New Faces in New Places: The Changing Geography of American Immigration*, edited by Douglas S. Massey, 25–50. New York: Russell Sage Foundation.

Matsuda, Mari J. 1989. "Public Response to Racist Speech: Considering the Victim's Story." *Michigan Law Review* 87:2320–81.

Mazama, Ama. 2001. "The Afrocentric Paradigm: Contours and Definitions." *Journal of Black Studies* 31:387–405.

McAdam, Doug. 1994. "Culture and Social Movements." In *New Social Movements: From Ideology to Identity*, edited by Enrique Laraña, Hank Johnston and Joseph R. Gusfield, 36–57. Philadelphia: Temple University Press.

– 1988. *Freedom Summer*. Oxford: Oxford University Press.

McCain, Patricia A. 1993. "Litigating for Lesbian and Gay Rights: A Legal History." *Virginia Law Review* 79:1551–641.

McCarthy, Thomas. 1999. "On Reconciling Cosmopolitan Unity and National Diversity." *Public Culture* 11:175–208.

McCormick, John P. 2003. "Machiavelli against Republicanism: On the Cambridge School's 'Guicciardinian Moments.'" *Political Theory* 31:615–43.

McCrudden, Christopher. 2008. "Human Dignity and Judicial Interpretation of Human Rights." *European Journal of International Law* 19:655–724.

McDaniel, S.A. 1985. "Implementation of Abortion Policy in Canada as a Women's Issue." *Atlantis* 10:74–91.

McDonald, Forrest. 1985. *Novus Ordo Seclorum: The Intellectual Origins of the Constitution.* Lawrence: University Press of Kansas.

McHugh, Peter. 1966. "Social Disintegration as a Requisite of Resocialization." *Social Forces* 44:355–63.

McNeill, John T. 1949. "The Democratic Element in Calvin's Thought." *Church History* 18:153–71.

McWilliams, Wilson Carey. 2011. "Emerson: The All and the One." In *A Political Companion to Ralph Waldo Emerson,* edited by Alan M. Levine and Daniel S. Malachuk, 43–52. Lexington: University of Kentucky Press.

Melson, Robert, and Howard Wolpe. 1970. "Modernization and the Politics of Communalism: A Theoretical Perspective." *American Political Science Review* 64:1112–30.

Meyer, David S., and Suzanne Staggenborg. 2008. "Opposing Movement Strategies in U.S. Abortion Politics." *Research in Social Movements, Conflicts and Change* 28:207–38.

Meyer, David S., and Nancy Whittier. 1994. "Social Movement Spillover." *Social Problems* 41:277–98.

Mickelson, Roslyn Arlin. 1990. "The Attitude-Achievement Paradox Among Black Adolescents." *Sociology of Education* 63:44–61.

Mill, John Stuart. 1972. "On Liberty." In J.S. Mill, *Utilitarianism, On Liberty, and Considerations on Representative Government,* edited by H.B. Acton. New York: Dutton.

Milton-Edwards, Beverley. 2005. *Islamic Fundamentalism Since 1945.* New York: Routledge.

Mintz, Steven. 1995. *Moralists and Modernizers: America's Pre–Civil War Reformers.* Baltimore: Johns Hopkins University Press.

Moffitt, Robert. 1992. "Incentive Effects of the United States Welfare System." *Journal of Economic Literature* 30:1–61.

Monahan, Patrick. 1987. *The Charter, Federalism and the Supreme Court of Canada.* Toronto: Carswell.

Montesquieu, Charles de Secondat, Baron de. 1989. *The Spirit of the Laws.* Edited and translated by Anne M. Cohler, Basia Carolyn Miller, and Harold Samuel Stone. Cambridge: Cambridge University Press.

Moos, Rudolf H. 2002. "Life Stressors, Social Resources, and Coping Skills in Youth: Applications to Adolescents with Chronic Disorders." *Journal of Adolescent Health* 30:22–9.

Morgan, Edmund S. 1988. *Inventing the People: The Rise of Popular Sovereignty in England and America.* New York: Norton.

Morland, J. Kenneth. 1969. "Race Awareness among American and Hong Kong Chinese Children." *American Journal of Sociology* 75:360–74.

Morrill, John. 1984. "The Religious Context of the English Civil War." *Transactions of the Royal Historical Society* 34:155–78.

Morris, Aldon D. 1984. *The Origins of the Civil Rights Movement: Black Communities Organizing for Change.* New York: Free Press.

Mumby, Dennis K., and Linda L. Putnam. 1992. "The Politics of Emotion: A Feminist Reading of Bounded Rationality." *Academy of Management Review* 17:465–86.

Murray, John Courtney, S.J. 2005. *We Hold These Truths: Catholic Reflections on the American Proposition.* Lanham: Rowman and Littlefield.

Nagel, Joane. 1994. "Constructing Ethnicity: Creating and Recreating Ethnic Identity and Culture." *Social Problems* 41:152–76.

Nagel, Joane, and Susan Olzak. 1982. "Ethnic Mobilization in New and Old States." *Social Problems* 30:127–43.

Nagel, Robert F. 2001. *The Implosion of American Federalism.* New York: Oxford University Press.

Najemy, John M. 2003. "Civic Humanism and Florentine Politics." In *Renaissance Civic Humanism,* edited by James Hankins, 74–104. Cambridge: Cambridge University Press.

Neal, Odeana R. 1995/96. "The Limits of Legal Discourse: Learning from the Civil Rights Movement in the Quest for Gay and Lesbian Civil Rights." *New York Law School Review* 40:679–718.

Nelson-Barber, Sharon. 1982. "Phonological Variations of Pima English." In *Language Renewal among American Indian Tribes: Issues, Problems, and Prospects,* edited by Robert N. St. Clair and William Leap, 115–32. Rosslyn: National Clearinghouse for Bilingual Education.

Newfield, Christopher. 1991. "Emerson's Corporate Individualism." *American Literary History* 3:657–84.

Newman, Saul. 1991. "Does Modernization Breed Ethnic Political Conflict?" *World Politics* 43:451–78.

Newton, Kenneth. 1997. "Social Capital and Democracy." *American Behavioral Scientist* 40:575–86.

Niblett, Robin. 2006. "Islamic Extremism in Europe." Statement Before the Subcommittee on European Affairs, United States Senate Foreign Relations Committee. http://www.globalsecurity.org/security/library/congress/2006_h/060405-niblett.pdf. Accessed 16 February 2012.

Nock, C.J. 1995. "On the Dissent Theory of Political Obligation." *Polity* 28:141–57.

Noll, Mark. 2002. *America's God: From Jonathan Edwards to Abraham Lincoln.* Oxford: Oxford University Press.

– 1985. "Common Sense Traditions and American Evangelical Thought." *American Quarterly* 37:216–38.

North, J.A. 1990. "Democratic Politics in Republican Rome." *Past and Present* 126:3–21.

Novak, Michael. 1998. "The Judeo-Christian Foundation of Human Dignity, Personal Liberty, and the Concept of the Person." *Journal of Markets and Morality* 1:107–21.

Nozick, Robert. 1974. *Anarchy, State and Utopia.* New York: Basic Books.

Oakland Board of Education. 1996. *Resolution of the Board of Education Adopting the Report and Recommendations of the African-American Task Force; A Policy Statement and Directing the Superintendent of Schools to Devise a Program to Improve the English Language Acquisition and Applications Skills of African-American Students.* Resolution No. 597-0063. http://linguistlist.org/topics/ebonics/ebonics-res1.html. Accessed 21 October 2011.

Offer, Avner. 2006. *The Challenge of Affluence: Self-Control and Well-Being in the United States and Britain since 1950.* Oxford: Oxford University Press.

Olson, Mancur. 1982. *The Rise and Decline of Nations: Economic Growth, Stagflation, and Social Rigidities.* New Haven: Yale University Press.

Olson, Su, and Robyn Walker. 2004. "The Women and the Boys." *Women in Management Review* 19:244–51.

Olsthoorn, Peter. 2005. "Honor as a Motive for Making Sacrifices." *Journal of Military Ethics* 4:183–97.

Oneal, John R., and Bruce M. Russett. 1997. "The Classical Liberals Were Right: Democracy, Interdependence, and Conflict, 1950–1985." *International Studies Quarterly* 41:267–94.

Organization for Economic Cooperation and Development. 2011. "Social Expenditure Database." http://stats.oecd.org/Index.aspx?datasetcode=SOCX_AGG. Accessed 27 December 2011.

Oswald, Debra S. 2007. "'Don't Ask, Don't Tell': The Influence of Stigma Concealing and Perceived Threat on Perceivers' Reactions to a Gay Target." *Journal of Applied Social Psychology* 37:928–47.

Padelford, F.M. 1913. "Spenser and the Puritan Propaganda." *Modern Philology* 11:85–106.

Paine, Thomas. 1986. *Common Sense.* Harmondsworth: Penguin Classics.

Painter, Nell Irvin. 2006. *Creating Black Americans: African-American History and Its Meanings, 1619 to the Present.* Oxford: Oxford University Press.

Pangle, Thomas L. 1988. *The Spirit of Modern Republicanism: The Moral Vision of the American Founders and the Philosophy of Locke.* Chicago: University of Chicago Press.

Passel, Jeffrey S., and D'Vera Cohn. 2008. *Trends in Unauthorized Immigration: Undocumented Inflow Now Trails Legal Inflow*. Washington: Pew Hispanic Research Center.

Paul, T.V. 2005. "Soft Balancing in the Age of U.S. Primacy." *International Security* 30:46–71.

Pech, Laurent. 2009. "The Law of Holocaust Denial: Towards a (Qualified) EU-wide Criminal Prohibition." New York University School of Law, Jean Monet Working Paper 10/09.

Perry, Theresa, and Lisa Delpit, eds. 1998. *The Real Ebonics Debate: Power, Language, and the Education of African-American Children*. Boston: Beacon Press.

Peterson, Peter G. 1999. "Gray Dawn: The Global Aging Crisis." *Foreign Affairs* 78:42–55.

Pew Forum on Religion and Public Life. 2010. "Muslim Networks and Movements in Western Europe." 15 September. http://www.pewforum.org/Muslim/Muslim-Networks-and-Movements-in-Western-Europe.aspx. Accessed 9 February 2012.

Pew Global Attitudes Project. 2006. "The Great Divide: How Westerners and Muslims View Each Other." 22 June. http://www.pewglobal.org/files/pdf/253.pdf. Accessed 9 February 2012.

Phelps, Edmund S. 1996. "On the Damaging Side Effects of the Welfare System: How, Why and What to Do." In *Equity, Efficiency and Growth: The Future of the Welfare State*. Edited by Mario Baldassarri, Luigi Paganetto and Edmund S. Phelps, 41–56. New York: Palgrave Macmillan.

Phinney, Jean S., Gabriel Horenczyk, Karmela Liebkind, and Paul Vedder. 2001. "Ethnic Identity, Immigration, and Well-Being: An Interactional Perspective." *Journal of Social Issues* 57:493–510.

Pico Della Mirandola, Giovanni. 1965. *Orations on the Dignity of Man*. Translated by Charles Glen Wallace, J.W. Miller, and Douglas Carmichael. Indianapolis: Bobbs Merrill.

Pierson, Paul. 1996. "The New Politics of the Welfare State." *World Politics* 48:143–79.

Pincus, Steve. 1998. "Neither Machiavellian Moment nor Possessive Individualism: Commercial Society and the Defenders of the English Commonwealth." *American Historical Review* 103:705–36.

Piore, Michael J., and Charles F. Sabel. 1984. *The Second Industrial Divide: Prospects for Prosperity*. New York: Basic Books.

Plato. 1992. *Statesman*. Translated by J.B. Skremp. Indianapolis: Hackett.

– 1974. *Plato's Republic*. Translated by G.M.A. Grube. Indianapolis: Hackett.

Pocock, J.G.A. 1981. "Virtues, Rights and Manners: A Model for Historians of Political Thought." *Political Theory* 9:353–68.

– 1975. *The Machiavellian Moment: Florentine Political Thought and the Atlantic Republican Tradition*. Princeton: Princeton University Press.

Polybius. 1889. *The Histories of Polybius*. Translated by Evelyn S. Shuckburgh. London: Macmillan.

Popenoe, David. 1993. "American Family Decline, 1960–1990: A Reappraisal." *Journal of Marriage and Family* 55:527–42.

Porter, J.R., and R.E. Washington. 1993. "Minority Identity and Self-Esteem." *Annual Review of Sociology* 19:139–61.

Preuss, J. Samuel. 1979. "Machiavelli's Functional Analysis of Religion: Context and Object." *Journal of the History of Ideas* 40:171–90.

Prinz, Aloys. 2005. "Why Is It So Hard to Restructure the Welfare State? An Explanation Based on Cognitive Economics." In *Reforming the Welfare State*, edited by Aloys Prinz, Albert E. Steenge, and Jörg Schmidt, 43–73. Münster: Lit Verlag.

Pritchard, Michael S. 1972. "Human Dignity and Justice." *Ethics* 82:299–313.

Publius. 1961. *The Federalist Papers*. New York: Mentor.

Putnam, Robert D. 2007. "*E Pluribus Unum*: Diversity and Community in the Twenty-First Century, the 2006 Johan Skytte Prize Lecture." *Scandinavian Political Studies* 30:137–74.

– 1995. *Bowling Alone: The Collapse and Revival of American Community*. New York: Simon and Schuster.

– 1988. "Diplomacy and Domestic Politics: The Logic of Two-Level Games." *International Organization* 42:427–60.

Rae, Gavin. 2010. "Kierkegaard, the Self, Authenticity and the Teleological Suspension of the Ethical." *Critical Horizons* 11:75–97.

Ramsey, Paul. 1947. "A Theory of Virtue According to the Principles of the Reformation." *Journal of Religion* 27:178–96.

Rawls, John. 2003. *A Theory of Justice*. Revised edition. Cambridge: Belknap.

– 1996. *Political Liberalism*. New York: Columbia University Press.

– 1975. "Fairness to Goodness." *Philosophical Review* 84:536–54.

– 1963. "The Sense of Justice." *Philosophical Review* 72:281–305.

Reynolds, Andrew. 2005. "Reserved Seats in National Legislatures: A Research Note." *Legislative Studies Quarterly* 30:301–10.

Richards, Peter Judson. 2002/03. "'The Law Written in Their Hearts'?: Rutherford and Locke on Nature, Government and Resistance." *Journal of Law and Religion* 18:151–89.

Riker, William. 1980. "Implications from the Disequilibrium of Majority Rule for the Study of Institutions." *American Political Science Review* 74:432–46.

Roberts, Kevin D. 2006. *African-American Issues*. Westport: Greenwood.

Roberts, Veronica. 2016. "Augustine's Ciceronian Response to the Ciceronian Patriot." *Perspectives on Politics* 45:113–24.

Robinson, David M. 1993. *Emerson and the Conduct of Life*. Cambridge: Cambridge University Press.

Robson, William B.P. 2006. "Out of Control: Reining in Soaring Federal Spending is a Critical Task for the Next Parliament." *C.D. Howe Institute e-brief.* Toronto: C.D. Howe Institute.

Rodgers, Daniel T. 1992. "Republicanism: The Career of a Concept." *Journal of American History* 79:11–38.

Romanow, Roy, John Whyte, and Howard Leeson. 1984. *Canada Notwithstanding: The Making of the Constitution 1976–1982.* Toronto: Carswell/ Methuen.

Romney, Paul. 1999. "Provincial Equality, Special Status and the Compact Theory of Confederation." *Canadian Journal of Political Science* 32:21–39.

Roof, Wade Clark. 1999. *Spiritual Marketplace: Baby Boomers and the Remaking of American Religion.* Princeton: Princeton University Press.

Rosaldo, Renato. 1999. "Cultural Citizenship, Inequality, and Multiculturalism." In *Race, Identity, and Citizenship: A Reader,* edited by Rodolfo D. Torres, Louis F. Mirón, and Jonathan Xavier Inda, 253–61. Oxford: Blackwell.

– 1994. "Cultural Citizenship and Educational Democracy." *Cultural Anthropology* 9:402–11.

Rosen, Michael. 2012. *Dignity: Its History and Meaning.* Cambridge: Harvard University Press.

Rothschild, Emma. 2001. *Economic Sentiments: Adam Smith, Condorcet, and the Enlightenment.* Cambridge: Harvard University Press.

Rousseau, Jean-Jacques. 1913. *The Social Contract and Discourses.* Translated by G.D.H. Cole. London: J.M. Dent.

Rowe, William L. 1964. "Augustine on Foreknowledge and Free Will." *Review of Metaphysics* 18:356–63.

Rudolph, Christopher. 2003. "Security and the Political Economy of International Migration." *American Political Science Review* 97:603–20.

Russell, Conrad. 1976. "Parliamentary History in Perspective, 1604–1629." *History* 61:1–27.

Russell, Margaret M. 1994. "Lesbian, Gay and Bisexual Rights and 'The Civil Rights Agenda.'" *African-American Law and Policy Report* 1:33–78.

Russett, Bruce. 1993. *Grasping the Democratic Peace.* Princeton: Princeton University Press.

Said, Abdul. 1977. "Pursuing Human Dignity." *Society* 15:34–8.

Saideman, Stephen M., and R. William Ayres. 2000. "Determining the Causes of Irredentism: Logit Analysis of Minorities at Risk Data from the 1980s and 1990s." *Journal of Politics* 62:1126–44.

Sambanis, Nicholas. 1991. "Do Ethnic and Nonethnic Civil Wars Have the Same Causes?: A Theoretical and Empirical Inquiry (Part 1)." *Journal of Conflict Resolution* 45:259–82.

Sandel, Michael. 1982. *Liberalism and the Limits of Justice.* Cambridge: Cambridge University Press.

Saskatchewan Human Rights Tribunal. 2008. "M. J. v. Nichols in the Matter of the Saskatchewan Human Rights Code S.S. 1979, c. S-24.1." 23 May. http://www.saskhrt.ca/forms/index/Decisions/05232008.htm. Accessed 19 July 2008.

Savage, Timothy M. 2004. "Europe and Islam: Crescent Waxing, Cultures Clashing." *Washington Quarterly* 27:25–50.

Saxonhouse, Arlene W. 2012. "To Corrupt: The Ambiguity of the Language of Corruption in Ancient Athens." In *Corruption: Expanding the Focus*, edited by Manuhuia Barchum, Barry Hindess, and Peter Larmour, 37–52. Canberra: Australian National University EPress.

Sayegh, Liliane, and Jean-Claude Lasry. 1993. "Immigrants' Adaptation in Canada: Assimilation, Acculturation and Orthogonal Cultural Identification." *Canadian Psychology* 34:98–109.

Schelling, Thomas C. 1984. *Choice and Consequences: Perspectives of an Errant Economist.* Cambridge: Harvard University Press.

Schiller, Herbert I. 1976. *Communication and Cultural Domination.* New York: International Arts and Sciences Press.

Schneider, Elizabeth M. 1993. "Feminism and the False Dichotomy of Victimization and Agency." *New York Law School Law Review* 38:387–99.

Schulman, Alex. 2009. "Stockholm Syndrome: Radical Islam and the European Response." *Human Rights Review* 10:469–92.

Schwartz, Barry. 1985. "Emerson, Cooley, and the American Heroic Vision." *Symbolic Interaction* 8:103–20.

Scodel, Joshua. 2005. ""None's Slave": Some Versions of Liberty in Donne's Satires 1 and 4." *English Literary History* 72:363–85.

Scott, Joan W. 1992. "Multiculturalism and the Politics of Identity." *October* 61:12–19

Segal, David R., Jerald G. Bachman, Peter Freedman-Doan, and Patrick M. O'Malley. 1999. "Propensity to Serve in the U.S. Military: Temporal Trends and Subgroup Differences." *Armed Forces & Society* 25:407–27.

Segal, Mady Wechsler, Meredith Hill Thanner, and David R. Segal. 2007. "Hispanic and African American Men and Women in the U.S. Military: Trends in Representation." *Race, Gender & Class* 14:48–64.

Seljak, David. 1996. "Why the Quiet Revolution was 'Quiet': The Catholic Church's Reaction to the Secularization of Nationalism after 1960." *Historical Studies* 62:109–24.

Sharrin, Andrea M. 1989/90. "Potential Fathers and Abortion: A Woman's Womb Is Not a Man's Castle." *Brooklyn Law Review* 55:1359–404.

Shaw, Charles Grey. 1914. "Emerson the Nihilist." *International Journal of Ethics* 25:68–86.

Shore, Zachary. 2006. *Breeding Bin Ladens: America, Islam and the Future of Europe.* Baltimore: Johns Hopkins University Press.

Shue, Henry. 1996. *Basic Rights: Subsistence, Affluence, and U.S. Foreign Policy.* 2nd ed. Princeton: Princeton University Press.

Silvestrini, Blanca G. 2004. "'The World We Enter When Claiming Rights': Latinos and their Quest for Culture." In *Latino Cultural Citizenship: Claiming Identity, Space, and Rights,* edited by William V. Flores and Rita Benmayor, 39–53. Boston: Beacon Press.

Simmons, A. John.1979. *Moral Principles and Political Obligations.* Princeton: Princeton University Press.

Simon, Herbert A. 1990. "Bounded Rationality." In *Utility and Probability.* Edited by John Eatwell, Murray Milgate, and Peter Newman, 15–18. New York: Macmillan.

Simpson, Jeffrey. 2011. "Quebeckers Want Power, Not Independence." *Globe and Mail.* 15 October.

Sisk, Timothy D. 2002. *Power Sharing and International Mediation in Ethnic Conflicts.* New York: United States Institute of Peace.

Skinner, Quentin. 2002. *Visions of Politics: Volume II Renaissance Virtues.* Cambridge: Cambridge University Press.

– 1990. "The Republican Ideal of Political Liberty." In *Machiavelli and Republicanism,* edited by Gisela Bock, Quentin Skinner, and Maurizio Viroli, 293–309. Cambridge: Cambridge University Press.

– 1984. "The Idea of Negative Liberty: Philosophical and Historical Perspectives." In *Philosophy in History,* edited by Richard Rorty, J.B. Schneewind, and Quentin Skinner, 193–221.Cambridge: Cambridge University Press.

– 1978a. *The Foundations of Modern Political Thought.* Vol 1. Cambridge: Cambridge University Press.

– 1978b. *The Foundations of Modern Political Thought.* Vol 2. Cambridge: Cambridge University Press.

Skrentny, John David. 1988. "The Effect of the Cold War on African-American Civil Rights: America and the World Audience, 1945–1968." *Theory and Society* 27:237–85.

Smith, Adam. 1982. *The Theory of Moral Sentiments.* Edited by D.D. Raphael and A.L. Macfie. Indianapolis: Liberty Fund.

Smith, Christian. 2010. *What Is a Person? Rethinking Humanity, Social Life, and the Moral Good from the Person Up.* Chicago: University of Chicago Press.

Smith, Steven B. 1989. "What Is 'Right' in Hegel's *Philosophy of Right?*" *American Political Science Review* 83:3–18.

Smyth, Lisa. 2002. "Feminism and Abortion Politics: Choice, Rights, and Reproductive Freedom." *Women's Studies International Forum* 25:335–45.

Solomon, R.C. 1970. "Hegel's Concept of 'Geist.' *Review of Metaphysics* 23:642–61.

Spencer, Margaret B. 1985. "Cultural Cognition and Social Cognition as Identity Factors in Black Children's Personal Social Growth." In *Beginnings:*

The Social and Affective Development of Black Children, edited by Margaret B. Spencer, Geraldine K. Spencer, and Walter R. Allen, 215–30. Hillsdale, NJ: Lawrence Erlbaum Associates.

Spencer, Margaret Beale, and Carol Markstrom-Adams. 1990. "Identity Processes among Racial and Ethnic Minority Children in America." *Child Development* 61:290–310.

Spencer, Margaret Beale, Dena Phillips Swanson, and Michael Cunningham. 1991. "Ethnicity, Ethnic Identity, and Competence Formation: Adolescent Transition and Cultural Transformation." *Journal of Negro Education* 60:366–87.

Spencer, Martin E. 1994. "Multiculturalism, 'Political Correctness,' and the Politics of Identity." *Sociological Forum* 9:547–67.

Spencer, Steven J., Claude M. Steele, and Diane M. Quinn. 1999. "Stereotype Threat and Women's Math Performance." *Journal of Experimental Social Psychology* 35:4–28.

Steele, Claude M. 1999. "Thin Ice: Stereotype Threat and Black College Students." *Atlantic Online* August.

Steele, Claude M., and Joshua Aronson. 1995. "Stereotype Threat and the Intellectual Test Performance of African Americans." *Journal of Personality and Social Psychology* 69:797–811.

Steinberg, Laurence, Sanford M. Dornbusch, and B. Bradford Brown. 1992. "Ethnic Differences in Academic Achievement: An Ecological Perspective." *American Psychologist* 47:723–29.

Stetson, Dorothy McBride. 2001. "Introduction: Abortion, Women's Movements, and Democratic Politics." In *Abortion Politics, Women's Movements, and the Democratic State: A Comparative Study of State Feminism,* edited by Dorothy McBride Stetson, 1–16. Oxford: Oxford University Press.

Steyn, Mark. 2006. *America Alone: The End of the World as We Know It.* Washington: Regnery.

Stinchcombe, Arthur L. 1965. "Social Structure and Organizations." In *Handbook of Organizations,* edited by J.G. March, 142–93. Chicago: Rand McNally.

Stolle, Dietlind, Stuart Soroka, and Richard Johnston. 2008. "When Does Diversity Erode Trust? Neighborhood Diversity, Interpersonal Trust and the Mediating Effects of Social Interactions." *Political Studies* 56:57–75.

Stonequist, E.V. 1935. "The Problem of the Marginal Man." *American Journal of Sociology* 41:1–12.

Stout, Harry S. 1977. "Religion, Communications, and the Ideological Origins of the American Revolution." *William and Mary Quarterly* 3rd series 34:519–41.

Sullivan, William M. 1982. *Reconstructing Public Philosophy.* Berkeley: University of California Press.

Swenden, Wilfried. 2002. "Asymmetric Federalism and Coalition-Building in Belgium." *Publius* 32:67–87.

Sztompka, Piotr. 2000. "Cultural Trauma: The Other Face of Social Change." *European Journal of Sociology* 3:449–66.

Tancredo, Tom. 2004. "Immigration, Citizenship, and National Security: The Silent Invasion." *Mediterranean Affairs* 15:4–15.

Tawney, R.H. 1977. *Religion and the Rise of Capitalism.* Harmondsworth: Penguin.

Taylor, Charles. 1995. "Irreducibly Social Goods." In *Philosophical Arguments,* edited by Charles Taylor, 127–45. Cambridge: Harvard University Press.

– 1993. *Reconciling the Solitudes: Essays on Canadian Federalism and Nationalism.* Edited by Guy Laforest. Montreal: McGill-Queen's University Press.

– 1992. *Multiculturalism and "The Politics of Recognition."* Edited by Charles Taylor and Amy Gutmann. Princeton: Princeton University Press.

– 1991a. "What's Wrong with Negative Liberty." In *Liberty,* edited by David Miller, 141–62. Oxford: Oxford University Press.

– 1991b. "Shared and Divergent Values." In *Options for a New Canada,* edited by Ronald L. Watts and Douglas Brown, 53–76. Toronto: University of Toronto Press.

– 1991c. *The Malaise of Modernity.* Toronto: Anansi.

– 1989. *Sources of the Self: The Making of the Modern Identity.* Cambridge: Harvard University Press.

– 1988/89. "Hegel's Ambiguous Legacy for Modern Liberalism." *Cardozo Law Review* 10:857–70.

– 1985. "Atomism." In *Philosophy and the Human Sciences: Philosophical Papers 2,* edited by Charles Taylor, 187–210. Cambridge: Cambridge University Press.

– 1979. *Hegel and Modern Society.* Cambridge: Cambridge University Press.

Taylor, Verta, and Leila J. Rupp. 1993. "Women's Culture and Lesbian Feminist Activism: A Reconsideration of Cultural Feminism." *Signs* 19:32–61.

Teitelbaum, Michael S., and Jay M. Winter. 1986. *The Fear of Population Decline.* London: Academic Press.

Telles, Edward E., and Vilma Ortiz. 2008. *Generations of Exclusion: Mexican Americans, Assimilation, and Race.* New York: Russell Sage Foundation.

Thomas, Scott M. 2010. "Religion and Global Security." *Quaderni di Relazioni Internazionali* 12:4–21.

Thomson, Irene Taviss. 1997. "From Conflict to Embedment: The Individual-Society Relationship, 1920–1991." *Sociological Forum* 12: 631–58.

Todd, Margo. 1987. *Christian Humanism and the Puritan Social Order.* Cambridge: Cambridge University Press.

Tönnies, Ferdinand. 1974. "Gemeinschaft and Gesellschaft." In *The Sociology of Community: A Selection of Readings,* edited by Colin Bell and Howard Newby, 7–12. New York: Frank Cass and Company.

Trenchard, Robert, and Thomas Gordon. 1995. *Cato's Letters, Or Essays on Liberty, Civil or Religious, Or Other Important Subjects.* Edited by Ronald Hamowy. Indianapolis: Liberty Fund.

Trinkaus, Charles. 1949. "The Problem of Free Will in the Renaissance and the Reformation." *Journal of the History of Ideas* 10:51–62.

Tubalado, Charity J. 2007. "The Immigration-National Security Nexus: Immigration in Contemporary France." *The Current* 10:59–80.

Tushnet, Mark V. 1987a. *The NAACP: Legal Strategy against Segregated Education, 1925–1950.* Chapel Hill: University of North Carolina Press.

– 1987b. "The Politics of Equality in Constitutional Law: The Equal Protection Clause, Dr. Du Bois, and Charles Hamilton Houston." *Journal of American History* 74:884–903.

United Nations. 2011. Department of Economic and Social Affairs. Population Division. *World Population Prospects: The 2010 Revision.* New York: United Nations.

United States. 2011. Department of Homeland Security. *Yearbook of Immigration Statistics: 2010.* Washington: U.S. Department of Homeland Security, Division of Immigration Statistics.

Uslaner, Eric. 2002. *The Moral Foundations of Trust.* Cambridge: Cambridge University Press.

Vaisse, Justin. 2008. "Muslims in Europe: A Short Introduction." Brookings Institution Center on United States and Europe, US-Europe Analysis Series. September.

Valentine, Gill. 1997. "Making Space: Lesbian Separatist Communities in the United States." In *Contested Countryside Cultures: Otherness, Marginalization and Rurality*, edited by Paul Cloke and Jo Little, 109–22. London: Routledge.

Vallières, Pierre. 1971. *White Niggers of America.* Translated by Joan Pinkham. Toronto: McClelland and Stewart.

Van den Brink, Bert. 2007. "Imagining Civic Relations in the Moment of Their Breakdown: A Crisis of Civic Integrity in the Netherlands." In *Multiculturalism and Political Theory*, edited by Anthony Simon Laden and David Owen, 350–72. New York: Cambridge.

Van Dyke, Vernon. 1977. "The Individuals, the State, and Ethnic Communities in Political Theory." *World Politics* 29:343–69.

Van Keersbergen, Kees. 2002. "The Politics of Welfare State Reform." *Swiss Political Science Review* 8:1–19.

Van Wormer, Katherine, and Robin McKinney. 2003. "What Schools Can Do to Protect Gay/Lesbian/Bisexual Youth: A Harm Reduction Approach." *Adolescence* 38:409–20.

Vernon, Richard. 2001. *Political Morality: A Theory of Liberal Democracy.* London: Continuum.

Vigdor, Jacob L. 2008. "Measuring Immigrant Assimilation into the United
    States." Center for Civic Innovation, Manhattan Institute, Report No. 53.
Vipond, Robert C. 1991. *Liberty and Community: Canadian Federalism and the
    Failure of the Constitution.* Albany: State University of New York Press.
Vose, Clement E. 1954/55. "NAACP Strategy in the Covenant Cases." *Western
    Reserve Review* 6:101–45.
Waever, Ole, Barry Buzan, Morton Kelstrup, and Pierre Lemaitre. 1993. *Identity,
    Migration and the New Security Agenda in Europe.* London: Pinter.
Waldo, Craig R. 2001. "Working in a Majority Context: A Structural Model of
    Heterosexism as Minority Stress in the Workplace." *Journal of Counselling
    Psychology* 46: 218–32.
Waldron, Jeremy. 1999a. *Law and Disagreement.* Oxford: Clarendon.
– 1999b. *The Dignity of Legislation.* Cambridge: Cambridge University Press.
Walker, Brian. 1997. "Plural Cultures, Contested Territories: A Critique of
    Kymlicka." *Canadian Journal of Political Science* 30:211–34.
Walsh, David. 2016. *Politics of the Person as the Politics of Being.* Notre Dame:
    University of Notre Dame Press.
– 1997. *The Growth of the Liberal Soul.* Columbia: University of Missouri Press.
Walsh, P.G. 1958. "Livy and Stoicism." *The American Journal of Philology*
    79:355–75.
Walton, Hanes, Jr, and William H. Boone. 1974. "Black Political Parties:
    A Demographic Analysis." *Journal of Black Studies* 5:86–95.
Walzer, Michael. 1981. "The Distribution of Membership." In *Boundaries:
    National Autonomy and Its Limits,* edited by Peter G. Brown and Henry Shue,
    1–35. Totowa: Rowman and Littlefield.
– 1969. *The Revolution of the Saints: A Study in the Origins of Radical Politics.* New
    York: Atheneum.
– 1963. "Puritanism as a Revolutionary Ideology." *History and Theory* 1:59–90.
Ward, Cynthia V. 1991. "The Limits of 'Liberal Republicanism': Why Group-
    Based Remedies and Republican Citizenship Don't Mix." *Columbia Law
    Review* 91:581–607.
Waring, Luther Hess. 1910. *The Political Theories of Martin Luther.* New York:
    G.P. Putnam's Sons.
Wasby, Stephen L. 1984. "Civil Rights Litigation by Organizations: Constraints
    and Choices." *Judicature* 68:337–52.
Weber, Max. 1930. *The Protestant Ethic and the Spirit of Capitalism.* Translated and
    edited by Talcott Parsons. New York: Charles Scribner's Sons.
Weissberg, Robert. 2005. "When God Goes Bad." *Society* 42:30–6.
Weithman, Paul. 1992. "Augustine and Aquinas on Original Sin and the
    Function of Political Authority." *Journal of the History of Philosophy* 30:353–76.
Wellek, René. 1943. "Emerson and German Philosophy." *New England Quarterly*
    43:41–62.

Williams, Robert R. 1997. *Hegel's Ethics of Recognition.* Berkeley: University of California Press.

Wilson, James Q. 1993. *The Moral Sense.* New York: Basic Books.

Wood, Gordon S. 1998. *The Creation of the American Republic 1776–1787.* Chapel Hill: University of North Carolina Press.

– 1966. "Rhetoric and Reality in the American Revolution." *William and Mary Quarterly* 3rd Series 23:3–32.

Woodhouse, A.S.P. 1951. *Puritanism and Liberty: Being the Army Debates (1647–49) from the Clarke Manuscripts with Supplementary Documents.* Chicago: University of Chicago Press.

Yancey, William L., Eugene P. Ericksen, and Richard N. Juliani. 1976. "Emergent Ethnicity: A Review and Reformulation." *American Sociological Review* 41:391–403.

Yang, Alan S. 1997. "Trends: Attitudes toward Homosexuality." *Public Opinion Quarterly* 61:477–507.

Young, Iris. 2003. "From Guilt to Solidarity: Sweatshops and Political Responsibility." *Dissent* Spring.

Young, Iris Marion. 1990. *Justice and the Politics of Difference.* Princeton: Princeton University Press.

Zirkel, Sabrina. 2002. "Is There a Place for Me? Role Models and Academic Identities among White Students and Students of Color." *Teachers College Record* 104:357–76.

Zolberg, Aristide R. 1968. "The Structure of Political Conflict in the New States of Tropical Africa." *American Political Science Review* 62:70–87.

Zook, Melinda S. 1999. *Radical Whigs and Conspiratorial Politics in Late Stuart England.* University Park: Penn State University Press.

COURT CASES

Brown v. Board of Education of Topeka [1954] 347 U.S. 483.

M.J. v. Nichols [2008] 63 C.H.R.R.D./45

Newdow v. United States Congress et al. [2002] 328 F. 3d 466.

Plessy v. Ferguson [1896] 163 U.S. 537.

R. v. Keegstra [1990] 3 S.C.R. 697.

R. v. Morgentaler [1988] 1 S.C.R. 30.

Roe v. Wade [1973] 410 U.S. 113.

Texas v. Johnson [1989] 491 U.S. 397.

Index